THE MOTION PICTURE IMAGE

FROM FILM TO DIGITAL

STEVEN BARCLAY

**Focal
Press**

Boston • Oxford • Auckland • Johannesburg • Melbourne • New Delhi

Copyright © 2000 Steven Barclay

Focal Press is an imprint of Butterworth–Heinemann.

 A member of the Reed Elsevier group

 Butterworth–Heinemann supports the efforts of American Forests and the Global ReLeaf program in its campaign for the betterment of trees, forests, and our environment.

Library of Congress Cataloging-in-Publication Data
Barclay, Steven, 1971–
    The motion picture image : from film to digital / Steven Barclay.
    p.   cm.
    Includes bibliographical references and index.
    ISBN 0-240-80390-6 (alk. paper)
    1. Cinematography.   2. Video recording.   I. Title.
    TR850.B36   1999
    778--dc21   99-045476

British Library Cataloguing-in-Publication Data
A catalogue record for this book is available from the British Library.

CONTENTS

Introduction   vii
1   Human Vision and Cinematography   1
2   The Camera and Exposure   19
3   Measuring Light and Assessing Exposure   35
4   Color Temperature   51
5   Filters   69
6   Sensitometry   83
7   Lenses and Depth of Field   99
8   The Laboratory   115
9   Formats and the Theater   131
10   Understanding Video   147
11   Film to Video   169
12   Digital Scanners and Film Recorders   183
13   The Digital Image and the Computer   193
14   Digital Cinema   205
Notes   213
Index   215

INTRODUCTION

Cinematography can be viewed as an art, a craft, an applied science, or a challenge of technology and logistics. It is very often unclear where one ends and the other begins. The challenge, however, is continuous and ever-changing, and we do not refer simply to the tasks themselves, but also to the technical aspects of the medium—the technologies which make it all possible.

Knowledge of the detailed workings of the various systems involved is not required in order to photograph or otherwise record moving images. For certain applications the non-technical method might be entirely acceptable, but when one considers the tremendous expenditures motion picture, television, and commercial productions entail, the entirely non-technical approach becomes questionable at best. Even productions such as short films or "student" films involve, at the very least, substantial applications of time and effort, and to approach even these projects with simply a hope for the best is selling oneself short.

As our analogy we might look to the test pilot flying a high-performance aircraft. What allows such a task to be successfully completed is an excellent understanding of the dynamics of flight, the engineering of the aircraft, and the inherent limitations of that aircraft and its numerous interconnected systems. The better the pilot understands and can apply this knowledge, the less likely it is control will be lost, or that the flight will end with the aircraft punching a hole in the desert.

This does not preclude the pilot from taking risks. Quite the opposite, it allows risks to be taken because there is a good measure of confidence in what the outcome will be. Likewise, for the director of photography every project is like test-flying a new aircraft. It is probable the cinematographer has not designed the project, or even been involved in the complete planning of it, but bringing the picture to life through a combination of technical and creative methods is the task at hand.

In the cockpit of cinematography there are times when one must take a stick and rudder approach, and the science and engineering of the whole enterprise become for a time, if not entirely secondary, then at least relegated to the background. This is when an intrinsic understanding of the basis, workings, and possible future of the images being shot can be of great value.

The logistics of production are myriad, and at times this facet becomes the primary influence on all aspects of a production. The photographic aspects are not excepted, and the limitations of time, funding, equipment, and personnel influence the decisions of a director of photography just as they would a general in the field, sometimes to a good end, sometimes to detriment, and more often than not leading to a kind of equilibrium where the desired result is attained to varying degrees.

The challenge of the technology itself involves making choices as the image is created, modified, and mastered, which could proceed through two or three steps, but might easily encompass many more. If one leaves the decisions at any of these junctures to someone else, the results may deviate from the intentions. Without a reasonably comprehensive understanding of the stages the image can or will go through, it can be difficult to exercise control, and therefore by default the decisions will be made by someone else.

As science advances, the technological details upon which the moving picture is based evolve. At times the evolution is rapid, but in general its course is not entirely unexpected. We use as our basis traditional film technology, since it remains the standard by which all other forms of imaging technology are judged (i.e., "photo-realistic"). By beginning with an extensive examination of film, we are laying the groundwork to discuss the electronic and digital systems. We are also essentially following the linear historical development of these respective forms of the motion picture.

If one's inclination is towards the artistic, and the scientific calculator programs look like ancient Egyptian calculus, it should be noted that one is only likely to leave the relative safety of the clear, often-trod path and strike off into the forest when one knows the lessons and something of the secrets of that place. The bewildering thickets and vines can then give way to new discoveries and new observations.

And the cinematographer must observe. The three-dimensional world forms the basis of the two-dimensional image in motion, but that world is tempered and changed within the mind. The image may be a fantasy, a daydream, a nightmare, or a delusion.

The cinematographer is attempting to exercise a mastery of the imaginative within the realm of reality—a mastery which always seems just beyond reach.

1

Ingenious Evolution

HUMAN VISION AND CINEMATOGRAPHY

While the means of recording images on film are clearly different from the way our eyes receive and process images, basic and reasonable correlations can be made regarding the camera and the eye. Furthermore, useful knowledge can be gained of both processes through a comparative analysis, resulting in a better understanding of the inherent disparity between how a scene is perceived by the eye and how an imaging system such as film reproduces it.

We can best explain the relative structure of the human eye by following the path of a parallel beam of light that is reflected from an imaginary object towards the viewer. Light, traveling from the outside of the eye to the inside, first enters the cornea, the lens on the surface of the eye which produces the initial focusing, and then passes through the pupil. Expansion or reduction of the eye's aperture is the initial light control, but this is not the only method of light regulation as we will see later. The iris alone cannot provide the necessary exposure control because it has a limited aperture range, approximately 4 1/2 stops. Camera lenses contain a similar variable aperture, a circle of intermeshed metal blades controlled by turning a calibrated ring. Most will have a range in the order of 6 stops, and it is for this reason that a shutter must be used to control exposure over a wider range of light levels.

After entering the pupil, the light continues through the lens of the eye. When comparing the eye's lens to the lens of a camera, a similarity is obvious, as both utilize the biconvex (both sides of the lens are curved outwards) design, which converges light rays into a real im-age—one that can be focused on a surface. The image focused on the retina is inverted and reversed, identical to that produced by a camera lens. Drastic differences can be noted at this point between the image capture and focus method used by the eye and that which is used by the camera.

The distance between the center of the lens and the point of con-vergence is the image distance. The eye has a fixed image distance because the lens cannot move backwards or forwards, and, likewise, the retina is stationary. Additionally, the eye has a curved sensory field, which relates poorly to the flat surface of film, although it should be noted that this design is in fact superior when used with a simple bi-convex lens, as it provides a sharper degree of focus across the whole surface of the retina. The camera also has a fixed image plane (the film), but the image distance is variable. The lens can be moved in relation to the film, thus allowing objects at different distances to be focused properly.

Given that the image distance is fixed in the eye, by both the lens and the retina, a unique focusing method is employed, the ingenious

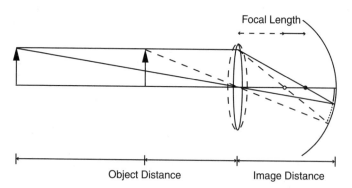

FIGURE 1.1 The varying thickness of the eye's lens causes near and far objects to focus clearly on the retina.

product of evolution. The eye maintains focus (accommodates) by modifying the shape of the lens, keeping the image focused on the retina through a system of lens curvature, where the ciliary muscles squeeze the lens to produce more or less curvature. Focal length is effectively increased when the lens is flat (less curved) and decreased when curved so that we can view distant scenes and near objects respectively (Figure 1.1).

The image is formed on the retina, the region of densely packed photoreceptors at the rear of the eye. It is made up of millions of rod receptors and cone receptors which are chemically active, i.e., capable of changing sensitivity. Rods are monochromatic, meaning they cannot perceive color, while cones are traditionally classified as three types based upon wavelength sensitivity. Therefore, our perception of brightness is controlled not only by the iris, but by chemical changes occurring within the photoreceptors in order to increase or decrease light sensitivity. This sensitivity change within the eye is necessary based upon the limited aperture range of the iris and the wide range of light levels typically encountered.

The central portion of the retina, which is located directly behind the pupil, is called the fovea, and contains all cones, while the outer area becomes increasingly populated with rods. Our vision is best in the foveal region, where the greatest detail can be perceived, while the level of detail is reduced in the peripheral regions. All of these light-induced electrical impulses travel along the optic nerve, the complex bundle of nerve fibers exiting the rear of the eye, terminating in the brain where the image processing takes place (Figure 1.2).

The rod and cone cells, the biological imaging systems within the eye, use light-reacting pigments to control ocular sensitivity. The cones (three varieties) have pigments that only react to certain wavelengths of light, which appears to explain color vision, while the rods have a pigment known as visual purple. When light strikes the rods or cones, a chemical reaction occurs which bleaches the sensitive pigment, and therefore limits the light absorption in these cells. An example of this process is the dark after-image that results from staring at an extremely bright object and then looking away, where the affected receptors do not respond to subsequent light stimulation (they form a black hole in our visual field) until they have resensitized. During photopic vision, a term used to identify the period of predominantly cone-based func-

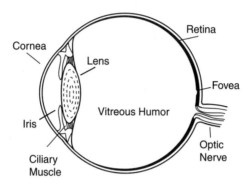

FIGURE 1.2 Simplified anatomical drawing of the human eye.

tioning (essentially bright daylight conditions) the rods are largely inactive. At an intermediate level, called mesopic vision, both rods and cones operate. If light is reduced to a point at which the rod cells are vitally necessary for proper vision, and therefore become the primary photoreceptors (when vision is said to be scotopic), rod cell pigmentation must occur rapidly in order to resensitize the eye.

Now that we understand how the eye chemically reacts to light we can explain the process of dark adaptation as it pertains to sight. When an observer passes from a bright area to a dark area, a period occurs where the observer experiences an underexposed image before the sensitizing rod pigment is completely activated. Because dark adaptation can take several minutes, depending upon the circumstances, it is usually more noticeable than light adaptation. True dark adaptation, what is generally called night vision, can take more than thirty minutes to occur in some cases. The rate at which the eye adapts, of course, is in direct correlation with the light level from which it has recently been exposed. Dark adaptation is much faster if we prepare for it beforehand, such as by avoiding bright lights or high levels of illumination.

The process of light adaptation, which occurs when passing from a dark area into a bright area, is much more obvious in its course. Because excessive light is damaging to the eye, and in particular the retina, adaptation must rapidly occur. The speed at which this happens, and the rate at which the receptors are bleached of their content, is a much more abrupt reaction. When the adaptation process involves extreme light level differences, the event can be highly undesirable. In fact, a common reaction to excessively bright lights is a painful headache. A less severe example of light adaptation would be the use of dark lenses over the eyes, such as sunglasses, where the adaptive process will alter the user's eyes for the modified viewing conditions, and the removal of them, albeit briefly, will create the perception of an overly bright surrounding.

The chemical changes in the receptor region are similar, although of a transitory nature, to the concept of switching film stocks for controlling sensitivity in the camera. However the film manufacturer must produce a variety of emulsions for specific applications, as the sensitivity technology is static. The exposure index of the film, once it has been manufactured, is only controllable through optical or mechanical means. We must remember, though, that we are not really changing the sensitivity of the film stock, only the light reaching the emulsion.

Video cameras, on the other hand, are quite capable of this feat (the rapid changing of sensitivity) without such mechanical or optical light-controlling devices. The video chip can be electronically modified by boosting the gain (increasing the amplitude of the electrical signal), thereby allowing the user to define specific exposure parameters based upon the sensitivity range of the imaging device. Normally in modern video cameras the image is received by a flat pixel array formed with discrete light-sensitive elements, not unlike our eye in many respects, so the signal amplification is similar to the rod cells increasing sensitivity in order to send a stronger electrical impulse to the brain. The technique is not without its drawbacks because increasing sensitivity in any electronic camera increases noise, which, in turn, produces undesirable picture qualities.

Comparatively speaking, our eyes experience a similar problem when faced with low light levels. Detail is restricted because the rod cells do not contribute to this function, which is the task of the cones, nor do the rods process wavelengths across the whole visual spectrum. As the light fades, when the eye can no longer fully adapt, our vision is essentially black and white.

The cone receptors of the retina can be divided into three types: red (ρ), green (γ), and blue (β), i.e., rho, gamma, and beta. A single cone is responsive to only a certain range of electromagnetic energy (light waves), although there is considerable overlap, and each one has a specific peak sensitivity (Figure 1.3). By this function our eyes can process light waves which are approximately between 400nm and 700nm (a nanometer being the equivalent of a millionth of a millimeter and a measurement of the wavelength). Ultraviolet radiation, below the 400nm range, is damaging to the eye but is not perceived. Infrared, at the opposite end of the scale, beyond 700nm, is also outside our range of perception and therefore it, too, is invisible (Figure 1.4). Relatively speaking, the human eye is most sensitive in the 550 to 555nm zone, the center of all visible light, which is not in the least surprising when we realize that the sun primarily emits this wavelength of energy. One may wonder, given the relationship between the eye's spectral sensitivity and the sun's output, how an off-planet being might perceive light on earth, particularly when that creature's eye may have evolved under the spectra of a red giant.

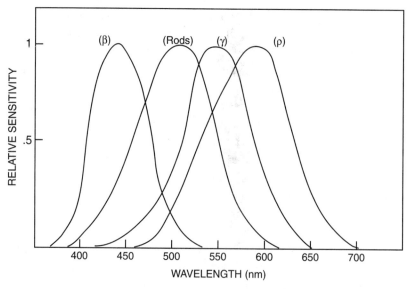

FIGURE 1.3 Relative spectral sensitivity of the eye.

We can perceive an enormous range of colors based on the fact that the stimulus signals from the three cones are combined. Exactly how these signals mix, and the associated processing that takes place in the complex neurological pathways of the brain is still open to debate, but the fact remains that red and green light can be mixed to produce the sensation of yellow light, and a multitude of other colors can be produced in exactly the same way—with mixtures. This, in fact, is the basis for using three dyes (cyan, magenta, and yellow) in color film, and red, green, and blue phosphors in television screens. The sensation of color itself, of course, only exists because the cone receptors are responsive to these wavelengths of energy. In the electromagnetic spectrum light is only another form of radiation, and would be as alien to us as gamma rays or cosmic rays if we did not possess the appropriate sensory system. If electromagnetic radiation outside the 400nm to 700nm range can be visually perceived, one's terrestrial origins may be in doubt.

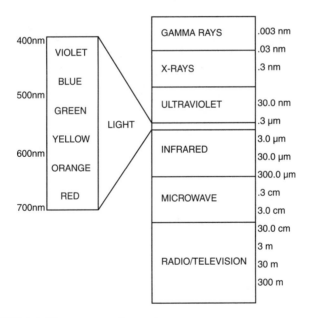

FIGURE 1.4 Electromagnetic spectrum.

Color perception, then, is determined by the spectral power distribution of the light source, the spectral reflectance of the object, and the resulting wavelengths (the stimulus) incident upon the retina. A blue car, for example, is reflecting mostly blue light and absorbing the green and red wavelengths. White reflects all colors equally, which explains why red, green, and blue phosphors are used at equal intensities to produce white on a television screen, and black is the result of total wavelength absorption. This, of course, objectively models color perception, but does not take into account the psychological factors, namely color constancy, which can make colors appear the same under a wide variety of illuminants.

If the source of light is emitting a very specific wavelength, any previously perceived color will probably be drastically modified. For example, if we illuminate a red object with light that contains only blue and green wavelengths, the object will appear black. Therefore, in order for an object to reflect a certain wavelength, that wavelength must be present in the incident light—the light falling on the object. Rarely will a light source be so deficient in the distribution of spectral energy that colors will be noticeably abnormal to the eye, as most typical fixtures are designed to provide relatively equal energy at all wavelengths.

Colors perceptibly change depending upon the time of day, or whether they are illuminated by a tungsten lamp or daylight. Yellow, for example, tends to look considerably different under tungsten illumination than in daylight. Higher or lower intensity light can also modify our interpretation of colors to a large extent. In other words, color perception is relative, and this can be illustrated by the fact that a color placed adjacent to or in front of its complementary color will appear to be more saturated. For example, blue will appear more saturated when in close proximity to yellow. Precise indication of a color can be done with a colorimeter and a chromaticity chart, although as stated before, the resulting perception is centrally based on the illuminant itself, which must be standardized before valid comparisons can be made. Even given such a quantifiable means of color description, the fact remains that color is a sensation, and there is no way of knowing exactly how each human perceives it.

Since the cinematographer is not interested in the color of individual objects, we simply desire a means of specifying an illuminant;

therefore the spectral composition of the light needs to be defined. The main concern, as we indicated earlier, is that our perception of color is affected by the illuminant, and this applies as much to film (even more so) as it does to the eye. Color film is manufactured to mimic the spectral response of the eye within the confines of practical engineering, so we can automatically assume a similarity in color with the original scene and our resulting picture. But film can only be designed for one color balance, so it is particularly susceptible to incompatible illumination, which will result in pictures having the wrong colors. Only under very specific spectral conditions will film faithfully record the colors as our eyes see them. There are many methods of describing an illuminant using various scientific systems and their accompanying charts, but for the cinematographer, Kelvin (K) is the only measuring system commonly used.

The eye cannot be assigned a specific balance because it adapts depending upon the spectral power distribution of the source. We accept, after color adaptation, almost all light sources as white. Generally speaking, due to a limit in adaptation, which is the reason why color perception is not the same under all lighting conditions, household lamps will naturally look somewhat yellow, more so if low wattage, while daylight typically appears to be more neutral. The perception of excessive blue in daylight is less frequently encountered but can be easily detected when viewing a scene that is reflecting mostly direct sunlight, such as a snow-covered landscape, where the shadows can appear very blue to the eye.

Logically, one might say, white as perceived by the eye can only be produced in conditions which have a source with a similar spectral composition as the sun, and therefore daylight yields a true white. In a scientific sense this is absolutely true, as standards in the photographic industry are closely related to daylight, the spectral composition our eyes can adapt within most easily.

All illuminant-related perceptions, though, due to adaptation, depend on certain conditions. For example, sitting in an interior with the lights on during twilight hours, we perceive daylight, or the last few minutes of it, as quite blue because the eye has changed balance under the tungsten illumination. If we were to step outside at this time and let the eye adjust to the new conditions, our perception would be the opposite—the lights inside the house would now appear amber.

The eye attempts under most conditions to balance the source; therefore compensation takes place and color adaptation occurs. A more technical way of describing a comparison, based on the video camera, is the process of automatic white balancing. The camera will modify the red and blue gain (as professional cameras use three separate charge-coupled devices, sensor arrays that are fused to an optical block which acts as a beam splitter to send specific wavelengths of light to each imaging device, thereby creating red, green, and blue channels) in order to reproduce white light (white balance).

Once the eye is balanced, i.e., perceives the light as neutral and unbiased, perceptually assessing the spectral composition of the illuminant for photographic purposes becomes nearly impossible. We will accept almost anything as white light, and therefore our conclusions will likely be erroneous when we attempt to define a source by eye.

However, the ocular region has its limitations. It cannot shift its balance for relatively pure spectral sources, such as a light fixture that contains most of its energy in one specific wavelength. It will not compensate, and the color produced will be the color perceived. If other light sources are visually apparent and within our field of view, the eye will tend to adjust to the most powerful one and then, in many cases, the other lights will be affected by this balancing. The eye also tends to neutralize colored light in order to render an untinted white, which is the reason why if we stay in a room with only one colored light source we might notice after a long duration that the light does not appear as strongly tinted.

Another discrepancy we rarely notice by eye is color reflection and natural filtering. If a colored surface is present in a scene, it may reflect light back in the color of the reflecting surface. This can be a problem when filming in a jungle, for example, when strong sunlight is filtered and reflected off the foliage and therefore becomes altered in spectral composition. Skin tones may take on a greenish tinge in this specific case and it is something which is very hard to detect by eye.

While assessment of an illuminant's spectral composition is not as crucial, for example, as proper film exposure, the fact that the eye is adaptable in its color response is not to be entirely ignored. Even given that light sources fit into certain known spectral energy distributions, we must realize that the eye is just as unreliable for color balance assessment as it is for exposure assessment. For the most part, though, color balancing film only becomes a problem when dealing with odd sources. Comparative judgment as it relates to color balance is usually relatively accurate, but if we want to objectively determine the distribution of spectral energy for a light source, we must use a meter specifically designed for that very task.

Once we can define a source accurately, we can use an assortment of filters to compensate for a poorly balanced illuminant, either over the source itself, as in a lighting fixture, or in front of the camera lens, correcting light which would render an abnormally colored image if left unfiltered. Video cameras can be electronically color balanced, which eliminates the need for optical filtering, but the proper controls and the requisite knowledge must be available to the user.

The eye perceives only brightness. It cannot measure an actual quantity. How light or how dark an object really is, objectively speaking, is strictly the concern of photometric measurements. Luminance, as we will see in Chapter 3, is such a measurement. Brightness can be interpolated with practice, particularly if we are dealing with a scene of limited contrast and we have already determined a photographic exposure, but it causes innumerable problems for the observer when the relationship is not comparative. We can all say a sheet of white paper is brighter than a sheet of gray paper and, if it is under similar illumination, it is a given fact. But, and this is where the problem of subjective perception plays a larger role, if we place the papers in totally different environments (different levels of illumination), it will be very difficult to decide which one is actually brighter because we are limited to purely perceptual means and this, as we noted above, is really only useful in a very restricted sense.

That, of course, is the very reason why determining an exposure for the film camera or the video camera is very difficult when only using the eye. Even given the fact (which is the case with cinematographers) that better judgment is obtained through the repetitive task of measuring light with a light meter, our capability to generalize an exposure before measurement is not based on the eye alone, but on the meter's previous result which we have visually associated with a specific lighting condition. We need a scientific basis from which to start.

The most critical topic regarding the perception of brightness is contrast. When we view a scene with our eyes we see a range of reflected light levels. How vast a range depends entirely on the lighting conditions and the specific objects within our field of view. Outside, for example, on a sunny day, we can expect the contrast to be quite severe. In the shade of a tree it will likely be very dark, while a white house nearby in the sunlight will likely be very bright. The difference between these two could be measured using various objective techniques, but for now, as we are discussing only subjective matters, it is best we explain just how the eye's adaptability hinders our decisions regarding how light or how dark each really is—an important distinction when making decisions regarding exposure and image tone.

Specific nomenclature is used to describe the three types of adaptation. The first, which is called general adaptation, is simply the ability of the photoreceptors to change sensitivity based on the ambient light and reflected light reaching the retina. It allows the eye to see an incredible range of lightness. The second, termed localized adaptation, is largely a result of the fact that each photoreceptor can modify its sensitivity individually. Faced with a very dark area and a very light area the eye does not have to compensate for one or the other. It can, in fact, compensate for both. This explains the reason why the range of contrast as perceived by the eye is far greater than that of film. The eye can adapt to a specific area, not just a general scene. The third type is called simultaneous contrast or lateral adaptation. It indicates the relativity of brightness perception as it relates to adjacent tones. Darker tones will always appear lighter against a black background and, conversely, darker against a white background (Figure 1.5). This aspect of the eye's operation can affect perceived contrast in all reproduced images, one particular example being a film presented in a theater, where the darkened room (the equivalent of a dark background) tends to perceptually gray the black shadows in the image. To a large extent the dark adapted eye is also responsible for this reduction in contrast.

Because contrast is largely responsible for the perception of intensity, we are typically hindered in deciding how much light is really being output from a source. Light dissipation (or fall-off), a common reality of using artificial and relatively weak sources of illumination for our subjects, is something which rarely can be detected with reasonable accuracy by the eye alone. We know that a light source is not giving off equal levels of light at all distances because of the inverse square law, which states that doubling the distance quarters the light

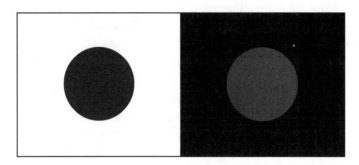

FIGURE 1.5 The circles are exactly the same tone.

level. Perceptually, though, just using the eye and no instrumentation, it is difficult to decide just how much light is lost with distance, particularly when we realize that the eye is adjusting every time we look into a new area. With small sources, such as desk lamps, it is very apparent that the light is confined around a zone, but with large sources it becomes more difficult to discern this effect.

Human vision has a remarkable level of contrast acceptance in bright ambient light, but when the light fades and the eye is forced to compensate by increasing the sensitivity of the rods, the eye loses this ability. It is for this reason that it is easier to judge photographic results under low light levels. The most difficult light to evaluate is one that is bright and contrasty. Our eyes tend to see these images in more gradations of tone, while the film emulsion, when developed and printed, will appear rather stark.

Film has a fixed range of possible exposures which can result in a viable image being recorded. It is incapable of recording an image as a duplication of visual perception because the exposure range is limited. What we perceive is *our* perception of reality, but the disparity between what the film can record and what the eye sees is the salient debate. When we realize the eye has the ability to accept a range of luminance, with adaptability in the order of 10 trillion:1 in a ratio of lightest subject to darkest subject, it is clear we are dealing with a phenomenal difference in operational capability. The only reason why this is not as troublesome as it seems is that the average daylight scene will rarely exceed 160:1 from lightest subject to darkest subject, so film can capture most of the details.

We referred earlier to the decrease in color perceived at low light levels, and here we might note that the eye also appears to have, in a sense, an increased exposure time when adapted to dim light. The effect of this is a delay in images reaching the brain. This can be illustrated by attempting to catch a rapidly moving ball at dusk. It will become increasingly more difficult as the remaining skylight fades because reaction time and accuracy are compromised due to this reduced temporal sampling.

Persistence of vision is another phenomenon which affects perception. If an image is flashed at a slow rate, say ten times a second, we can easily detect the dark periods between the flashes, but as the flashing increases, eventually a point will be reached where the picture will appear to be a continuous, steady projection because the eye retains previous images for a fraction of a second. Based on the fact that the realism of the motion picture image is due to the rapid projection of discrete frames, persistence of vision is an important part of the illusory experience. Without this ability, the eye would recognize the periods of darkness between the images when the projector is pulling down a new frame into the gate and the spinning shutter is cutting out the projector light. Many projectors use shutters that increase the frequency of flashing to 72 cycles per second (Hz) or more in order to produce less visual flicker.

It is interesting to note that an improperly calibrated projector, i.e., one that is fitted with a lamp of excessive output (a common problem in small theaters), will increase the perception of flicker because a brighter image produces less persistence of vision. A television or computer monitor with excessive screen brightness can produce similar results, and the only remedy is to increase the refresh rate.

The complete integration of the visual system, particularly the instantaneous focus process and the very wide angle of view, due in large part to the very short focal length (roughly 17mm) of the eye, means that depth of field is not really applicable in terms of human vision. A person without visual defects can usually focus from six inches to infinity, until with advancing age the lens loses its flexibility and close focusing becomes impossible without the aid of man-made optical devices. In reality, of course, we can only focus at one distance, but the speed at which our focus adapts is not perceptible so everything appears to be properly focused. We can see now why we do not relate well to depth of field, but it is a primary compositional concern for the cinematographer, and can be most easily assessed by examining the scene through the camera's viewfinder. It can be used to great effect when it is necessary to create separation between subjects and their backgrounds.

The perception of depth itself is largely created by the fact that we have two separate eyes viewing the same scene. Each eye is actually seeing a slightly different image, so a system of stereoscopic vision is utilized. The subsequent processing of these disparate images in the brain adds to the effect. The dual nature of vision should never be underestimated in perceiving dimensions, as depth perception is seriously hindered by the covering of one eye.

For example, if we look at the corner of a book held sideways at arm's length (use the paper side only) with the point facing roughly in the middle of our nose, we can see the effect of reduced depth perception when one eye is closed. The triangular edge looks almost flat, and then seems to pop into dimension when the other eye is opened. Interestingly, the closing of one eye can help the cinematographer visualize a scene as it will appear on film because depth perception is compromised; thus it mimics more accurately the resulting two-dimensional film image.

When looking at faraway scenes with one eye covered there is little difference from our normal vision because the stereoscopic effect is substantially reduced at far viewing distances (there is little disparity between the images). It is for this reason that a closer correlation exists between visual perception and the reproduced two-dimensional image when filming distant scenery.

Perspective (the primary visual indication of depth, used by painters for centuries) contributes greatly to three-dimensional awareness. This explains why pictures, either drawn or photographed, can viably mimic reality. The closer one is able to reproduce an image in perspective, the more real it will look to the eye. The camera can generally do this task better than a painter, although this may not always be the case because the artist can use enhancing illusory effects. The application of light and shadows is one of the primary tools in making two dimensions look like three not only for the painter, but also for the cinematographer.

Dimension is also created by object scale and placement within the frame. By placing an object in front of another object, one automatically assumes the object doing the blocking must be closer, just as an identical object that is half the size must be twice the distance. In motion pictures an added level of realism is provided by the movement of the camera and the movement of objects within the scene itself, both of which create (individually or in tandem) a more compelling effect of dimension than is possible with a static image.

We can, with little conflict, watch two-dimensional images on a movie screen and our brain is easily fooled into believing a dimension of depth exists, where in fact none exists. Watching such an image with one eye enhances the effect even more, which is not surprising given the fact that our eyes are inherently two-dimensional receivers just as a camera lens is, and can only perceive true depth through the stereoscopic nature of sight and the fusion of both images in the brain. The stereoscopic nature of vision ultimately reveals the flat screen, yet in cases where such a screen fills almost the entire field of view the depth effect is far greater, while a smaller screen, such as that produced by a television, cannot create the same level of realism because we can see the surroundings.

When a cinematographer evaluates a scene using only the eye, these numerous factors must be taken into account in order to assess the most probable outcome. The ability to visually preconceive the scene's resulting film image is one of the most important abilities of a professional cinematographer.

Throughout the course of the chapter we have enumerated the problems of perceptually assessing a scene for cinematographic purposes based on the subjective nature of the eye's response. For these very reasons it is obvious that we cannot be expected to conjure up answers to the vital questions regarding exposure, reproduced tone, and color balance using our eyes alone. Many precision instruments have in fact been invented for the sole purpose of assisting in the interpretation of images on the objective level.

As far as exposure is concerned we employ the exposure meter, the two main types being the incident meter (a measure of ambient illumination) and the reflected meter (a measure of luminance or reflected light), both giving, respectively, vital information for exposure and tonal assessment. In the rendition of proper color balance, we utilize a color temperature meter, measuring wavelengths of light with either a two-cell or three-cell type, providing the user with color temperature in Kelvin or, in some cases, the filter specifications necessary for balancing the stock.

The contrast question, an important piece of the puzzle of cinematography, can be evaluated and understood with a simple device such as a contrast viewing glass, available either in-camera in the form of neutral density filters switchable in the viewfinder or in a hand-held configuration—all equally designed to restrict the eye's ability to see into shadows and therefore approximate the response of film. There is also more complex instrumentation which can directly indicate the actual luminance, such as the spot meter. All of these devices can be used either alone or in conjunction with each other in order to gauge how the film will reproduce the image.

It is really the understanding of what the eye is *not* telling you that matters. This determination is made with all of your meters, leading to educated and artistic decisions regarding color, exposure, and contrast. What is visualized must be analyzed on a more precise level than one may initially realize. As we improve our skills we tend to rely less on our meters and more on intuition, but it is reassuring to know we can always verify our decisions scientifically.

2

A Mechanical Eye

THE CAMERA AND EXPOSURE

We must now delve into the machinery which has traditionally made repetitive image capturing possible: the motion picture camera. On a rudimentary level the motion picture camera is not much different than a still camera, except, of course, that it must expose twenty-four pictures a second. The subsequent projection of these sequential images results in the perception of motion and the resulting term—movies. Even when we consider the fact that we are now in an age of widespread digital camera systems, the design of the motion picture camera still retains its simplicity of operation and the superior image characteristics of film. As long as film maintains a qualitative advantage, the motion picture camera will be required. The complete replacement of film may be looming on the horizon, but how far off that horizon is and how long it will take us to get there we cannot yet tell.

As we are mainly discussing the camera in order to provide an explanation for its operation, i.e., the movement and basic design, along with an understanding of how to calculate the proper exposure when given all the necessary variables, we will therefore focus on the mechanical processes taking place that contribute most directly to this function. Rather than explain every motion picture camera system currently in use, it makes far more sense to use a typical camera as the subject of technical operation and to simply allow the differences between manufacturers, subtle and not so subtle, to remain the quest of further inquiry. It is easier if we sequence the process from the front of the camera, where the image is formed by the lens, and then provide an explanation of the mechanics.

As image-forming light rays pass through the front optics of the lens, then through the iris, and exit the rear optics of the lens, they continue on their way into the camera body in order to expose the film. Inside, essentially in the space between the back of the camera lens and the film plane, a spinning mirror rotates. The mirror (typically a twin-bladed variety) has two purposes: one is to reflect the image into the viewfinder, thereby allowing the camera operator to view the scene, and the other is to block the light from the film during the pull-down phase of the movement (it works as a shutter). Some cameras also have a focal plane shutter (like a still camera) which acts in synchronization with the rotating mirror; this is the case with the Panavision Panaflex.

While the spinning mirror rotates, the image is reflected into a ground glass which contains frame line markings. The image, now superimposed with the frame lines, is passed through the viewfinder's optics to the operator's eye (Figure 2.1). The quality of the reflex design can usually be determined by the brightness of the image in the viewfinder. If the finder image is not bright enough it can be difficult to focus by eye and precise framing can be burdensome to achieve. Although most cameras have a system of frame line illumination to improve the visibility of the framing in low lighting conditions, it will be of little help if the image is too dark to begin with. A bright and orientable viewfinder—meaning it can be rotated on its axis without changing the image orientation to the viewer—is usually a given on all professional cameras.

The real benefit of the reflex system is that the viewfinder is providing an image which is the same as that which is being exposed (though of course the two events, the reflecting and the exposing, are not in fact simultaneous). Lens defects, focusing problems, and optical flare can all be assessed with accuracy (assuming the ground glass is properly aligned and the viewfinder optics have not been damaged in any way) because the operator is using a system that does not rely on a separately attached viewfinder which attempts to approximate the camera's view.

Due to the fact that the mirror shutter is segmented (if it was solid it would never expose the film, always providing an image to the viewfinder), it allows an exposure to take place when the mirror is not

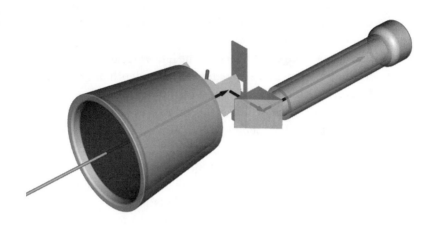

FIGURE 2.1 The light is being reflected into the viewfinder.

FIGURE 2.2 The light is exposing the film.

aligned to the viewfinder, i.e., during unimpeded light flow to the film (Figure 2.2). Conversely, when the film is blocked by the shutter, the viewfinder receives the image. Substantial and very apparent flicker is seen through the reflex viewfinder when the camera is running because the eye is only seeing the image less than half of the time. The flickering is a detriment of the reflex viewfinder system, but the ability to view the actual image as formed by the lens is far more important for the operator, who must assess such matters as depth of field, framing, and, in certain situations, even provide follow-focus by eye.

Certain cameras which still use the reflex design do not have a spinning mirror but a fixed pellicle mirror instead. A design of this type allows an image to be provided to the viewfinder at all times, but at a loss of light available to the film and, one might add, the possible loss of image quality by not having light pass unimpeded from the lens to the film. In professional cameras the pellicle mirror system is uncommon, although some cameras can be converted for such a setup. The pellicle system is really only useful when the operator desires an absolutely flickerless image or when a video assist monitor will be used for operating, such as with remote cranes or dangerous stunts, where a flickering image would seriously impair the operator's judgment of focus and framing on a small video screen in uncontrolled and possibly changing viewing conditions.

Now we must follow the path of the film from its storage in the magazine. Starting in the feed side, where the film is wound emulsion-in and winds clockwise, it passes through a set of light-trapping rollers, designed to keep light out of the magazine during the loading phase, and then into the camera body. The film is guided between the aperture plate and the pressure plate by a precisely machined slot, where it is intermittently pulled through frame by frame by two pull-down claws. As each frame is cycled through the aperture plate for exposure, a set of registration pins locks each frame into position by entering into the perforations at the bottom of the frame (the top of the aperture plate); this occurs when the claws are at the bottom of their stroke. While the film is stationary, for that brief moment between the reciprocating claws, the exposure takes place. After each frame is exposed (the actual exposure time varies with shutter setting and frames per second), the two registration pins disengage and the pull-down claws (now at the top of their stroke) advance the film to the next frame.

The film is drawn through the camera on a powered sprocket wheel, performing both feed and take-up, where the exposed film is drawn up (or back) into the magazine through a series of rollers designed to reduce tension and allow precise loop sizes. Some magazines also have motors which maintain an equilibrium in film tension within the magazine. While this is an oversimplification of the process, it does explain the fundamental mechanics of a typical 35mm motion picture camera.

The shutter angle and the speed at which the film travels through the gate are indicative of the exposure time in a motion picture camera. The standard frame rate is 24 frames per second. It should be noted that any deviation from this speed is considered to be a special effect. The theater projector is running at 24 fps; therefore if we were to capture our images at 12 fps, we would find our on-screen movement to be fast, while at 48 fps the movement would appear to be slow—roughly half of what it should be. Faster film speed creates slower motion, i.e., more frames produced during a specified interval, which take longer to project at 24 fps, while slower film speed, i.e., fewer frames produced during a specified interval, creates faster motion.

The shutter angle is quoted in terms of the cut-out portion of the shutter. It is normally a spinning reflex mirror with two sides that contain 90 degrees, or sometimes less (Figure 2.3). A 180 degree shutter angle creates an exposure time of 1/48th of a second or, if rounded off, 1/50th of a second. A shutter angle of 172.8 degrees produces exactly 1/50th of a second. Even though most cameras are set to 180 degrees, it is common practice to still use 1/50th of a second for an exposure time regardless of the slight difference.

If we change the speed of the film through the camera we change our exposure. For example, at 12 fps the exposure time is 1/25th of a second, or double the time of the standard 1/50th of a second. If we increase film speed through the camera, such as 48 fps, we lose half of our exposure from the original 1/50th of a second and therefore arrive at 1/100th of a second.

If we change the shutter angle of the camera, but not the frames per second, we still modify the exposure time. Therefore in actual usage we must be aware that both camera speed and the shutter angle affect exposure, regardless of whether one changes and the other does not. The opening of the shutter is the portion we measure to determine the degrees. The angle of a camera shutter can be verified by

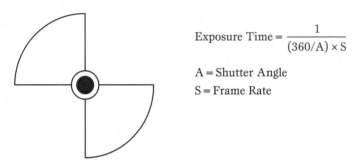

$$\text{Exposure Time} = \frac{1}{(360/A) \times S}$$

A = Shutter Angle
S = Frame Rate

FIGURE 2.3   A camera shutter at 180 degrees.

close visual inspection through the camera's lens port opening. The Panaflex is an exception to this method, as the mirror shutter angle is fixed and the focal plane shutter controls the actual exposure time.

If the shutter is closed down from 180 degrees, exposure time is reduced and therefore less light is able to reach the film. A 90 degree shutter opening creates an exposure time of 1/96th of a second, rounded to 1/100th of a second, while a 144 degree opening produces 1/60th of a second. Based on this fact, we can also correlate a light loss in stop notation, such as a 144 degree shutter being a loss of 1/3 of a stop and a 114 degree opening being a loss of 2/3 of a stop, while a 90 degree shutter is a complete loss of a whole stop in terms of exposure.

Now that the basis of exposure time in the motion picture camera (a combination of shutter angle and frames per second) has been studied, the problems that shutter angle changes can create and why this feature has limited practical use for the cinematographer except in special situations must be expounded.

Shutter angle is not really usable for adding more exposure due to the obvious reality that most cameras have a maximum shutter angle of 180 degrees (or possibly 200), which is the recommended angle for normal use, so unless we start out at a smaller shutter angle and change to a larger one, it is not really possible to use this feature. Therefore, we cannot add to the exposure if we use the standard 180 degree angle, but only subtract. The possibilities, unfortunately, are just as restricted in reducing exposure, but for entirely different reasons.

The narrower the shutter angle, the sharper the image. The reason is simple: the exposure time is reduced. We can relate to the still camera analogy, where faster shutter speeds are recommended for photographing rapid movement because they reduce the time the film is being exposed and therefore produce a sharper image. In regular photography this is a desirable feature. Unfortunately, when we project frames from a motion picture film that have been captured using very short exposure times, the images do not blend as well from frame to frame as they do for longer exposure times. If the camera does not move during the take and very little movement is taking place on the screen the lack of image blending is not noticeable, but in cases of fast movement or rapid camera panning the results will be very detrimental to the audience's perception of smooth movement. Larger shutter angles produce longer exposure durations, so the result is a pronounced blur for each frame. While blur may seem to be the last thing a cinematographer would want, it is, in actuality, preferred. By having a slight amount of blur in each frame, the images, when projected, will blend together into a smoother overall effect of motion.

Typically, in normal cinematography, the shutter angle and the frames per second will be fixed at their usual settings: 180 degrees and 24 fps. On occasion, though, it may be necessary to modify one or both of these variables when the situation calls for it. Special circumstances might include high-speed photography, time-lapse photography, or the filming of television and computer screens. Additionally, in-shot speed changes are sometimes required, usually for a particular effect in television commercials or music videos where the shutter can be used to compensate for the exposure change caused by the frame rate modification.

High-speed photography, for example, requires the camera to run at an increased frame rate in order to present slower movement on-screen when projected at 24 fps. By doubling the frame rate, we can slow movement down to half of normal speed when projected, but at a loss of 1 stop of exposure. In this case, we can see an obvious and direct relationship between the exposure loss when an increase in frame rate occurs. If we quadruple the frame rate we lose 2 stops of exposure. For odd and fractional frame rates it is best to calculate the loss with a formula for accuracy. Another factor which must be taken into account is the shot duration. At 96 fps (360 feet per minute) there is less than three minutes of running time per 1000-foot roll of 35mm film, or roughly one minute for a 400-foot roll.

Time-lapse photography is the complete antithesis of high-speed photography. We need to capture a single frame with long intervals of time between each one. To denote the speed in frames per second would be invalid in this case because most likely we would not even be working with a speed of one frame per second. It may be a frame a minute or a frame an hour. Generally custom-fitted cameras are used for this task, as it requires the application of an intervalometer, and substantial pre-planning is necessary.

Due to the proliferation of CRTs, particularly with the expanding use of computers, many cinematographers are required to film televisions, monitors, and a variety of new display devices such as LCDs. In order to produce images that are free from a scan bar, synchronization is a necessity, which invariably involves both frame rate and shutter angle modification.

Assuming we know the frame rate of the source, such as NTSC television, where we are attempting to match the exposure time of the camera with the field rate of television, i.e., 1/59.94th of a second, several options exist. We can run the camera at 29.97 fps with a 180 degree shutter angle, or in the case of a feature film, 23.976 fps and a 144 degree shutter angle. Neither method will entirely eliminate the scan bar, but it should be minimized and quite thin. For absolute precision, when a pristine video image needs to be captured direct from the monitor, a video/film synchronizer is recommended. These devices, which are available from a variety of manufacturers, will set the camera motor at exactly 23.976 fps with a 144 degree shutter angle, and also add a phase control button which will roll the scan bar off the monitor.

For computer screens, where the refresh rate is frequently unknown, a more complex speed control will be required. These systems can allow an operator to check the monitor directly through the viewfinder of the camera while changing the frame rate. Once the frame rate has been determined, the black scan bar can be rolled away from the picture area. In this case any monitor can be utilized regardless of its refresh rate. Given the frame rate and shutter angle modifications, one must never forget that the exposure time is invariably changed, so when calculating a final exposure all variables must be taken into account.

In the case of frame rate changes in-shot, an electronically controlled shutter can be utilized, a relatively common feature on any microprocessor-controlled camera. By programming the camera to perform a specified speed change while maintaining precise exposure compensation with the shutter, many creative possibilities are available for the cinematographer. The primary benefit is the ability to compensate for the change in exposure time when changing frame rates in-shot without affecting depth of field, which is a common problem when one relies on the lens aperture control.

For example, if the director needed a shot that started out in real time (24 fps) but ended in slow motion (96 fps), a 24 fps starting frame rate could be used with a 45 degree shutter angle. When indicated, the camera will increase its speed up to 96 fps, while the shutter simultaneously compensates for the loss of exposure by changing its angle in synchronization with the frame rate from 45 degrees to 180 degrees. In this example the exposure time remains at a constant 1/192 of a second throughout the shot. The effects of exposure loss from a faster frame rate have been cancelled out by increasing the shutter angle. The shot, then, will be perfectly exposed from one end of the speed ramp to the other, and the viewer will be unaware of any visual clues that might indicate how it was done.

These factors are the variables used to understand and define a unified exposure formula as it relates to cinematography. First, however, an explanation of the f-stop must be provided. The f-stop is the mathematical means of indicating how large the lens aperture is, and most still photography lenses do indeed have f-stop markings. In practical use the f-stop is not entirely accurate, so on motion picture lenses the T-stop, which is determined by actual testing of the lens, is used instead. These are the ubiquitous numbers printed on every motion picture camera lens. Aperture control (the T-stop) is the most common method of controlling exposure in a motion picture camera.

The T-stop ring on a lens controls the iris, a meshed circle of light alloys (typically titanium) designed to restrict light flow into the camera. When the lens is wide open (at the lowest aperture number), usually at T-2 or T-1.4, the lens is passing all the light that technically can be passed through it, meaning it cannot pass any more light than that which the engraved maximum aperture stop indicates. The maximum aperture is derived from a simple formula based on the division of the focal length (mm) by the effective diameter of the lens opening in millimeters. For example, a 100mm lens that has an effective diameter of 25mm would be considered to have a maximum aperture of f-4. It is essentially a ratio between the focal length of the lens and the iris opening. A notation of speed, as it relates to lenses, is based on this information, so a lens that has a starting aperture of f-4 would be regarded as slow, while an f-2 would be considered fast, i.e., it passes more light.

From a physical standpoint, each f-stop (or T-stop) allows twice as much light or half as much light to pass through the lens. At this point, an explanation of how the f-stop numbers were mathematically acquired is of some importance. The starting f-stop is the square root of the number 1, which is, of course, 1. We then double the 1 and get 2, calculate the square root, double the 2 to 4, get the square root of 4, then 8, and so on to 16, 32, 64, etc., calculating the root as we go. If we take the square root of 1, 2, 4, and 8 we arrive at 1.0, 1.41, 2, and 2.82. These are the numbers that are subsequently printed on the lens itself. It should be noted that these numbers are rounded off, not consistently either, so the numbers that are normally marked on the lens are actually not mathematically accurate as far as precision is concerned. A lens with f-5.6 engraved on it is really 5.65, 11 is really 11.3, and so on. It is largely irrelevant except when we are dealing with formulas that require the exact number.

Modern and invariably complex lens design dictates that a formula that relies on a simple mathematical calculation such as the division of the focal length by the effective diameter of the lens opening in order to determine the maximum aperture is not always correct. How much light is actually getting through the elements is far more critical than a basic mathematical method. Lenses that contain multiple glass elements, sometimes as many as ten or more, such as zoom lenses, experience a drop in actual light transmission. Based on this fact, lens designers began engraving T-stops instead, which are accurate photometric measurements made at the rear of the lens. By using such a method manufacturers are able to produce lenses that are calibrated in direct relation to actual performance.

It is for this reason that most motion picture lenses are calibrated in T-stops. If the lens in use is calibrated in f-stops, the actual aperture may not correspond to the engraved number, and with a zoom lens the difference could be noticeable, in certain cases possibly a whole stop when using a long focal length.

Although most light meters will give a measurement as an f-stop, we still use T-stops for the lens setting. It may seem confusing at first, but the indications are the same for measurement purposes. As we stated earlier, the T-stop is just a more accurate method of defining an f-stop on a lens.

At this point two more factors need to be explained in order for the cinematographer to fully implement the multi-variable exposure formula. The first of these variables is exposure index (EI), which indicates the ability of the film stock to react to light. It is a rating that the manufacturer places on a specified emulsion after extensive testing. A higher number denotes a faster film (a more sensitive emulsion) while a low number denotes a slow film, or a less sensitive emulsion. Typical exposure indexes one might encounter are 50, 100, 200, and 500. Certain films, particularly black and white, may have two exposure indexes for different lighting conditions, i.e., daylight and tungsten, and in some cases, for a variety of reasons, a cinematographer may prefer to only use the manufacturer's exposure index as a starting point for further testing.

The numbers ascend and descend in 1/3 stop increments, or a factor of 1.26, i.e., the cube root of 2. If we double the number, we double the film speed. Thus 200 EI is half the sensitivity of 400 EI, or conversely, 400 EI is twice the sensitivity of 200 EI. We can also see an obvious relationship exists between f-stops and exposure index because there is a proportional similarity: a factor of 2. For example, if we are using a film with an exposure index of 100 with our lens set at f-5.6, and we decide to switch to 400 EI for the next shot, we will need to subtract 2 stops of exposure from our original f-stop. Assuming the shutter angle remains the same, the lens should now be set at f-11. Since the film is now four times faster, the aperture must be reduced by a similar factor: 4.

Other designations exist, such as in Germany where a system based on DIN indicates film sensitivity. Essentially each digit corresponds to a jump of 1/3 of a stop, with 21 being the equivalent to 100 EI. Given this example we can see that 18 DIN would be 50 EI.

The final variable, the last piece of the algebraic puzzle, is the light level. The light falling on the scene is the incident light, the so-called illumination, so by using a light meter which can measure such a value properly, we can determine how many footcandles of light are available. A footcandle is essentially the same as a candela, with a footcandle being derived from the amount of light produced one foot from the candle source. This is defined as one footcandle.

Now we have the ability to calculate exposure as it relates to the camera. The answer to such a formula is given as an f-stop, so we can directly change our lens aperture for the correct exposure. Most light meters can now calculate the f-stop, but it is helpful to understand the mathematics involved.

The variables are the exposure index of the film stock, the shutter angle of the camera, the frame rate of the camera, and the footcandles measured. These are incorporated into the formula:

$$T = \sqrt{(E(A/360/S)/(25/F))}$$

Exposure Index = E
Shutter Angle = A
Frames Per Second = S
Footcandles = F

On the following pages are several examples illustrating the multi-variable exposure formula with preset variables. When using a calculator with direct algebraic notation capability, the user may directly enter the formula with actual values in substitution for the letters. For standard calculators the formula must be done in steps. A scientific calculator program follows.

$$T = \sqrt{(E(A/360/S)/(25/F))}$$

Example 1,

E = 500	172.8/360/24 = .02
A = 172.8	500 × .02 = 10
S = 24	25/100 = .25
F = 100	10/.25 = 40
	$\sqrt{40}$ = 6.3

1/10th Calculation:
log 40/log 2 = 5.321...
Integer is 5, thus $\sqrt{(2^5)}$ = 5.65
Decimal is 1/10th = .3

Example 2,

E = 200	172.8/360/24 = .02
A = 172.8	200 × .02 = 4
S = 24	25/50 = .5
F = 50	4/.5 = 8

$\sqrt{8}$ = 2.82   *or*   log8/log2 = 3
$\sqrt{(2^3)}$ = 2.82

Scientific Calculator Program: Multi-Variable Exposure
(for Casio scientific and graphing calculators)

```
"Exposure Index"?→E:
"Footcandles"?→F:
"Shutter Angle"?→S:
"F.P.S."?→P:
(E(S/360/P)/(25/F))→A:
log A/log 2→B:
Int B→Z:
"Stop":
√(2^Z)▲
"Tenth":B-Z
```

EXPOSURE CHART (172.8 @ 24 F.P.S.)								
STOP	1.4	2	2.8	4	5.6	8	11	16
25(EI)	100fc	200	400	800	1625	3250	6500	12800
32	80	160	320	640	1290	2580	5160	10000
40	64	125	250	500	1000	2000	4100	8200
50	50	100	200	400	800	1625	3250	6500
64	40	80	160	320	640	1290	2580	5160
80	32	64	125	250	500	1000	2000	4100
100	25	50	100	200	400	800	1625	3250
125	20	40	80	160	320	640	1290	2580
160	16	32	64	125	250	500	1000	2000
200	12	25	50	100	200	400	800	1625
250	10	20	40	80	160	320	640	1290
320	8	16	32	64	125	250	500	1000
400	6	12	25	50	100	200	400	800
500	5	10	20	40	80	160	320	640
640	4	8	16	32	64	125	250	400
800	3	6	12	25	50	100	200	400
1000	2.5	5	10	20	40	80	160	320

TABLE 2.1 Exposure chart.

SHUTTER ANGLE (Degrees)	EXPOSURE TIME (@24 f.p.s.)	COMPENSATION (1/10ths)	
180	1/48	.058	(0)
172.8	1/50	0	
170	1/51	–.02	(0)
160	1/54	–.11	(1/8)
150	1/58	–.20	(1/4)
140	1/62	–.30	(1/3)
130	1/66	–.41	(1/2)
120	1/72	–.52	(1/2)
110	1/78	–.65	(2/3)
100	1/86	–.78	(2/3)
90	1/96	–.94	(1)
80	1/108	–1.11	(1 1/8)
70	1/123	–1.30	(1 1/3)
60	1/144	–1.52	(1 1/2)
50	1/173	–1.78	(1 2/3)
40	1/216	–2.11	(2 1/8)
30	1/288	–2.52	(2 1/2)
20	1/432	–3.11	(3 1/8)
11.2	1/771	–3.95	(4)

TABLE 2.2 Exposure time and compensation with modified shutter angle.

The Camera and Exposure

FRAMES PER SEC.	EXPOSURE TIME (@172.8 degrees)	COMPENSATION
120	1/250	–2 1/3
96	1/200	–2
76	1/160	–1 2/3
60	1/125	–1 1/3
48	1/100	–1
38	1/80	–2/3
30	1/60	–1/3
24	1/50	0
19	1/40	+ 1/3
15	1/30	+ 2/3
12	1/25	+ 1
9.5	1/20	+ 1 1/3
7.5	1/15	+ 1 2/3
6	1/12	+ 2

TABLE 2.3 Exposure time and compensation with modified frame rate.

3

Hats at High Noon

MEASURING LIGHT
AND ASSESSING EXPOSURE

It is unrealistic to expect acceptable or consistent exposure results without a certain degree of exactitude regarding the measurement of light. Given the level of importance in providing quality images in any production, almost every director of photography will have at least one incident light meter on the set, and in many cases this will be supplemented by a spot meter.

When using any light meter it is important that one understand the terms which describe the different types of measurement. Light which is incident, or falling on the scene, is called illuminance. Incident light meters, therefore, strictly measure illuminance and are unaffected by scene reflectance. Luminance, on the other hand, is the measure of light reflected from a surface or a self-illuminated object, so it is directly related to the reflectance of a scene. Reflected light meters provide luminance measurements.

It is critical to differentiate between the two, as many meters can provide both measurements with the removal, or addition, of a hemispherical diffusion attachment and by adjusting the direction the meter is pointed in. Obviously the specific meter manual should be consulted regarding the proper setup for such a conversion, and it should be duly noted that when the meter is in the reflected light mode it is important that the incident light values are not used, i.e., footcandles or lux.

Whether analog or digital, all meters use the same basic principle of a light-sensitive photocell. Older and invariably less complex meters usually have a simple scale and registering needle. Many of these also have calibrated rings that can be turned to provide various exposure calculations once a measurement has been taken. The negative aspect of needle-indicating meters, beside the obvious fact that they are mechanical, is that precision is compromised. In comparison to newer electronic meters, which are accurate to 1/10th of a stop, the analog meter is relatively imprecise. However, a light meter of this design is still perfectly acceptable and is useful even if only as a backup. Although malfunctions are rare, the meter's calibration is not guaranteed forever. All meters should be regularly checked for calibration using either another meter (and it is a good idea to own at least two in the event that one fails) or by sending it back to the manufacturer every few years.

Digital meters have an advantage over analog meters in that they are far more sensitive and react instantaneously. This is in large part due to the superior silicon blue and silicon photodiode cells. These meters also have an added degree of exactitude because mechanical parts, such as dials and indicator needles which are generally the source of calibration errors, have been eliminated. Another very attractive feature is the integration of a microprocessor chip which performs all the exposure calculations given the user input values. Depending on the model, this can range from the most basic of photographic exposure parameters to the highly specialized. For example, some of the latest light meters designed specifically for cinematography can include in the exposure calculation the shutter angle of the camera. Meters which are capable of such computations almost eliminate the need for mathematically calculating exposure variables, but they do not provide every frame rate or shutter angle, so formulas are still useful.

The measurements that light meters provide will vary according to both the design (whether reflected or incident) and the intended use. Light meters which can be readily converted (those which can be configured to read both incident and reflected light) will indicate an f-stop given the exposure index and frames per second. F-stops are commonly used in these types of meters because they can be used interchangeably regardless of the mode. When employing meters that do not have a frame rate function or the appropriate scale, an exposure time of 1/50th of a second is used as a substitute. In a situation where the closest exposure time available on a meter is 1/60th of a second, closing the aperture by 1/3 of a stop from the meter reading will give the correct exposure. Of course, this only applies to 24 frames per second and a 180 degree shutter angle.

In the case of some specialized incident meters, direct illuminance measurements are also available. Technically, the hemispherical attachment, which is normally covering the photocell for incident readings, must be replaced by a flat diffuser disk to directly read footcandles or lux. A footcandle is defined as the light output produced from a candle at a distance of exactly one foot—the term essentially explains itself. Lux, which is a metric measurement, is the amount of light from the same standardized source at exactly one meter. One footcandle is equal to 10.76 lux, so one can easily convert between the two values by multiplying the footcandle answer by 10.76 to get the lux equivalent, or dividing the lux answer by 10.76 to get the footcandle equivalent. Most electronic meters that provide such a measurement have the ability to switch between lux and footcandles. While a footcandle measurement is far from an absolute necessity for calculating exposure, there is still an advantage in that exposure charts and mathematical equations can be used more readily, and the measurement is entirely independent of photographic terminology. It is for this reason that the footcandle measurement is very useful for lighting.

Reflected meters, which can be either a general wide-angle type or a narrow-angle spot meter, will normally provide f-stops or, in some cases, an exposure value (EV). There are a few spot meters which directly measure luminance, such as candelas per square meter (cd/m^2) or candelas per square foot (cd/ft^2), but these meters are not really designed as exposure meters because the spectral sensitivity of the cell is based on the Commission International de L'Eclairage (CIE) photopic luminosity curve. In other words, they are matched to the spectral response of the eye and therefore are used primarily for assessing screen brightness (luminance).

Light meters designed for photographic exposure purposes have a spectral sensitivity which attempts to mimic that of film, and many of these meters employ some degree of custom filtering to produce a closer approximation. While it is rare, there are situations where the approximating spectral response of the meter compared to that of the film stock may produce unacceptable results. This can occur when a light source is limited to very narrow wavelengths, with an output of uncommon spectral power distribution, which may affect the accuracy of an incident reading, or when using a spot meter to take measurements from spectrally pure colors. Under these circumstances the disparity between the spectral response of the meter and that of the film might be drastic enough to produce incorrect exposure. It is preferable to make preliminary test exposures if in doubt before actually shooting the scene. Errors in exposure under these circumstances can also be caused by forgetting to make the appropriate compensation if heavy filtering is employed on the camera, i.e., when an odd illuminant is being used.

The underlying concept in the calibration of all light meters is the mid-scale or 18 percent gray card; this card has a reflectance of exactly 18 percent. Perceptually the card is a middle gray, and was derived from an average between a typical light tone and typical dark tone in a normal scene. Since film can only record a finite range of exposures (the so-called exposure range), the key to proper exposure is providing a method of getting the average reflectance object to be exposed approximately in the middle of the film's exposure curve. By calibrating light meters to 18 percent gray, which is the average reflectance of a normal scene, and assuming the recommended exposure index is used, one can be guaranteed of proper mid-scale tone placement. There is a limitation to how literal the concept can be taken, and as we will see it is largely dependent on the meter type itself.

Incident meters are designed to always produce a mid-scale gray reading regardless of the scene tones, whereas reflected meters are only accurate when the area of measurement is exactly 18 percent gray. If the measured area does not contain mostly mid-tones, the reflected light reading will only be approximate. In fact, the only reason why typical reflected light meters work at all for regular photography is because they have a wide acceptance angle, usually 30 to 50 degrees, which allows an averaging of the scene to take place. Because the reflected meter is completely dependent on either a gray card or user interpolation for accuracy, the incident meter is generally more popular with cinematographers. For this reason we will explain this type of meter first, and the two types of reflected meters, the wide-angle and the narrow-angle spot, second.

The incident meter, in fact, is simply a reflected meter with a diffusing sphere placed over the photocell. Since this type of meter is measuring illumination, it is pointed at the camera from the subject's location or, in some cases, at the light source. The ability of this meter to register an exposure at 18 percent gray is based on the principle that the diffuser over the photocell should reflect 82 percent of the incident light and allow only 18 percent of the light to hit the photocell. We can see this is the case when examining any hemispherical diffuser, as they are always constructed from white translucent plastic. In effect, we have converted our reflected light meter into a portable, self-reading gray card.

Therefore, the incident meter will always give an 18 percent gray reading based on the illumination. It is unbiased by scene factors such as bright skies or dark trees, and will always place objects of a given reflectance in their relative steps. Lighter tones, such as many faces, will be approximately 1/2 to 1 stop over mid-scale gray, while white surfaces will be about 2 stops over mid-scale gray, and dark surfaces around 3 stops under mid-scale gray. The advantage of this design is that we can get consistent results without having to resort to complex multiple measurements or averaging techniques.

On occasion, when the subject is either excessively dark or light, and showing detail is important in the final projected print, modification of the incident meter's measurement must be applied. When the subject is darker than normal, compensation can be made by opening the lens aperture 1/2 to 1 stop, which will provide better detail in the darker tones. A scene with lighter than normal tones will require the opposite: the aperture should be reduced by at least 1/2 to 1 stop in order to allow more detail in the highlights. This is necessary because the incident metering method does not take scene reflectance into account.

Most incident light meters have both a hemispherical (dome) attachment for general use and a flat diffuser disc for measuring lights. When the subject is absolutely flat, as in a painting or photograph, the flat disc can be used for exposure purposes. The hemispherical diffuser was designed to produce a more accurate method of exposure determination with normal subjects, as it allows all the light falling onto the dome to be measured. By having a three-dimensional light collector, the meter can take into account other lights being used in the scene at different angles and, more importantly, the ambient fill light that is naturally reflected from the scene or produced with supplemental lighting units. Fill light will add to the exposure when the ratio of key to fill is low, such as 2:1 or 3:1. It is for this reason that the hemispherical attachment is recommended for exposure purposes.

The measuring technique one uses for an incident meter can affect the resulting exposure to a large degree. It has been noted that an incident meter can be made to read virtually any stop depending on how it is angled or shaded with the hand. Given the fact that as little as 1/3 of a stop change in exposure is detectable by eye when viewing projected color film, this might appear to present a problem. The most commonly recommended method of measuring incident light is by using the hemispherical collector, as noted before, and then simply aiming the meter at the camera from the subject. In practice, many tend to turn the meter's dome in the direction of the key light as the angle of the light becomes greater from the camera's longitudinal axis.

In fact, there is a serious limitation as to how literally one can take the advice of measuring towards the camera because the key light can be coming from any direction. For example, when dealing with a single source that is directly opposite the camera lens, such as a backlight, the basic metering technique will entirely expose for the shadows (the hemisphere is blocked from the back), so in this case if we want our backlight to be our exposing light (key), the meter must be pointed at the light and not at the camera. The logic of this last example is exemplified if one imagines dollying from the shadow side of the subject to a sidelight position, as this technique will allow such a move without an undesirable exposure at the end of the shot; whereas if we expose for the shadow side, as the camera moves around to the side of the subject, overexposure will occur. The reality is that the key light can be coming from anywhere so one must, to a certain degree, favor this key light measuring method over the strictly academic process of aiming the meter at the camera. Therefore, the metering technique is based on the scene itself and which light is defined as the key source.

Exteriors require a different methodology altogether when using an incident meter because contrast is typically a problem. Using the sun as a backlight or sidelight will reduce the contrast by exposing more for the shadows, which is the natural result of pointing the meter towards the camera in such a situation. If the sunlight is coming from behind the camera, i.e., front light, very harsh modeling of the subject can occur, not only because the sun generally produces a most uncompromising light quality (except early or late in the day), but because we are measuring the direct light, and this in turn produces the darkest shadows. Shielding the top of the hemisphere can also help when shooting exteriors, as under these circumstances the midday sun will hit the top of the meter and cause a higher reading. This can create dark eye sockets and odd facial shadows, and the only effective remedy is a reflector board or a daylight-balanced lighting fixture of high output. Hats at high noon can be a hopeless cause unless, of course, your main actor is supposed to look like a raccoon.

The basic reflected light meter is used from the camera position and pointed at the subject. Very rarely is this type of meter used by professionals because the wide acceptance angle creates doubt in what exactly is being measured, and therefore produces difficult scene interpretation by the user. The spot meter solves this problem by the addition of a reflex viewfinder and a very narrow acceptance angle, usually 1 degree. Verification of exact subject values can be readily determined by using such a meter.

Spot meters are very effective luminance measuring instruments, but in order to use them correctly a few principles must be understood. The most basic way of explaining a spot meter would be to simply state that it measures the subject matter, whatever that may be, and exposes it at exactly 18 percent gray. It may seem somewhat confusing why this happens, but it will gradually become obvious how this works and why it works. Since the reflected light meter is designed to only produce a correct exposure when the area being measured is exactly 18 percent gray (it will give the same exposure as an incident meter), it can be assumed that when the meter is pointed at an area that is not mid-scale gray it will be modified by the degree of reflectance from the subject. This is precisely what happens, and is the reason why spot meters and reflected meters cannot correctly indicate a mid-scale exposure without a gray card. Therefore, if the area measured is lighter or darker than the standard 18 percent gray, these meters will be simply providing the exposure to place that sampled tone at mid-scale.

Assuming the measured object is not 18 percent gray one must extrapolate a correct exposure based on the gray scale. For visualizing tone placement the gray scale is a superb tool, as it is based on a specified incremental system. By starting with 18 percent as middle gray, one can simply double this number to create the next higher reflectance tone, i.e., a factor of 2. If we remember that each f-stop more in exposure is double the light, it makes sense that each tone should be twice the reflectance or half the reflectance in order to create a proportionately accurate scale in whole stops. In practice, most gray scales are produced by taking the cube root of 2, i.e., 1.26, and multiplying (or dividing) 18 by 1.26 in order to get 1/3 stop increments between the reflectance values. In the case of 1/2 stop increments, one can use the square root of 2 as a substitute, e.g., $18 \times 1.41 = 25$ percent, and so on.

Another way of looking at it, in logarithmic terms, is by finding the log (base 10) of 90 percent, i.e., .05, and adding .1 (the log of 1.26) to .05, which is the reflectance density of our original 90 percent white. Since .1 is the equivalent of 1/3 of a stop, we can produce the same scale using this method. If the number of significant digits is limited to one to the right of the decimal point, the scale appears as 0, .1, .2, .3, .4, .5, through 1.1, 1.2, 1.3, and so on (see Figure 3.1).

The gray scale contains three sets of numbers, where one series is the reflectance of the sample, another the f-stop difference between mid-scale (18 percent) gray and the sample, and the last set the reflectance density $D(r)$. In order to convert from one value to the other, a simple set of formulas can be applied. For example, to convert a reflectance percentage to a reflectance density, calculate the log of the reflectance, e.g., log of .18 equals .74 $D(r)$. In order to find the reflectance percentage from a reflectance density, one must use the antilog (10^x) function, e.g., $100/(10^{D(r)})$; $100/(10^{.74})$ equals 18 percent. When converting density to f-stops a formula is not necessary, as each .1 (log) is the equivalent of 1/3 of a stop. For example, the difference between .74 and .44 is exactly 1 stop, i.e., .74–.44 = .3 (log), or 1 full stop.

An understanding of the gray scale allows one to use a spot meter very effectively. For example, when measuring a surface of 72 percent reflectance (an average white), if a reading is taken literally without regard for the previously enumerated facts, it is obvious that the meter is simply providing a mid-scale exposure for this tone; therefore it is valid to assume that the exposure as given will be approximately 2 stops underexposed, because a tone of 72 percent is exactly 2 stops higher in reflectance value. Moreover, if the lens aperture was, in fact, set to this exposure, the white area would appear to be more gray than white on the final print. In a mathematical sense, the meter incorrectly placed this tone 4 times darker. The error is derived from the

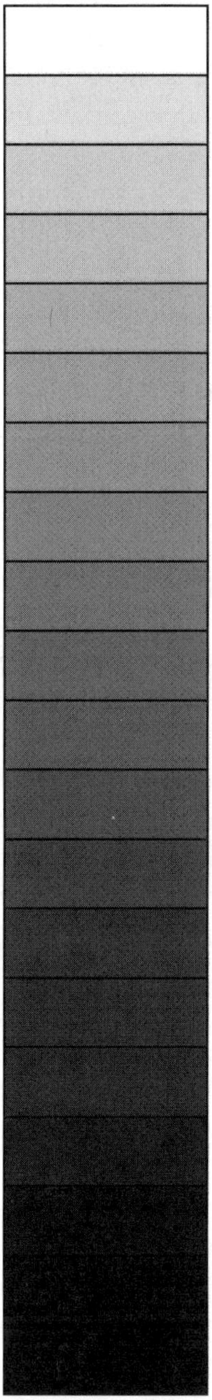

	+ 2 1/3	90 %	D(r) .05
	+ 2	72 %	D(r) .1
	+ 1 2/3	57 %	D(r) .2
	+ 1 1/3	45 %	D(r) .3
	+ 1	36 %	D(r) .4
	+ 2/3	28 %	D(r) .5
	+ 1/3	23 %	D(r) .6
	N	18 %	D(r) .7
	–1/3	14 %	D(r) .8
	–2/3	11 %	D(r) .9
	–1	9 %	D(r) 1.0
	–1 1/3	7 %	D(r) 1.1
	–1 2/3	5.7 %	D(r) 1.2
	–2	4.5 %	D(r) 1.3
	–2 1/3	3.6 %	D(r) 1.4
	–2 2/3	2.8 %	D(r) 1.5
	–3	2.25 %	D(r) 1.6
	–3 1/3	1.79 %	D(r) 1.7
	–3 2/3	1.40 %	D(r) 1.8
	–4	1.125 %	D(r) 1.9

FIGURE 3.1 Gray scale.

fact that a 72 percent white surface is reflecting exactly 4 times the light as a surface of 18 percent. In this example, in order to properly expose the tone in relation to mid-scale gray, we must add 2 stops (log4/log2) of exposure to the meter's indication, e.g., change the stop from T-8 to T-4.

When measuring a darker subject, for example, something that has a reflectance of 2.25 percent, the spot meter will still be indicating a reading to expose this tone at 18 percent gray, as it did unerringly in the last example. If this tone is a dark shadow in the scene, it can be guaranteed that if the lens is set to this given stop the whole image will appear overexposed and, consequently, all the shadows will be a medium gray. To properly expose this tone in its normal place, so that everything else in the scene will appear correctly, one must subtract 3 stops of exposure from that which is indicated, e.g., change the stop from T-4 to T-11. 2.25 percent is 8 times darker than 18 percent, so a change in aperture by a factor of 8 is necessary.

To counteract the inability of the spot meter to provide the correct exposure without a gray card, we must use our own visual interpretation of the tone and decide how many stops brighter or darker the measured area will be in relation to 18 percent gray. In the last two examples the reflectance of the tone was given, but in real scenes this fact will not be known and therefore it becomes to a large degree a matter of subjectivity. Of course, this explains why having a gray card or an incident meter is very handy, as it eliminates the uncertainty of how light or how dark scene tones are in relation to a medium gray.

A basic rule to follow with spot meters (and this is the key to their effectiveness when a gray card is not being used) is that if an object is brighter than 18 percent gray we must open our lens aperture accordingly, while if the object is darker than 18 percent gray (of lower reflectance) we must close our lens aperture accordingly. It is for this reason that the spot meter in the hands of an inexperienced operator can create confusing and difficult exposure interpretation. The fact that the meter is calibrated to indicate an exposure at 18 percent gray regardless of the actual measured tone must be clearly understood.

Using the same method as before, however not viewing it in the same sense of attempting to provide a proper scene exposure through interpretation of measured reflectance, but rather specific tone placement, which may or may not agree with a mid-scale exposure, the user is given a very simple method of guaranteeing that certain subjects are exposed at a specific point on the film's exposure curve. The fact that we can use a spot meter to determine the exposure of any subject at mid-scale gray, without calculation or real effort, allows unprecedented control over the placement of subject tones. For example, if a silhouette is required for a particular shot, it is easier and far more precise to use a spot meter. To create such an image, the subject is measured from the camera and the resulting f-stop, which will be indicative of a mid-scale exposure, is selectively modified by closing the lens aperture at least 4 stops from that which is indicated. By changing our stop in this fashion the subject tone itself will expose 4 stops below mid-scale, which will render a nearly black image—a silhouette. The incident meter could be used in the same situation also, but since it does not take scene reflectance into account, if the subject is lighter than normal the resulting 4 stops of underexposure from the incident meter's indicated lens aperture may not completely darken the subject and produce the desired silhouette.

The real benefit of the spot meter, or any accurately used reflected light meter, is the ability to make comparisons to a gray card or an incident measurement of the same scene, which will indicate precisely where the individual scene tones will be placed relative to your exposure. Shadow detail is frequently of concern, and when dealing with windows or practical lamps, spot meters are crucial for making an accurate assessment. By measuring the darkest and the brightest tones in a scene we can also determine if the exposure range of the film stock can capture all the details.

The spot meter used with an 18 percent gray card can be as effective as an incident meter, although the angle the gray card is held at can affect the overall accuracy and a second person is usually required to hold the card. If the spot meter has a multiple memory function, taking the first reading from the gray card can then allow the user to compare further readings to the original exposure measurement in the same way that a separate incident reading can be compared. It cannot be understated that spot meters are a boon in situations of duress.

Light meters are also used to determine lighting ratios and luminance ratios. A lighting ratio is defined as the difference between the key light and the fill light, or key plus fill and fill alone, as it is assumed that fill light will add to the overall exposure if the ratio is low enough.

In order to determine lighting ratios, one must use an incident meter, or a spot meter and a gray card. Whether the results are produced in footcandles or f-stops is irrelevant, as a ratio can be easily determined based on the difference between the two measurements. This can be done by first measuring the key, and then blocking the key light with your hand in front of the meter's dome so that only the fill light is hitting the sensor. For example, by taking a key reading of 80 foot-candles and a fill reading of 20 footcandles, a ratio of 4:1 is procured.

In other words, our key light is four times as powerful as our fill light. If you are using a meter that only has f-stops, another method must be employed. Between each stop a factor of 2 exists, i.e., twice as much light or half as much light. A difference of 1 stop is a 2:1 ratio, while 2 stops creates a 4:1 ratio and 3 stops produces an 8:1 ratio. If we remember that between each stop is a factor of 2, and 1/3 of a stop is 1.26 whereas 2/3 of a stop is 1.6, virtually any ratio can be computed.

In using these ratios we can create a mental file for image contrast. A ratio of 2:1 can be considered low contrast, meaning the shadows are weak and show much detail. If the ratio is expanded to 4:1, it can be assumed an appreciable drop in shadow definition will occur in certain areas of the scene, particularly those that are not reflecting significant amounts of light; and at 8:1 or higher, the scene will start to look considerably contrasty. In using such a system the cinematographer can easily relate a ratio to a desired look.

A lighting ratio is a somewhat overly academic process, and over time most will agree it is a useful but not imperative system of lighting. In certain cases, though, particularly when working on locations where the lighting rigs must be taken down every day, having a lighting ratio can simplify the matching of light setups from day to day.

A luminance ratio, which should not be confused with a lighting ratio, is simply the difference between two measurements taken with a reflected type meter, such as a spot meter. For example, if the results of our measurements yield f-2.8 and f-5.6, we know the ratio is 4:1. A 7 stop range, a more typical result during exterior measurements, would be a luminance ratio of 128:1 (2^7). Such a ratio is very useful for determining if the film emulsion has the exposure range available to reproduce the scene accurately, which makes it extremely useful for determining the probable results before the film is actually exposed.

While film exposure tends to be used as an objective term, subjectivity is added into the equation when one considers that lighting and exposure are interrelated. Nonetheless, there are very obvious and important objective considerations that must be accepted in order to produce an image which can even begin to be defined as properly exposed, but these, as implied, are mainly relegated to purely technical concerns.

Clearly, in order to provide usable images, the cinematographer must be cognizant of the basic limitations of the film stock. Severe underexposure or overexposure will not be conducive to producing the best looking prints, and there are different reasons for both. When an image is underexposed, in the most serious of cases, the negative will print too low on the printer lights, and this will invariably create prints with smoke-gray blacks instead of the rich black tones produced from a normally exposed negative. Conversely, in the case of extreme overexposure it may not be possible to print the image correctly either, although this is generally easier to correct than the former example. A print of good quality, therefore, is the product of a correctly exposed negative.

Determining a correct exposure involves more factors than just objective light measurement, because experience and intuition affect the decision-making process to a large degree. In most cases it is impractical to painstakingly measure every tone in a scene, so for purposes of speed it is wise to accept a limitation on this technique. It can also be said that creativity will lag if emphasis is placed entirely on the technical concepts of tone reproduction, and furthermore, calculated experimentation is the key to improving subjective judgment and the on-screen results.

Clearly, by applying scientific principles to your assessment of a scene, and following an objective system of exposure determination, one can very easily produce a justifiably proper exposure. In itself, this is not a particularly challenging task given the right tools and equipment, but the salient issue is whether the results are not only technically acceptable but creatively acceptable. Therefore, one must admit, correct exposure is also based on creative decisions, and so one must begin to think in terms of lighting, not simply technically correct exposure. In other words, the scene may contain a variety of light levels, but likely only one of which coincides with our so-called "exposure level." The other areas will therefore expose differently, either lighter or darker, but this is what adds realism to the picture. If everything were similarly exposed, in a flat, evenly lit fashion, the result would be bland and uninteresting. The use of light and shadow is the key to producing depth and separation in two dimensions, be it by a flicker, a glint, or a murky gloom.

Exposure is also relative to the scene and the individual shots within the scene. A still photographer can think in terms of a single photograph, but the director of photography must take into account a much larger concept during production. Shots are edited together to form the final motion picture, and rarely is anything shot in sequence, so having shots match from cut to cut is imperative. They must appear consistent within the framework of the scene, so a certain degree of editorial respect must be followed. Shots that cannot be matched within the scene present difficulties for both the editor, who may reject a poorly exposed one in favor of another, and the color timer, who is left with the grim prospect of getting this material consistent.

A brief description of a few theoretical scenes can elucidate the requirements. Given a medium-sized room with one key light providing a strong overhead illumination and no supplemental fill light except the natural bounce from the walls, if the main subject (actor) is sitting under the source and we measure the light with an incident meter, we can determine our basic exposure. If that was the only shot in the scene, and we had none other in the same location, it would really be as simple as that—unless of course we purposely wanted the subject darker or lighter than normal, essentially changing the dynamics of the scene through under- or overexposure. If, for example, we want to have the actor bathed in a very bright light, and this is the intention of the director, then we can go ahead and purposely overexpose our subject. How many stops over normal exposure is purely a creative decision. Basically this is an example which proves we do not always inexorably follow the mid-tone exposure principle, and there are many more like it.

Now assume, using the same setup as before (but normally exposed), that we introduce another character into the same shot, but in a different location. If the director called for a two-shot, where both actors are visible at the same time, it seems more than likely that common sense would dictate that the same exposure should be used in order for proper exposure to be made with the original subject under the key light. That assumption would be correct, of course, but what about the other actor who may not be under the key? Well, we still expose for the key, and wherever the other actor may be in the room is irrelevant, because he or she is not under the same illumination and therefore should not be exposed as such. This may seem quite obvious and basic, but where this presents a problem is in contrasty, low light level scenes where the other actor may literally be standing in the inky shadows by the walls. If we decide to cut to a close-up before the character has moved into the light, assuming he or she will for the dialogue shots, the exposure must match the wider angle two-shot, which may have been (as far as the actor who was not under the key goes) virtually nonexistent. Obviously we could introduce fill light, or another source, allowing us to show more detail in the second actor's close-up, but that has to be decided before we shoot any establishing shots, which will typically show the whole room.

In the example just noted, we are, for the sake of continuity, forced to expose the close-up the same as the wide angle. Now, one may decide the shot is too dark and cheat with other lights for the close-up, which is very common, but it must be done in a subtle fashion because any serious lighting difference will be noticeable. In other words, the tones must remain proportional within the shot. In this example we have not followed the principles outlined in the mid-scale gray procedure. Instead we have made an intuitive decision based on logic. If we had set our exposure according to an incident measurement of this area of the room, a rather severe mismatch between the two-shot and the close-up would have occurred.

Exposure is a sliding scale, a scale which can be shifted according to the requirements of the scene. While many use the terms over- and underexposure as definitions of the circumstances enumerated earlier, it can be a confusing way of defining such a decision for many because it seems to imply an error. In fact it is just another method of indicating tone placement and the subsequent choice of tonal shift as decided by the director of photography. Since an exposure decision for one tone will affect all the other tones in the scene, it can be a very practical description.

When shooting night scenes (at night), where we must have a dark and contrasty image, if we decide that the faces must be at least 2 stops underexposed, we can measure these subject tones with our spot meter and then close down the lens aperture 2 stops from the indicated reading. In this fashion we have created the required exposure for the scene based on tone placement and, in effect, have underexposed the whole scene in order to get these results. Somewhere else in the same scene a street lamp may be lighting a row of parked cars to a light level which actually may be the recommended exposure, but this is perfectly realistic if the current shot is taking place in the shadowy areas away from the lights. Contrast, then, is the tool one uses to create the mood of an image, and exposure is just part of that creative process. It has been said many times before, but it is still a very important statement: *Meters only measure light, they do not decide how you are going to expose your film.*

Our goal, when we set the T-stop on the lens, is to be able to visualize the scene as it will look when it is reproduced on the theater screen or the television monitor. We do not have the capability of viewing a film image instantly, and therefore substantial faith is required during the initial image gathering process.

4

Furnace of Light

COLOR TEMPERATURE

The perceived color of objects within a scene is largely dependent on the illuminant. We are not perceptually aware of this fact because our eyes adapt to the light source so well, and only in extreme cases are we certain that colors are being abnormally portrayed. Film is not so forgiving, as it can only accurately reproduce color under very specific spectral conditions. Matching the appropriate illuminant to the film's color balance is relatively straightforward, but defining the spectral quality of a particular light source is not so simple.

Illuminants can be described using a spectral power distribution graph, which will indicate the power (radiance) in relation to the wavelength. Because we are only interested in visible radiation, a very narrow band of electromagnetic radiation, typical measurements are made from 400nm to 700nm (light).

The spectral power distribution graph shown in Figure 4.1 indicates the wavelength in nanometers on the x-axis and relative power on the y-axis. By plotting power in relation to wavelength a curve can be formed (these are generally normalized at 550nm). A graph such as this can be produced by using a spectroradiometer measuring in at least 10nm bands, although greater precision is possible when using narrower bands. The benefit of knowing the spectral power distribution of an illuminant is that the spectral characteristics are well defined; however, due to the impracticality of identifying an illuminant by its spectral power distribution, color temperature is frequently used instead.

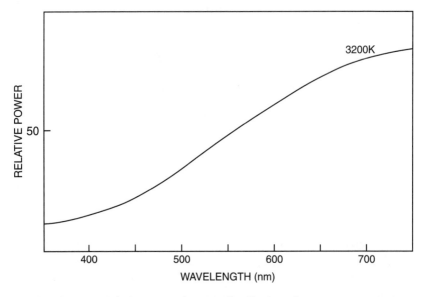

FIGURE 4.1 Relative spectral power distribution of a tungsten halogen lamp.

The concept of color temperature was derived from scientific experimentation involving approximate black body radiators such as metal filaments and bars, eventually leading to the realization that the spectral power distribution of the emitted light was directly related to the temperature at which the object (black body) was heated. The Kelvin scale, a temperature designation established by Lord Kelvin, is used to indicate a color temperature, where the degree symbol is omitted and a capital K is used as an abbreviation.

While the term in photographic applications is used to define the spectral power distribution of light, it is, in fact, the temperature in Kelvin of the black body radiator. It is derived from the comparison of a light source to a black body radiator which emits a visibly similar light, where the temperature of the black body radiator defines the color temperature of the source in question. Due to the lack of an ideal black body radiator the actual values are approximations based upon testing.

What can be determined by these experiments is that black body radiators (also known as Planckian radiators) at different temperatures emit varied but predictable spectral power distributions (Figure 4.2). Assume, for ease of clarification, that we are using a metal bar as our radiator. When initially heated it will exhibit a noticeable reddish tinge, and eventually over time it will turn orange, then yellow, and if the furnace can be truly superheated, possibly blue. Essentially the hotter the object gets, the bluer the light becomes and the greater the energy output.

The reason why this spectral energy shift occurs can be directly attributed to the fact that as the object becomes hotter the wavelengths become predominantly shorter. Accepting that higher numbers in a temperature scale are higher temperatures, we can define 9500K as bluish light and 3200K as reddish light. In describing a light source using color temperature, we are essentially defining the spectral power distribution, but, as we will soon realize, there is a limitation to this classification system.

The two most common light sources are tungsten and daylight, having associated color temperatures of 3200K and 5500K respectively. Tungsten lights are found in both the studio and the home. Those designed for professional lighting applications contain a small amount of halogen vapor to extend the life of the filament, and this feature is also found on some consumer products. The light produced by tungsten halogen lamps (and non-halogen tungsten) has a considerably different spectral power distribution from daylight, as indicated by the color temperature difference. Rich in long-wavelength radiation, tungsten halogen lamps emit light predominantly in the red and orange end of the spectrum, while daylight has far more blue content. Because tungsten filaments cannot be heated beyond a certain temperature (3750K) without melting, there is a limit placed on their maximum color temperature. The output is also dependent on the age of the lamp itself and the supply voltage, where older lamps and lower voltage combine to cause a decrease in color temperature.

Daylight is not just direct sunlight, but actually a product of both skylight and sunlight, where skylight is largely the result of short-wavelength radiation scattered by the atmosphere. Thus, the contribution of skylight generally produces a higher overall color temperature. The quoted 5500K is given as an average, and rarely will the cinematographer find this to be entirely accurate, particularly when the color temperature of daylight changes quite drastically over the course of a day. Therefore, regarding color temperature, we have only defined one relatively fixed light source (tungsten), and one highly variable light source (daylight).

Even given the variability of daylight many assumptions can be made without technically determining the color temperature with a color temperature meter. When the sky is clear, and it is not early morning or late afternoon, a color temperature of anywhere from 5500K to 6300K can be a reasonably accurate prediction. In overcast conditions, particularly thick and high cloud cover, the color temperature can increase substantially, in some cases to as high as 7300K. In this case, skylight is providing most of the illumination. When filming in the shade during the afternoon the color temperature will also be significantly higher (6000 to 7000K) due, in large part, to the lack of direct sunlight.

From sunrise to sunset, even on a clear day, the color temperature will change. During the early morning hours the sunlight will be filtered by the thicker atmosphere, giving the light a yellowish color (3600K to 4100K). Generally between early morning and noon a color

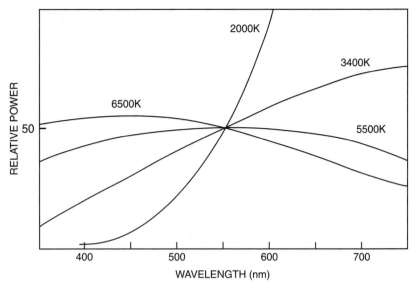

FIGURE 4.2 Relative spectral power distributions of black body radiators.

temperature of 4300K to 5500K is common, while true afternoon will be slightly higher (6000K). As the sun continues to descend the cycle is repeated again, though sunset is normally perceived as more reddish-orange (3000K) than sunrise.

Because it is impractical to design a color film emulsion for every light source, the color balance of film had to be limited to several standards, which are 3200K, 3400K, and 5500K. Film which is designated 3200K is intended to be used with tungsten halogen sources, while 3400K stock (not available in color negative stocks in the motion picture industry) is balanced for photofloods, a source used mainly in still photography. The 5500K film is designed to be used in daylight or with lights that approximate daylight output, such as metal halide lamps (HMIs).

Based on these circumstances several broad judgments can be made in reference to film stocks. Daylight-balanced film is rarely high-speed, i.e., fast-reacting, because the light levels are assumed to be far greater with sunlight or artificial daylight sources, which are far more efficient than their incandescent counterparts. Tungsten-balanced stocks, on the other hand, are available in a wide range of exposure indexes because far more control can be exercised over light levels when using studio-based lighting units and, furthermore, with the addition of a proper filter a tungsten stock can be balanced for daylight.

As stated earlier in the text, an emulsion must be color balanced for a very specific illuminant in order to reproduce accurate color. In the case of tungsten halogen sources the color temperature is fixed or easily controllable. Given the inconstant nature of color temperature when dealing with exteriors, an average is used, heretofore stated as 5500K, and provides the color temperature for which daylight stocks are balanced or tungsten stocks are corrected to when shooting in daylight. In practice, daylight-balanced film stock is not used as often as a 3200K film stock, but at any rate, the result is the same when a conversion filter is employed on the latter.

The only period of the day when light can be accurately stated to be neutral (white light) is during the middle portion of a day. The differences in color qualities between a sunrise, a sunset, or an overcast day are visually apparent, despite the eye's ability to adapt, and as exterior scenes usually contain a combination of skylight, sunlight, shadows, and reflected light, the eye tends to average these, favoring whichever predominates. In other words, despite the fact that the eye can adjust and compensate for color temperature variations, a sunset takes place amidst the ambient, overall illumination of skylight, and this is the color temperature which most heavily weights the average, not the orb of the sun itself or the atmosphere around it. Therefore, a pronounced disparity between the film image and our visual perception out of doors is not readily apparent even given the fact that film has a fixed color balance. This is not to say the color effect is precisely accurate, as there are atmospheric conditions which can result in a greatly exaggerated color bias, but for the most part 5500K-balanced film will suffice.

Given the practical nature of using filters for color balancing emulsions to illuminants, an extensive range of color conversion filters and light balancing filters have been produced. The usage of these selectively designed filters permits color balancing to be accomplished under almost any conditions.

The application of Wratten (Eastman Kodak) filters gives the cinematographer the ability to control color balance with the utmost precision when necessary. Whether the light is corrected at the source, as with lighting filters, or corrected at the camera, as with camera filters, it makes little difference, although in some cases there is little choice, i.e., the sun. Generally it is easier, and faster, to apply a filter over the lens rather than filter all the lights. It is for this reason that film manufacturers provide two exposure indexes on most films, where one is tungsten and the other is daylight, e.g., 5279 EI 500T/320(85B). By using any correctly chosen filter, precise control over color temperature can be obtained.

In order to properly utilize a stock that is balanced for 3200K in 5500K conditions, an 85B filter must be used. By doing so, the light reaching the film will be spectrally altered by the filter and will render a color temperature which corresponds to the film balance; the accuracy of this depends on the real color temperature of the source. Because the 85B filter is amber in color cast, it subtracts out the blue in daylight and provides a compatible balance for tungsten film (Figure 4.3). The tungsten-balanced stock is less sensitive to red light and, therefore, without the predominantly long-wavelength content of tungsten illumination, or the color converting 85B, the projected (uncorrected) print will produce a bluish picture.

56

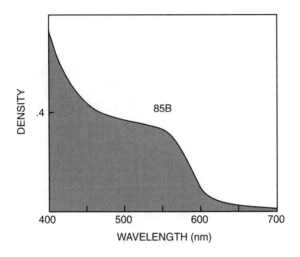

FIGURE 4.3 Density curve of 85B.

Daylight stocks, as we indicated earlier, have relatively equal spectral sensitivity, so the usage of a daylight-balanced film in a tungsten illuminated setting, as in a studio, would produce an excessive orange color cast on the projected print. If an 80A is used as a conversion filter, it will subtract out most of the long wavelengths in tungsten illumination, producing acceptable color reproduction (Figure 4.4). There is no practical reason to be doing this, as it makes far more sense to use 3200K film in a studio, where invariably the bulk of the lights available will be tungsten halogen anyway, and therefore no filter will be necessary.

There are rare circumstances when film that is balanced for tungsten light is used in daylight conditions without the appropriate filter. While a color conversion filter might not be used for creative reasons (in this case, cooler, bluer results), normally its omission is the result of light levels where adequate exposure is not possible, and the conversion filter, normally an 85B, is removed to allow more light to reach the film. Given that exposure time is more or less fixed on a motion picture camera, the only option, assuming force processing is out of the question, is to remove the filter. Surprisingly, the film will still be

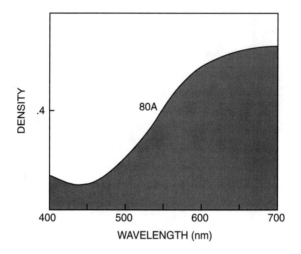

FIGURE 4.4 Density curve of 80A.

acceptable if the laboratory compensates when printing the negative, yet the degree of correction is not unlimited by any means, and in severe cases it will be impossible to produce a correctly color balanced print.

Based on this ability to correct such drastic color balance differences, it would seem that the cinematographer can ignore color temperature discrepancies when given such an option. This, of course, depends on what one considers a discrepancy and, more importantly, the degree of color correction possible in post production. A film to video transfer allows more control over such matters, whereas color timing in a film laboratory is somewhat limited. However, even given the degree of choice in such a decision, it should be stressed that the more one relies on the laboratory timer or video colorist, the less control one will have over the final result. In other words, it is possible to ignore color temperature to a large degree, but then the decisions regarding color balance will not always be your own.

Conversely, the concepts of color balancing and color temperature can be taken too far. Other than shadow length, there will be few clues as to time of day if the natural variance in color temperature is completely eliminated. Exceptions to this case are when scenes need to be matched over several days and the light must appear the same from shot to shot. Fine-tuning, though, should be left to the laboratory, video transfer, or other digital process, as there must be a sane limit to what can be accomplished on the set with filters and lighting gels.

In the case of mixed sources where a scene contains both tungsten lamps and daylight, but daylight is providing the exposure and color balance, such as that provided by windows on location, a creative decision must be made. If the tungsten sources are visible in the scene (which can be the case when using practicals), leaving them uncorrected probably provides the most realistic rendering because the eye adapts its color balance for the predominant illumination and the visual effect is appreciably orange anyway. It should be remembered that the luminance level of the lamp will also determine to a large degree the color results. An analogy to this situation can be made with car headlights: the lights will appear nearly white at night because our eyes have adjusted to the illuminant, but during the day they will appear quite orange. In the case of non-visible tungsten sources where there is apparently little motivation for its light (as in a previously established shot), the appearance will probably confuse the audience and seem rather odd. But this, too, will depend to a substantial degree on the scene itself.

By using color temperature one can indicate with reasonable accuracy the light output of a source, but it should be noted that there is a limit placed on the exactitude of this method because it can only be applied to sources which approximate a black body radiator, and secondly, it is not objective: we are strictly making a visual comparison during the assignment process. It may be true that tungsten halogen lamps and, for practical purposes, the sun, are reasonable matches for black body radiators, as they produce a spectral power distribution that is nearly identical to the light output of a similarly heated black body radiator, but as the light source is further removed from the heat/light relationship of a Planckian radiator, the results are almost useless.

When we consider the fact that not all light sources produce energy through the heating of filaments, e.g., studio quartz or household tungsten, the validity of color temperature designations becomes extremely questionable, particularly when dealing with non-black body radiators, i.e., non-incandescent sources. Therefore, lights that are based on gas discharge technology, such as fluorescent, are impossible to classify according to these guidelines. Unfortunately, it is common practice to use a correlated color temperature with such sources. This is done through the very questionable practice of comparing the light output of a black body radiator to the output of a non-black body source in order to render a comparable color temperature, normally quoted as a correlated color temperature.

The problems associated with using correlated color temperature in cinematography are manifold. Due to the fact that we are matching the two sources by eye, the discrepancies in spectral power distribution that are not evident visually will become readily apparent when filmed.

A fluorescent light that is given a correlated color temperature of 5500K may, indeed, visually match daylight, but excessive spectral energy in the green region will not be detectable to our eyes. When printed, the film will invariably cause the subject to have a very noticeable greenish tinge, which will probably not be appreciated unless you happen to be working on a science fiction film. It is for this reason that correlated color temperatures are not a good indication of reproduced color quality, and one should be wary of taking the figures literally (see Figures 4.5 and 4.6).

Fluorescent lights present a unique problem on location, but there are several methods of using them effectively. Given the type, such as cool white, warm white, warm white deluxe, etc., one can simply consult an appropriate chart and determine the recommended camera filters based on the color balance of the film. The problem, though, is usually much worse, as typically daylight will be entering into the room through windows. In this case it is usually safe to assume a cool white or cool white deluxe lamp, which means at least an 85 series filter to start with (if you are using 3200K film), while secondly, some degree of magenta or red color compensating filter will be required to subtract the excess green.

The unfortunate problem with this scenario is that the windows will still require plus-green over them in order to match the existing cool white fluorescent. So another choice might be to place filters directly over the fluorescent tubes, such as minus-green (magenta), and then shoot with a high-speed daylight film; however, this is just as

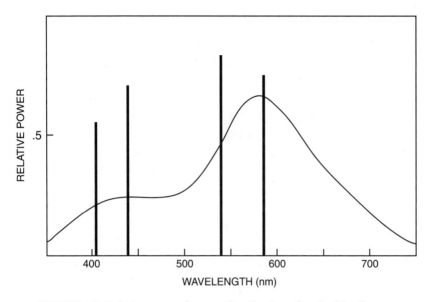

FIGURE 4.5 Relative spectral power distribution of cool white fluorescent. The discrete power spikes are caused by mercury vapor within the tube.

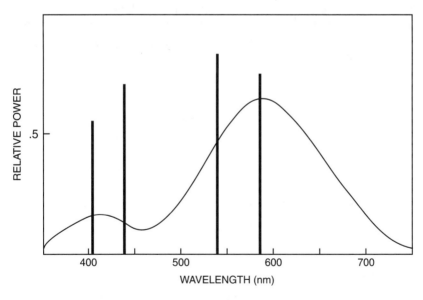

FIGURE 4.6 Relative spectral power distribution of warm white fluorescent. The discrete power spikes are caused by mercury vapor within the tube.

time-consuming, if not more so, as putting filter material over the windows. The problem is compounded by the fact that any supplemental lights must be matched to the existing fluorescents (plus-green) or at least filtered for daylight (in the case of tungsten halogen) when corrective measures have been made directly to the existing source. In the case of HMIs no daylight correction will be necessary, but plus-green will still be necessary in the latter case.

Where a mixture of tungsten and daylight along with fluorescent occurs, it can be nearly impossible to correct all the sources effectively. This is frequently a problem in museums, where skylights may be providing a general ambient daylight, and display cases are lit by a mixture of fluorescent lamps and photofloods. In this case it is usually best to balance for daylight if this is providing the base exposure, and then use a CC15M or CC30M on the camera lens. The photofloods will appear somewhat orange, but it is usually acceptable.

Concern over gas discharge sources is not unfounded, as virtually all of the lamps now used in large-scale commercial lighting applications fall into the category of high-intensity discharge (HID), such as mercury vapor, sodium vapor, and metal halide. These lamps produce light through an electrical current passing through a gas-filled quartz tube. The sealed tube usually contains mercury or various metal halides which are ionized by the electrical arc. Therefore the spectral power distribution of this source is dependent on the types of metals within the tube. Like fluorescent lamps, these lights can only be given a correlated color temperature, and the result of using such a source as your primary light (key) for filming can be very questionable unless certain precautions are taken.

There are several different methods of approaching the problem of gas discharge lamps. The first priority is to determine what type of lamp you are dealing with. There are several practical methods of narrowing down the possibilities. The initial assumption, of course, must be that the lamp is, in fact, a gas discharge variety. A method of verifying that you are dealing with a gas discharge lamp is to determine if there is a warm-up time. Any light which requires a warm-up time, where the full output is not obtained until the lamp has been turned on for a few minutes, is definitely a gas discharge variety, i.e., HID.

The visual color of the light output is another method of identification. If the light is yellow-orange, it is likely to be high-pressure sodium. These do not produce a continuous spectrum of light. Lights which appear relatively neutral, or cause tungsten lights nearby to look orange, are probably metal halide. Mercury vapor lamps, now less common (as they have been largely superseded by metal halide), are typically deficient in long wavelength content, producing very pale skin tones.

Another factor to consider is location. Metal halide is usually restricted to situations where the level of light must be high and the area to be lit is large. Such circumstances are usually limited to large indoor or outdoor stadiums. Mercury vapor and sodium vapor are more frequently used for parking lots and roadways. Placing filters over the camera lens is the only quick method of correcting such sources, while in certain circumstances, though rarely, it is possible to gel the lights instead.

Shooting a film test is necessary for critical verification. Determining the filters necessary is not complicated, as many charts are available that will provide such corrections based on the general type or even, in certain cases, the exact brand. Correction of the light output, unfortunately, is not the only concern, as these sources are also prone to potentially serious exposure problems related to discontinuous output which is not detectable by the eye, but can be a serious problem when filming. This is caused by the supply frequency, where a 60Hz supply will cause 120 pulsations a second. Between these pulses—two for every cycle—a significant reduction in light output can occur. Because many newer installations of these types of lights are frequently run from electronic ballasts, flicker may not always be a problem. The general rule, though, is that the exposure time should match the supply frequency, e.g., 1/60th of a second at 60Hz (144 degree shutter).

Metal halide lighting fixtures constructed for the specific purpose of professional film and video lighting applications are typically referred to as HMIs, and are designed to provide a color-correct daylight source (5500K), producing three times the luminous efficacy of the standard tungsten halogen lamp at a substantially reduced temperature. While the problem of flicker exists for these light sources when run from magnetic ballasts, newer electronic ballasts eliminate this detriment. Many manufacturers now provide flicker-free ballasts, allowing a greater range of freedom when different camera frame rates and shutter angles are being used.

Color temperature meters are the instruments we use for ascertaining color temperature. They are not as common as light meters, but have a place in the bag of any cinematographer. The two-color meter, which has two filtered photocells (red and blue), can indicate the color temperature of most typical sources, such as daylight or tungsten halogen. For more precision, when measuring fluorescent lights or high-intensity discharge types, a three-color meter is preferred. These meters will indicate color temperature with greater accuracy, because three photocells (red, green, and blue) are utilized. Any undesirable spectral irregularities, such as those found in fluorescent lights, will not be detected by a two-cell color temperature meter. When measuring discontinuous spectrum light sources a three-cell meter is necessary in order to obtain accurate results. Most meters will directly provide color temperature in Kelvin notation, and some of the newer models even correlate a proper filter given the film balance.

Color temperature is a subject which frequently causes undue concern for the nascent cinematographer, as a fear exists that if rigorous filtering techniques are not followed the footage will be unacceptable, with the result of a long day's work being a howl of laughter during dailies when the cast realizes they have been transformed into green-skinned oddities. Generally speaking, a basic understanding of film color balance, light sources, and basic conversion filtering is all that is necessary to exercise control over this sometimes overly emphasized technical issue.

Where a filter is required, such as those enumerated earlier, calculations are unnecessary because the sources are known, but in circumstances where it is not so obvious what type(s) of sources you are dealing with, it is best to determine the color temperature.

With the ability to measure color temperature (and assuming the meter only provides such a measurement, without automatically calculating the necessary filters), a method must be available to determine the correction necessary when the illumination does not match the film's balance and it is important that it does.

The first formula involves the conversion of our Kelvin measurement into a reciprocal megakelvin, for purposes of calculation, where the reciprocal megakelvin is defined as MK^{-1}.

$10^6/T_k = MK^{-1}$
$1,000,000/5500K = 181.8\ MK^{-1}$

Film–Actual Temperature = Filter
(MK^{-1})　　(MK^{-1})　　　　(Wratten)

After converting all of our variables into reciprocal megakelvin values, a formula for determining the proper filter when using tungsten-balanced film in typical daylight might appear as thus:

Film@3200K–Actual@5500K = 131 (MK^{-1})
$(MK^{-1}\ 312.5)$　　$(MK^{-1}\ 181)$　　　　　　(85B Wratten Filter)

The opposite scenario, converting daylight-balanced film to tungsten light, should appear as follows:

Film@5500K–Actual@3200K = –131 (MK^{-1})
$(MK^{-1}\ 181)$　　　$(MK^{-1}\ 312.5)$　　　　　(80A Wratten Filter)

Example, converting a 4300K source for tungsten film balance:

Film@3200K–Actual@4300K = 80 (MK^{-1})
$(MK^{-1}\ 312.5)$　　$(MK^{-1}\ 232)$　　　　　　(85C Wratten Filter)

Another useful formula, and one that is often overlooked, is the Unknown Filter.

Measured Kelvin With Filter–Actual Kelvin Alone = Filter
(MK^{-1})　　　　　　　　　(MK^{-1})　　　　　　(MK^{-1})

4300K Actual With Filter–5500K Actual Kelvin = Filter 81EF
$(MK^{-1}\ 232.5)$　　　　　　$(MK^{-1}\ 181)$　　　　　$(MK^{-1}\ 52)$

When we want to change the color temperature of a specific fixture we can also use filters, and these filters are known as lighting filters, as opposed to camera filters. The formula for converting color temperature using common filters produced by many manufacturers, though some may not directly correlate because of slight differences, is as follows:

Light + Filter = New Light Color Temperature

In order to get an answer in Kelvin we must convert the solution using this simple formula:

$1/MK^{-1} \times 1,000,000 = $ Kelvin

3200K Light + 1/2 CTO Filter = 393.5 (MK^{-1})   2540K
(MK^{-1} 312.5)   (MK^{-1} + 81)

The filter(s) noted in Table 4.1 are only useful when correcting over-blue daylight or for matching shots that were filmed with unbiased light. When using tungsten-balanced film, any filter under the standard correction (85B) will give cooler results, i.e., 85C or 81EF. For warmer results during the day, when using daylight-balanced stock, an 81EF or 81C can be used.

Scientific Calculator Programs: Color Temperature

```
"Film Balance"?→B:
"Actual Color Temp"?→K:
"Filter Needed":
(10^6/B)-(10^6/K)

"Light Color Temp"?→F:
"Mired Shift of Filter"?→M:
"Kelvin Temp":
1/(1/F×10^6+M)×10^6

"Measured Color Temp with Filter"?→A:
"Actual Only"?→Z:
"Filter Shift":
(10^6/A)-(10^6/Z)
```

QUICK REFERENCE CHART (Tungsten Balanced Film)			QUICK REFERENCE CHART (Daylight Balanced Film)		
Source (K)	Filters(s)	Filter Factor	Source (K)	Filters(s)	Filter Factor
7500K	85B + 81EF	2.5	7500K	81EF	1.6
6500K	85B + 81B	2	6500K	81B	1.25
5500K	85B	1.6	5500K	None	0
4300K	85C	1.6	4300K	80D	1.25
3850K	81EF	1.6	3850K	80C	2
3200K	None	0	3200K	80A	4

TABLE 4.1 Quick reference filter chart.

APPROXIMATE COLOR TEMPERATURE OF SELECTED SOURCES	
Candle Flame	2000K
Incandescent 100 Watt	2900K
Tungsten Halogen (Studio Quartz)	3200K
Tungsten Photoflood	3400K
HMI (Metal Halide)	5500K
Xenon Arc	6500K
Sunlight (Early Morning)	4300K
Average Daylight	5500K
Sunlight (Late Afternoon)	4300K
Overcast Sky	6800K
Typical Daylight	6000K
Thick Shade	7500K

TABLE 4.2 Approximate color temperature of selected sources.

| WRATTEN COLOR CONVERSION AND LIGHT BALANCING FILTERS | | | | | |
| AMBER/YELLOW FILTERS | | | BLUE FILTERS | | |
Designation	(MK⁻¹)Shift	Filter Factor	Designation	(MK⁻¹)Shift	Filter Factor
85B	+131	1.6	80A	−131	4
85	+112	1.6	80B	−112	3.2
85C	+81	1.6	80C	−81	2
81EF	+53	1.6	80D	−56	1.6
81D	+42	1.25	82C	−45	1.6
81C	+35	1.25	82B	−32	1.6
81B	+27	1.25	78C	−24	1.6
81A	+18	1.25	82A	−18	1.25
81	+10	1.25	82	−10	1.25

TABLE 4.3 Wratten color conversion and light balancing filters.

5

A Question of Wavelengths

FILTERS

Filters are used as a convenient way to control light. The most basic of these will change the spectral characteristics of light through the absorption of certain wavelengths, or as in the case of a neutral density filter, equal absorption in all wavelengths in order to provide an overall reduction in light. Color filters are usually either corrective, such as color conversion filters for color temperature concerns, or basic creative color effect filters.

Color compensating filters are used for very specific spectral corrections. The most common application is for light sources that have excessive energy output in a narrow area of the spectrum, as in the case of fluorescents. Applying magenta or red color compensating filters in varying densities and combinations can provide correction at the camera for such a light. It should be noted that the density values given for these filters are not indicative of the exposure compensation.

In black and white cinematography color filters can be used for contrast control, where tones can be lightened or darkened in a film. If we want a tone to appear lighter the addition of a color filter of similar hue will render this effect, while a darker result can be provided with a complementary filter. For example, when shooting an exterior with trees and grass, a dark green filter will make these areas appear lighter gray on the projected film print, while a magenta filter will produce the opposite: a darker gray. These results can be easily understood when we remember that magenta absorbs green light (it is used to correct fluorescent lights) and therefore the reflected light from the grass and trees will be attenuated by this color, thus creating a reduction in exposure in the areas of the film corresponding to the green subjects.

In general most correction filters are noted with their Wratten equivalents, e.g., 85, 85C, 81EF, etc., for ease of identification or, in the case of fluorescent filters, with a manufacturer's code, for example the FL-B. Color compensating filters are identified by the density and the color, an example being CC30M. Color effects filters (essentially any color filter without a Wratten equivalent) are normally classified according to a descriptive color, for example coral, straw, tobacco, sepia, etc. Color filters for contrast control in black and white film are normally Wratten filters, such as 8, 15, 21, etc., or equivalents, but any color filter will work in this case.

Specialized filters can usually be classified as diffusers, fogs, star, or graduated types. Off in a category by itself, but never to be underestimated, is the venerable polarizer. Many filters are also available in combinations where the characteristics of two filters have been combined into one, as the use of more than two or three filters at one time is not recommended in most cases.

Neutral density filters are used to reduce the light entering the camera without having to change the lens aperture and are extremely useful for controlling depth of field and exposure. They are indicated by the density, which is the log of opacity. Of course, opacity is the filter factor. So a neutral density filter with a filter factor of 2 would be designated as .3 (log of 2). These are commonly combined with color conversion filters, such as the 85 series, where the filter will then be denoted 85N3, i.e., an 85 in combination with an ND.3. When using combined filters it is important that proper exposure compensation is provided for the effects of both.

Ultraviolet filters are used to reduce the effects of excessive ultraviolet radiation which can sometimes have an undesirable influence on the quality of the image, and are very useful when shooting exteriors. Tungsten-balanced film with an 85 filter does not require the use of a UV filter, but daylight-balanced film can benefit from its application, e.g., 1A, 2B, or 2E. Wide scenic shots are usually the most affected by the purplish-blue haze created by ultraviolet light. Certain types of UV filters can have an effect on colors in a scene because they are absorbing visible light in the blue region (400-420nm) of the spectrum. Therefore, if a subtle warming of the scene is not desired, it is best to avoid UV filters which provide excessive correction.

Specialty filters are more difficult to define because the effect is largely dependent on the brand, but several generalizations can be made regarding these types. Low-contrast filters are designed to reduce the contrast of a scene and can be useful when shooting exteriors with available light. The only problem with some low-contrast filters is their somewhat detrimental flaring of highlights. It is also crucial that no stray light gets into the mattebox when using these filters, as the image will appear overexposed.

Fog filters are basically self-explanatory, but depending on the type, such as a double fog, the effect can be quite different. For creating a natural fog effect it is still better to use a fog machine in most cases, particularly when a heavy effect is necessary. Fog filters are more useful for establishing shots, where the problem of matching shots together is typically not an issue.

Diffusers are used for a subtle reduction in sharpness, which is very useful for eliminating too much detail in faces when a close-up shot is required. We must remember that when projecting film for theatrical presentation faces can be extremely large and reduction of resolution may be necessary for aesthetic reasons. For standard-resolution television production this is a debatable issue, due, in part, to the lack of resolution inherent in the system. Diffusers are available in a wide range of grades, but extensive testing is necessary in order to determine the on-screen effect as there are no standardized designations except those within a manufacturer's product line. Exposure compensation is not necessary with normal optical diffusers, but some varieties, such as those which use fine mesh nets to subtly bend the light rays before entering the lens, may require compensation. A word of caution should be given in the case of all filters which reduce image sharpness, such as fogs and diffusers: the effect is permanent, so choose wisely.

Star filters are used to create well-defined light streaks on glaring highlights and are usually defined by the number of points produced. Like most highly specialized filters, they have limited application in motion pictures, the effect being more readily applied to still photography, although in certain cases these might be interesting to use.

Graduated filters combine the color or neutral density function of a standard filter with a lessening of the effect towards the middle or bottom of the filter. Some have abrupt transitions between the two portions, while others have a smooth transition for blending better within the frame. They are limited in application to establishing shots, or shots where the camera is fixed, as the effect will be noticeable when the camera pans or tilts. Sunsets and skies can be selectively enhanced by such a filter, but caution should be exercised, as an extreme effect can look unrealistic and a visible change may be detectable in varieties which do not have a gradual demarcation line.

Polarizers are filters which can eliminate reflections from glass and glare from nonmetallic surfaces. In certain cases they can improve the color of the sky because skylight is partially polarized. Normal light is unpolarized, the waves vibrating randomly on multiple axes. Polarized light, on the other hand, vibrates in a single plane only. When light is naturally polarized, such as the effect that can be seen when filming through car windshields, a polarizer allows for the selective reduction of reflections. The filter will only permit light which is parallel to its axis to pass through and blocks perpendicular light waves (Figure 5.1). The orientation of the filter, then, determines the degree of absorption. Since the polarizer is modifying the amount of light pass-

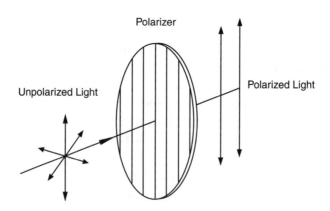

FIGURE 5.1 Polarizer.

ing through the lens while doing this, an exposure compensation must be allowed, usually at least 1 full stop. A simple method of determining the added exposure necessary is to use a light meter, as the amount will vary according to how the polarizer is rotated in the mount. When a dark blue sky is desired, the polarizer can significantly improve the color saturation if the camera is oriented at ninety degrees to the direction of the sun. Like the graduated filters mentioned earlier, the camera should not move during these shots as the effect will change with direction.

The quality of filters is largely dependent on the manufacturer and the materials used. Any filter that is specifically designed for professional use, and has an appropriate price, will usually have acceptable optical and spectral characteristics. Most filters are glass or glass laminate. Gelatin filters, made from thin sheets, are a far less expensive alternative and are typically only used with cameras that have a filter holder behind the lens where the size of the filter is quite small. Dirt and dust contamination is a significant problem with gelatin filters because of the filter's close proximity to the film. Several duplicates should be available in case someone accidentally touches the surface and ruins it.

There are many choices available when deciding on the placement of filters. The most basic method involves placing a filter directly on the lens itself with the threads provided, which is common in most photography, or using much larger rectangular or square filters, which are mounted in a mattebox. The benefit of using the second technique, beyond the fact that almost all professional motion picture cameras are already fitted with a mattebox and sunshade to keep stray light out of the lens, is the speed at which filters may be removed and replaced and the fact that the inherently larger size means they can be used with virtually all lenses irrespective of the front thread diameter. Since most motion picture camera lenses are rented only for the duration of a production, and most directors of photography do not own such lenses but frequently own filters, compatibility is a prime issue. Most matteboxes, if they are large enough, can be fitted with adapter trays for virtually all common square or rectangular filters. The common sizes are 4×5.650, 5×6, and 6.6×6.6 inches. The 4×4 size is also relatively common, particularly when a lightweight mattebox is required, as in hand-held camerawork.

When a circular filter is required, as in a polarizer or diopter (more will be discussed on diopters in Chapter 7), these are usually either 4.5 inches or 138mm and are mounted in a corresponding filter holder in the rear of the mattebox. This allows the filter to be rotated to the desired degree, and then fastened. Some matteboxes also have sliding filter holders for such filters as diffusers and grads, where placement relative to the scene is important.

Most matteboxes will hold a minimum of two filters at a time, although multi-stage versions can hold even more. When using filters in such a configuration several important considerations should be made regarding the setup of the mattebox. The first and foremost is the use of a rubber ring where the lens and the mattebox meet in order to keep light from hitting the filters from behind and creating spurious reflections. The second is the use of a sunshade extension when filming outdoors in bright sunny conditions. The third, which is not as imperative, is the use of masks over the front of the mattebox to keep stray light out. When using multiple filters at the same time it is usually preferable to reduce the space between them as much as possible with an appropriate filter holder, or by using a tilting version, which will help reduce the possibility of double reflections when a light shines directly into the lens, as in the case of car headlights.

Determining the exposure compensation for filters can be done either by testing with a light meter, or by simply following the manufacturer's recommendations. It is important, though, that the terminology is understood when different designations are given. The easiest to understand is a stop notation where one can simply add the additional exposure using the lens aperture, the simplest and most common method of compensating. Filter factor is another common method of defining the necessary compensation, and this is the same as opacity. A filter factor is derived from the reciprocal of the transmittance. A factor of 2 equals 1 stop, a factor of 4 equals 2 stops, and so on. 1/3 and 2/3 of a stop are 1.26 and 1.6 respectively. When several filters are used, multiplication of the separate filter factors will provide the correct compensation. Density is normally only used with neutral density filters and can be determined from the log (base 10) of the filter factor, i.e., opacity. A density of .1 equals 1/3 of a stop, .2 equals 2/3 of a stop, .3 equals 1 full stop, and so on. When using multiple filters, which are noted by their densities, the values should be added together.

An easy way of testing a filter yourself is by using a light meter with a flat diffuser. Placing the meter on a flat surface, position the filter in question over the light sensor so it covers the whole diffuser, and take a measurement. Remove the filter and take another measurement without moving the meter or tilting it in any way. A spot meter can also be used, but one must use a surface of consistent light reflection such as a gray card or white card. Some meters may not respond with the same values, especially when a direct comparison is made, due to minor differences in spectral sensitivity, but the results should be quite close. Use the formula below for determining transmittance, opacity, and density. It is simple with footcandles as your unit of measurement, but f-stops work as well and, in fact, can provide opacity without the need for calculation.

Transmittance/Opacity/Density:

(fc) with filter/(fc) without filter = % Transmittance
50 fc /125 fc = 40 % Transmittance

1/Transmittance = Opacity (Filter Factor)
1/.4 = 2.5 Opacity (Filter Factor)

Log (Base 10) of Opacity = Density
Log of 2.5 = .4 Density

In this example we can see that the filter reduces the exposure by 1 1/3 of a stop (see Table 5.1 for comparisons between different values), so when calculating your exposure this must be taken into account; therefore the lens aperture should be opened by 1 1/3 stops to compensate.

When using f-stops instead of footcandles, simply reverse the order of the calculation; that is, measure without the filter and then with the filter. If this is not done, then the reciprocal of the answer must be calculated to find the opacity. In most cases it is probably easier to mentally calculate the difference between the stops; however, in either case the fractional stops must be known (when necessary) in order for the formula to be exact, e.g., 6.3, 7.1, etc.

f-stop²/f-stop² = Opacity
16² (256)/2.82² (8) = 32

1/Opacity = % Transmittance
1/32 = 3.125 %

Log (Base 10) of Opacity = Density
Log of 32 = 1.5

Below is a formula for calculating the light loss on a specified filter, working equally well for lights or camera. It is usually best to follow the manufacturer's provided number when determining transmittance. The formula calculates light loss in 1/10th stops.

Log(1/(T × .01))/Log 2 = Light Loss
Transmittance % = T

LOG (Density)	FILTER FACTOR (Opacity)	STOPS
0	1	0
.1	1.25	1/3
.2	1.6	2/3
.3	2	1
.4	2.5	1 1/3
.5	3.2	1 2/3
.6	4	2
.7	5	2 1/3
.8	6	2 2/3
.9	8	3

TABLE 5.1 Relationship between log, filter factor, and stops.

While camera filters are invaluable for the cinematographer's work, lighting filters provide an equally important method of controlling light. These filters are typically supplied as thin sheets of gelatin which can be clipped into appropriate holders and then placed in front of the light source. All gelatin filters designed for lighting applications are relatively heat resistant, but if mounted too close to the fixture, melting will likely occur. In cases where one must work quickly, and the lamp is of relatively low wattage, it is possible to clip gels directly to the barndoors, but this is not recommended when the light will be on for long periods of time. More durable versions made of thick plastic exist for mounting over windows and doorways where the thin sheeting would not normally be acceptable, and have the added advantage of lasting longer, although fading and scratching can be a problem if the filter is in use over a long period of time.

Conversion filters are the most common, and are designed to convert either a 3200K source to daylight, or a 5500K source to tungsten halogen (3200K). CTBs are blue filters, which perform the former function, while CTOs are orange filters which are used in the latter case. In the case of converting 3200K to 5500K, as in using tungsten halogen fixtures for exterior shooting, a substantial loss of light will occur. For example, a Full Blue CTB only transmits 36 percent of the light, reducing an 80 footcandle source to 28 footcandles. This, of course, is the reason why HMIs are a superior light source for exteriors; they are already of the correct color temperature (5500K) and produce far more light for the wattage.

Lighting filters are usually classified as 1/2, 3/4, Full, etc. to indicate the degree of correction, but because of differences between manufacturers one must verify the actual results with either a color temperature meter or by consulting the appropriate swatchbook. Special conversion filters are available for fluorescent fixtures, and these are used either to correct the excessive green, as in the case of a 1/2 minus-green filter (magenta). If supplemental tungsten halogen lights are being used, and it is desirable to match the existing fluorescent sources, a plus-green filter can be utilized, assuming, of course, that the camera will be fitted with the necessary filter.

Color effect filters are also widely available and are given such names as flame, salmon, lilac, moss green, etc. They are used when the choice of color is purely based on aesthetic reasons and not color temperature conversion purposes. The range of colors can be used to great effect when trying to simulate certain conditions such as moonlight or torchlight.

Lighting fixtures may be fitted with neutral density filters to reduce the overall light output for the same reason that they are used on the camera. Most lights, though, are available with an assortment of wire scrims serving the same function, so it is usually less common to find these on the set. Still, they are a useful supplement to the usual plethora of colored gels.

Last, but not least, is the vast collection of diffusion materials. These filters are crucial for softening the light output from any fixture without having to resort to a piece of white foamcore or a soft-sided reflector board to bounce the light. Available both in gels and a variety of cloth-like materials with different characteristics, they allow one to choose just the right amount of diffusion necessary. Many lights are too harsh when used without diffusion media, so these filters are a most valuable addition. Fluorescents are the exception to this rule.

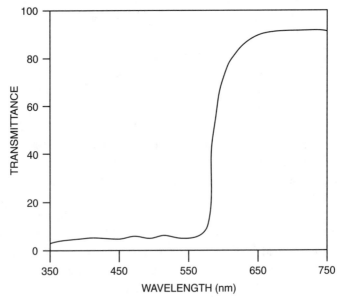

FIGURE 5.2 Spectrophotometric curve for a red filter.

When making a choice regarding a lighting filter for effect, it is advantageous to make a test exposure using the same color negative film that is intended to be used during production, and then project the results. In critical applications it is always a good idea to test the results beforehand. Obviously, once you make a decision you must keep using the same gel for the duration of the scene or the color will not match from shot to shot.

An actual film test is the best choice in any circumstance, but a certain degree of information can be gleaned from the spectrophotometric data supplied by the manufacturer. These graphs will indicate which wavelengths are absorbed by the filter based on the correspondingly low transmittance rate of these wavelengths. The wavelengths having the highest transmittance will create the perceived color. Figure 5.2 represents a filter that attenuates all wavelengths below 550nm, thus appearing red to the eye.

Due to the fact that most manufacturers provide a transmittance number indicating the total light loss as a percentage, a formula for calculating the attenuation in stops is very useful, and furthermore, because most light meters are calibrated in 1/10th incremental stops, the answer is provided as such, where the decimal is the fractional part of the whole stop.

Scientific Calculator Program: Filter Light Loss

```
"Filter Percent Transmittance"?→T:
"Light Loss":
1/(T×.01)→A:
log A/log 2▲
```

LIGHTING FILTERS	
EFFECT ON 3200K - CTO	EFFECT ON 3200K - CTB
Full CTO + 167 2083K	Full CTB −131 5500K
3/4 CTO + 131 2252K	3/4 CTB −100 4706K
1/2 CTO + 81 2538K	1/2 CTB −68 4100K
1/4 CTO + 42 2816K	1/3 CTB −49 3800K
1/8 CTO + 20 3003K	1/4 CTB −30 3500K
EFFECT ON 5500K - CTO	EFFECT ON 5500K - CTB
Full CTO + 167 2900K	Full CTB −131 10000+K
3/4 CTO + 131 3200K	3/4 CTB −100 10000+K
1/2 CTO + 81 3800K	1/2 CTB −68 8770K
1/4 CTO + 42 4500K	1/3 CTB −49 7518K
1/8 CTO + 20 4900K	1/4 CTB −30 6578K

TABLE 5.2 Lighting filters.

COLOR COMPENSATING FILTERS (Density)					
Cyan	Magenta	Yellow	Red	Green	Blue
CC05C	CC05M	CC05Y	CC05R	CC05G	CC05B
CC10C	CC10M	CC10Y	CC10R	CC10G	CC10B
CC20C	CC20M	CC20Y	CC20R	CC20G	CC20B
CC30C	CC30M	CC30Y	CC30R	CC30G	CC30B
CC40C	CC40M	CC40Y	CC40R	CC40G	CC40B
CC50C	CC50M	CC50Y	CC50R	CC50G	CC50B

TABLE 5.3 Color compensating filters.

WRATTEN COLOR CONVERSION AND LIGHT BALANCING FILTERS						
AMBER/YELLOW FILTERS			BLUE FILTERS			
Designation	(MK^{-1})Shift	Filter Factor	Designation	(MK^{-1})Shift	Filter Factor	
85B	+131	1.6	80A	−131	4	
85	+112	1.6	80B	−112	3.2	
85C	+81	1.6	80C	−81	2	
81EF	+53	1.6	80D	−56	1.6	
81D	+42	1.25	82C	−45	1.6	
81C	+35	1.25	82B	−32	1.6	
81B	+27	1.25	78C	−24	1.6	
81A	+18	1.25	82A	−18	1.25	
81	+10	1.25	82	−10	1.25	

TABLE 5.4 Wratten color conversion and light balancing filters.

COOL WHITE FLUORESCENT	FILTER(S)	COMPENSATION
3200K FILM	85C, CC30M	−1
5500K FILM	82C, CC30M	−1 1/3
WARM WHITE FLUORESCENT	FILTER(S)	COMPENSATION
3200K FILM	CC30M	−2/3
5500K FILM	80C, CC30M	−1 2/3

TABLE 5.5 Camera filters necessary to balance fluorescent lights.

6

The Study of Emulsions

SENSITOMETRY

While the visual examination of images is acceptable for simple analysis, sensitometry provides a rigorous method for determining the response of photographic emulsions to light using highly controlled exposure and processing techniques. Important qualities such as latitude, exposure range, and contrast can be determined using data obtained from such testing. Therefore, the understanding of sensitometry, and its related data, allows the cinematographer to determine the characteristics of any film stock. However, one must be aware of the fact that these sensitometric tests are absolute, and therefore do not indicate the actual results obtained in the camera. For now, though, we are only interested in the ideal.

In order to adequately understand the principles of sensitometry, a brief explanation of the structure of film must be provided, both before and after development. A color negative film before development consists of three main parts: the emulsion (light-sensitive silver halide crystals suspended in gelatin, generally of a flat shape called a T-grain), the triacetate film base (made from highly processed organic and non-organic materials), and the remjet backing (antihalation layer) which is a resin coating designed to minimize light reflections from the film base (this is removed during processing).

Color negative films have three distinct emulsion layers which react to different wavelengths of light. The first layer is sensitive to blue light, the second is sensitive to green light, and the third is sensitive to red light. Below the blue-sensitive layer a non-permanent yellow filter layer eliminates the inherent blue light sensitivity in the two subsequent layers. Between the green-sensitive layer and the red-sensitive layer is a gel interlayer, and a protective coat is placed over the whole tri-pack emulsion. In many cases the light-sensitive layers are actually made from double or in some cases triple coated emulsions, which are designed to further improve the response characteristics (Figure 6.1).

The blue-sensitive layer contains a colorless coupler which forms a yellow dye, the green-sensitive layer contains a colorless coupler and yellow-colored coupler which forms a magenta dye, and the red-sensitive layer contains a colorless coupler and a pink-colored coupler which forms a cyan dye. The remaining colored coupler in the green-sensitive layer and red-sensitive layer provides color masking, reducing the undesirable blue absorption of the magenta dye (yellow-colored coupler), and green and blue absorption of the cyan dye (pink-colored coupler). These residual couplers produce an overall orange hue in processed color negative films, especially in areas that were not exposed.

When color negative film is exposed in the camera the emulsion layers react to light, and dependent upon the wavelengths, the silver

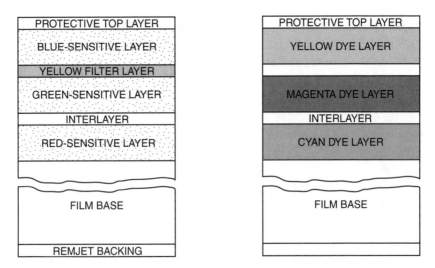

FIGURE 6.1 Film layers before and after processing.

halide crystals in each layer react accordingly, forming a latent image. Before development the remjet backing is removed. Then the action of the developer converts the exposed silver halide crystals into metallic silver and dye clouds are formed around the metallic silver grains in each layer by the oxidized developer and coupler. The development is stopped at a precise time and an accelerator prepares the film for bleaching. When the film is bleached the yellow filter layer is removed and all the metallic silver present is converted back to silver halide. The final step before washing is the fixer, which removes both the unexposed silver halide and the silver halide which has been converted from metallic silver. The result is three dye layers, i.e., yellow, magenta, and cyan, and no silver content. In a color negative image more exposure produces higher density, while less exposure produces lower density. Colors, of course, will be in their complementary form. Red subjects will be cyan, green subjects magenta, etc. (see Figure 6.1).

In order to provide a suitable sensitometric strip one must use a sensitometer. These instruments are designed to expose a length of film with precisely varying exposures. Generally, most sensitometers consist of a series of specifically selected (equal absorption) neutral density filters (normally a tablet or strip of 21 steps or more) which are of equal logarithmic increments, such as log 1.26 (.1) for 1/3 of a stop, log 1.41 (.15) for 1/2 of a stop, a light source (of proper color temperature for the film balance), and a shutter to control the exposure time. The exposure time should match actual common usage, which in the case of negative motion picture films implies 1/50th of a second.

Sensitometric exposure is defined as $H = E \times T$, where T is the time in seconds, E is the illuminance (measured in lux), and H is the exposure (lux-sec). When creating a D log H curve, we must convert our lux-sec exposure (H) to log H by using the logarithmic function (base 10). For example, if E equals 20 (lux) and T equals .02 (1/50th of a second), the lux-sec exposure (H) is .4 (.39), i.e., $\bar{1}.6$ log H. In order to convert our negative log to a bar log, which is the common notation, the decimal is moved one space to the right of the first non-zero digit, and the number of decimal spaces it is moved provides the bar number (in the above example this is 1). The original number is rounded if necessary, and the log of this number is the mantissa (the positive part of the log), as in the above example where the log of 4 is .6. Thus the bar notation for .4 is $\bar{1}.6$.

When a sensitometric strip is exposed and developed (any processing errors will invalidate the test) it will yield a range of densities produced by the step tablet in a single exposure. The results are measured with a densitometer, an instrument designed to determine optical density, invariably in a logarithmic form. Status densitometry refers to the spectral response of the instrument. In the case of measuring density in negative films this is *Status M* (printing density). When determining density in positive films, *Status A* is used. Both measurements are accomplished with a specified filter set, a standardized illuminant, and a photocell of proper sensitivity. Typical densitometer measurements of color negative films are called integral densities, indicating that all three layers are measured, as compared to analytical density, where only one dye layer is measured. Diffuse density measurements are used in order to simulate the conditions obtained through contact printing, whereas specular density measurements are suitable for optical printers.

Based on the fact that developed film is made up of three separate dye layers which are yellow, magenta, and cyan, a densitometer must have separate red, green, and blue filters in order to indicate the density of these layers. The yellow dye will absorb blue light, the magenta dye will absorb green light, and the cyan dye will absorb red light. For example, if blue light is directed through the film, the density of the yellow dye layer can be determined. Density is measured in a logarithmic form, that is, the log of the opacity, where opacity is defined as the reciprocal of the transmittance: $25/100$ is .25, $1/.25$ is 4, and log 4 is .6; i.e., $D = \log (1/\text{trans.})$. The result indicates the density of the yellow dye layer, and is referred to as the density to blue light, or D(b). A high degree of transmittance due to limited blue light absorption of the yellow dye layer would indicate that this layer received very little exposure (forming less dye), while a low degree of transmittance due to substantial blue light absorption would indicate that this layer received significant exposure.

By producing a graph which indicates the relationship between exposure (log H) and density (D), a characteristic curve can be produced. The D log H curves shown in Figure 6.2 provide the graphical representation of this data plotting. The x-axis indicates the lux-sec exposure (H) as log H (in many cases this can be a relative log). Each logarithmic step, i.e., 1.0 to 2.0, is 3 1/3 camera stops, based on the

86

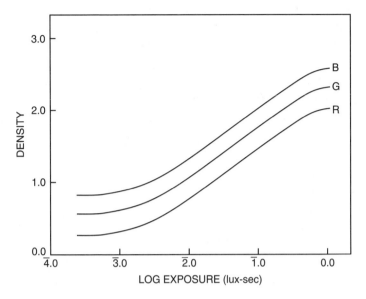

FIGURE 6.2 Characteristic curves for a color negative film.

antilog of 1.0 (the difference between the two), producing the number 10 (2^3.3), i.e., log10/log2. It is also on this axis that the mid-scale gray will sometimes be identified.

Density runs vertically on the y-axis, also shown in a logarithmic form. As the log H exposure increases, as shown on the x-axis, the density increases. In the case of the color negative film shown in Figure 6.2 there are three individual characteristic curves. The curves are labeled by the filters respectively employed in the densitometer, so that the dye layer being measured is the complementary color of the densitometer filter. Therefore, R indicates the cyan dye layer, G indicates the magenta dye layer, and B indicates the yellow dye layer. The displacement of the curves is caused by the color masking (residual colored coupler) in the film, as more blue and green light is absorbed by the orange mask (providing higher overall density in the blue and green curves) than red light, which is more readily transmitted.

A characteristic curve has essentially three main parts: the shoulder, the straight line portion, and the toe. The shoulder is the upper part of the curve, beyond the straight line region, and represents an area of high density. It can be identified by the gradual decrease in slope. Beyond this region it is called maximum density (D-max). No further density changes can occur beyond D-max. The toe is the portion of the curve which represents an area of low density, that which received the least exposure. Below the toe, the area of no density change, is minimum density (D-min). The straight line section is the longest of the three sections and has a slope which remains constant, making it easier to identify. The straight line region is the only linear portion of the curve, meaning if the density were determined for each stop, i.e., log H .3, in this straight line region, we would notice proportional density changes for each stop more or less exposure. As the slope begins to gradually flatten at either end, in the shoulder and the toe, the density changes become smaller and smaller until a maximum or minimum is reached. The emulsion eventually loses the ability to record a highlight or a shadow that falls outside its exposure range (Figure 6.3).

The longer the straight line portion, the more accurate the stock will represent the tones in the scene, as less compression will occur. However, another factor must be taken into account, and this is the

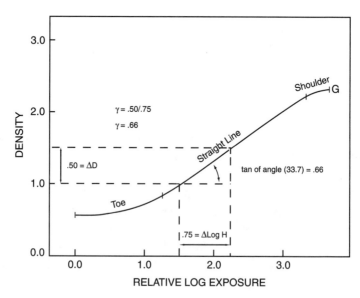

FIGURE 6.3 Calculating gamma based on the slope of a characteristic curve.

slope of the characteristic curve. A 45 degree slope would indicate exact reproduction—the input and output are identical. A steep slope (more than 45 degrees) will expand the input while a shallow slope (less than 45 degrees) will compress it. Thus the straight line of the characteristic curve indicates contrast. Therefore, film stocks which are low contrast must have shallow slopes, where the density changes are less for the respective step in exposure, and high-contrast stocks must have steep slopes, where the density changes are more for the respective step in exposure. Negative stocks fit into the former category, while positive stocks fit into the latter category.

Gamma is a method of mathematically indicating contrast, and is strictly associated with the slope of the straight line region. Terms such as steep and shallow are not definitive means of describing the slope of the linear portion of the characteristic curve, nor do they clearly indicate the relationship between exposure and the resulting density. Consequently, gamma calculations are frequently used for this purpose. The formula for gamma (γ) is $\Delta D / \Delta \log H$, which is the difference between two density points on the straight line region and the corresponding log H points. Gamma can also be calculated by finding the tangent of the angle that the straight line region forms with the horizontal axis (see Figure 6.3). Using this method, a slope of 72 degrees in the straight line region will produce a gamma of 3.0, while a slope of 33 degrees will yield a gamma of .65. Upon determination of gamma, density may be calculated from any log H point in the straight line region by multiplying the log H by the gamma. Conversely, the log H may be calculated from any density value in the straight line region by dividing the density by the gamma.

Most negative films used for motion picture production have a gamma of around .65, an indication that the density will only be roughly two-thirds as much as the change in log exposure. The advantage is that the subject tones are compressed, creating an extended exposure range, and are then expanded by printing onto a high-contrast positive stock, which has a gamma of around 3.0. Even though the print stock has a limited log H range in comparison to the negative, due to the steep slope and therefore high gamma value, this is acceptable because the negative has already compressed the image. Therefore the positive stock only requires the log H range necessary to reproduce the density range of the negative.

To calculate the system gamma of an image that originated on a negative film and was reproduced on a positive film, simply multiply the respective gamma values, i.e., .65 × 3.0 = 1.95. Such a result may seem high, but due to the considerable flare created by both the camera and the projector, this value is required in order to maintain acceptable contrast. When using an optical process during printing, i.e., an optical printer, one should expect additional flare beyond that obtained by the camera and the projector.

Projection prints are designed for viewing in darkened theaters, so they must expand the original negative density in order to present a

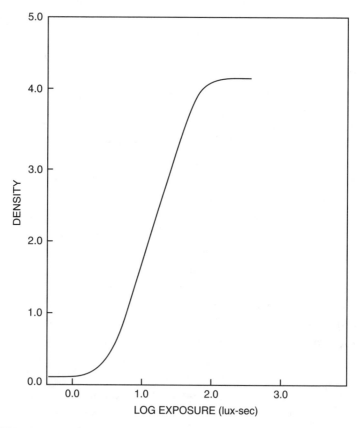

FIGURE 6.4 Characteristic curve of a color positive film.

desirable black and proper tone separation. The apparent contrast is reduced when projecting an image in a darkened room (due to the eye's dark adaptation), and this can be illustrated by the fact that the perceived black level of a print will vary with the level of the ambient illumination. It is for this reason that high gamma values are associated with prints and reversal films (Figure 6.4).

Gamma is also a concern when intermediates are to be produced, such as interpositives and internegatives. Since any change in the original tones of the negative during the duplication process will introduce compounding errors, it is imperative that the intermediate stocks have a gamma close to *unity*, where the gamma value is 1.0, producing a slope of exactly 45 degrees (the tangent of 45 is 1), so that the input will be the same as the output. Clearly this is desired to maintain the integrity of the original negative.

Following the standard procedure of multiplying the gamma of each element in the process, we can accurately predict the end result: system gamma. Taking our negative gamma of .65 and multiplying this number by the interpositive gamma, which is, for all practical purposes, 1.0, and the internegative gamma, also 1.0, we conclude that the gamma has not changed from our original negative. As expected, this is precisely why such duplicating stocks are used. When the internegative is printed onto a positive stock with a gamma of 3.0, where we multiply $.65 \times 1.0 \times 1.0 \times 3.0$, the end gamma is 1.95. Positive stocks also expand the mid-tone area (straight line) more than the shoulder and toe, where the toe contains the highlights and the shoulder the shadows. Therefore, compression of density takes place at both ends of the curve.

While this information is of scientific interest, more important to the cinematographer is how well an emulsion can reproduce a wide range of subject tones. This can be determined by the exposure range, which is defined roughly as the log H distance between the two points on the characteristic curve where a change in density is possible. By making a point at both locations, two vertical lines can then be drawn down to the horizontal axis, and the distance between these lines indicates the exposure range. D-min and D-max can be considered the extremes of such a range, but this is unrealistic to use, so it is common practice to use a smaller range (see Figure 6.5).

The advantage of knowing the exposure range of a film stock is

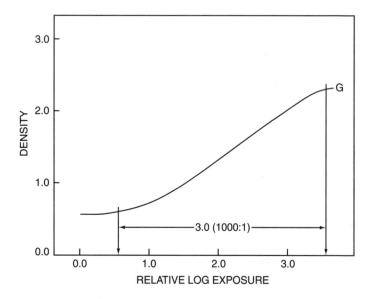

FIGURE 6.5 Log exposure range of a color negative film.

that one can predict within reason if a scene can be accurately reproduced. If the scene being exposed had a luminance ratio of 4096:1,
essentially 12 stops (2^{12}) between the lightest and the darkest subject, or a log range of 3.6 (based on the log of 4096), we can determine
if the scene will fit within the exposure range of the stock by comparing the subject luminance ratio to the useful log H range of the stock.
For example, if the horizontal axis revealed a log H range of 3.0 for the
emulsion in question, the ratio between the highest luminance tone
and the lowest luminance tone in a scene could be 1000:1 (antilog of
3.0) and will still be exposed on the characteristic curve. In the preceding example, the scene would exceed the exposure range of the stock,
as 3.6 is greater than 3.0. On the other hand, if a scene's luminance
ratio between the darkest subject and the lightest subject was only 7
stops (2^7), or a log range of 2.1 (based on the log of 128), then the
film would be considered to have exposure latitude, meaning an error
is permissible.

Reversal films have considerably less exposure range than negative stocks. This is caused by the steep slope and subsequent high gamma

(usually around 1.7) necessary to present a projected image with acceptable contrast. Due to the expansion of the original subject tones a reversal film cannot reproduce high-contrast subjects in the same way as negative film. Likewise, the exposure latitude is limited. Additionally, color reversal films are impossible to color correct in the event of an improper color balance without producing an intermediate, because they are intended to be directly projected. Therefore it is not recommended that a cinematographer utilize reversal stock unless it is imperative for convenience or cost purposes, or if a special look is desired which can only be achieved by using such a film.

Exposure latitude is the acceptable exposure error allowable in a particular stock. If the luminance range of the scene is in excess of the exposure range of the stock then there is no latitude. However, if the luminance range of the scene is 2.40, 250:1, or 8 stops, and the log H range of the negative is 3.0, or 10 stops, then the exposure latitude is 2 stops total (.6), or 1 stop of under- and overexposure, assuming the tones are properly placed in relation to mid-scale gray (Figure 6.6). If the darkest tone is set at the bottom of the curve (which can be done very accurately with a spot meter by determining how many stops below mid-scale gray black is produced) the latitude is all in the top of

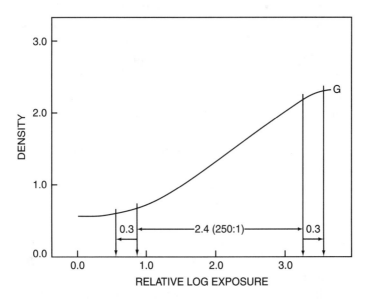

FIGURE 6.6 Latitude example of a color negative film.

the curve (2 stops), while conversely, if we set our exposure by the brightest portion of the scene, we would have latitude in the lower part of the curve (2 stops). Under normal circumstances the exposure range of a typical scene will rarely exceed 200:1, and most negative stocks, particularly emulsions designed specifically for cinematography, have an exposure range of at least log H 3.0, which means a total latitude of 2 1/3 stops is available, or a little more than 1 stop of overexposure and underexposure.

By using a D log H curve one can illustrate the effect of under- or overexposure. When the exposure for a scene is set for mid-scale (roughly the middle of the characteristic curve) it can be expected that the whole exposure range of the film is being used to its maximum ability, assuming a scene of equal proportions of shadows and highlights. When underexposure occurs, either intentionally or by error, the mid-scale gray tone will begin to slide down towards the toe. In this situation better highlight detail will be captured on the negative, but at the expense of the shadows (see Figure 6.7). When a film is overexposed the mid-scale gray tone begins to move up the curve, towards the shoulder, creating excessively bright highlights and increasingly better shadow detail in an uncorrected, one-light print (see Figure 6.8). Due to the latitude of most negative stocks, a 1 stop error will never present a problem, but excessive exposure errors could lead to a loss of either shadow detail or highlight detail. Printing the image up (lighter) or down (darker) can solve the problem to a large extent, but if the detail was not captured on the original negative, no amount of printing correction can solve the problem.

Of similar concern is the effect that push and pull processing can have on the characteristic curves. Some cinematographers extend or reduce development times in the laboratory to yield a better negative. This can be done for a variety of reasons, either to obtain a special look, or to produce more density in an underexposed image. One must realize, of course, that the results will be different than those obtained through normal development. When film is pushed the contrast is increased; moreover the emulsion layers respond differently to longer development times, which can create color balance problems that may not be correctable in printing (crossed curves). More density may be created on the negative, but at the expense of increased grain. When a film is pull processed (shorter development time) the contrast is re-

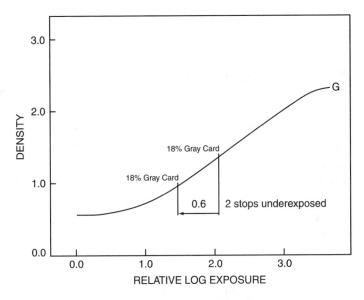

FIGURE 6.7 Underexposure relative to mid-scale gray.

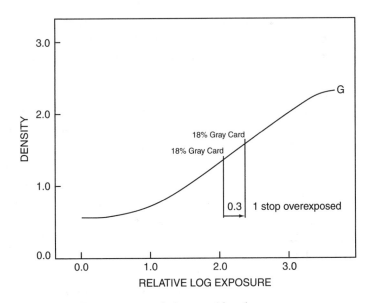

FIGURE 6.8 Overexposure relative to mid-scale gray.

duced, but likewise, as in the former case, with questionable color results (lower saturation) on the print.

Typically of less concern, due to its rarity, is reciprocity failure, although it is possible in certain high-speed applications. Reciprocity failure indicates that the sensitivity of a film stock is not the same at all levels of illuminance and exposure times. There are certain occasions when two identical exposures (lux-sec) will not provide the same density results on the same emulsion. It is normally assumed that any combination of illuminance and time can be used to provide a similar density as long as the exposure (H) remains constant. The term reciprocity failure indicates that this is not always the case when extremely short or long exposure times are used. For example, at exposure times shorter than 1/1000th of a second or longer than 1 second, reciprocity failure is likely to occur.

The effect of reciprocity failure is a negative with less density, which means an underexposed image. To avoid this problem additional exposure is necessary. Determining the exposure compensation is best done by testing, but usually rating the film stock at a two-thirds lower exposure index is a good starting point, for example, 500 to 320. Another problem that must be addressed is the fact that in a color negative film each layer is affected differently, so filtering is usually necessary. In general, the blue-sensitive layer is the least affected by reciprocity failure, so typically a yellow color compensating filter CC10Y (absorbs blue light) will be recommended to reduce overexposure in this layer when a correction is made.

Due to the ideal nature of a D log H curve produced by a sensitometer, and its limitations in respect to real image gathering, most cinematographers are more interested in the image that comes out of the camera. Sensitometry has the accuracy and repeatability of a laboratory experiment, which suits the manufacturer quite well because of the need to check the consistency of emulsions, but in order to get a real sense of the characteristics of a particular film stock one must use more practical techniques. Actual field testing with a camera is the only way to determine the qualities of a film, as objective methods of sensitometry can only be taken so far.

The optical quality (inherent flare) of a lens, imprecise exposure times, and poorly calibrated lenses can all contribute to a significantly different D log H curve than one which is published by a manufacturer using far more rigorous methods. Based on this fact, one may assume (and correctly) that in order to yield real results, actual results, the camera and lenses that will be used during production must be utilized when testing a film, and the film must be printed and projected in a similar method as that which is used in theaters, if this is ultimately the final presentation. In the case of a film to video transfer, where the image will not be printed at any stage, it is best to view the tests in a supervised telecine session, where one can determine the results on a properly calibrated monitor and professional video format.

The basic test usually consists of a gray scale, a color chart, and a large gray card, along with a representative subject (model), the latter providing invaluable information related to skin tone qualities and acceptable contrast when shooting a series of different tests. Generally a set of exposures ranging from 4 or 5 stops underexposed to 4 or 5 stops overexposed are initially shot. Changing lights around after completing the basic test can be done to determine subjective considerations regarding highlights, shadows, and the reproduction of important tones. After the film is developed it is imperative that it is printed at one-light (centered controls on the timing) so that the effects are not cancelled out by corrective printing measures. The same roll can then be printed with additional timing to determine the limit of correction possible when an image is under- or overexposed. Valuable information can be gleaned from such a test, and provides for both subjective and objective assessment.

An unfortunate problem with such testing methods is that the results are dependent, to a large extent, on the film laboratory. Different labs will likely develop the negative similarly (one hopes) but may not produce the same prints due to differences in printer settings. Even given a standard, such as the Laboratory Aim Density (LAD) system, there is little chance of duplicate results between two different laboratories. Therefore, the test has a validity which only holds for a particular facility.

Variability is the bane of all such testing, and can be caused by a myriad of problems, such as improper light meter calibration, incorrect aperture markings, developing differences (chemical impurities, lack of replenishment, and machine cleanliness), and, invariably, how the print is timed, to name but a few.

These are only the absolutely necessary stages of the photographic process in a motion picture film. Inevitably any release prints that are destined for substantial numbers of theaters will not be struck from the original negative, so intermediates will be necessary. At any stage in the duplication process errors can occur. To accurately test any film, the whole process of negative, interpositive, internegative, and final printing must be taken into account.

7

Bending Light

LENSES AND DEPTH OF FIELD

In categorizing lenses general terms such as prime lens and zoom lens are commonly applied, with specific definitions in the former being short focal length, medium focal length, long focal length, macro, and telephoto, and in the latter ratios such as 4:1 or 6:1, indicating the ratio between the minimum focal length and the maximum focal length. Additionally, the term "variable prime" is now used by some manufacturers to indicate a limited range zoom lens. Further classifications according to design and purpose, such as spherical and anamorphic, see frequent usage where one must differentiate between a standard lens and one which squeezes the image in the horizontal dimension. Special lenses, which may not be so indirectly identified, are extenders, diopters, slant focus lenses, shift and tilt lenses, and periscopes or borescopes. All lenses are chosen by the director of photography for a specific reason, based largely on compositional considerations, aesthetic concerns, and technical factors.

Prime lenses form the bulk of available optics, and have traditionally been associated with superior optical quality. The common focal lengths will vary depending upon the format, but in the case of standard 35mm, wide-angle lenses may be considered to span from 17.5mm to around 27mm. Anything below 17.5mm is usually considered an extreme wide-angle lens. From 27mm to 75mm is the range of medium focal length lenses or so-called normal lenses, and beyond 75mm, up to about 150mm, one would use the term long focal length. Telephoto lenses fill the gap beyond this, where focal lengths up to 1000mm are possible.

In 16mm, lenses that one might consider to be wide angle are 9mm to 16mm, with medium focal lengths generally in the range of 16mm to 40mm, and long focal lengths from roughly 50mm to 100mm. The designation telephoto is most fitting for lenses in excess of 100mm. When compared to 35mm, it is obvious that to yield a similar field of view in 16mm requires roughly half the focal length. This has implications when considering depth of field, as we will see later. In the case of Super 16, where such designated lenses must be used in order to cover the whole aperture, further variations exist between regular 16mm and Super 16 due to the greater horizontal dimension of this format.

35mm anamorphic presents the opposite situation, as the image is squeezed 2:1 in the horizontal axis by the anamorphic lens, creating a very wide field of view when unsqueezed in the viewfinder or theater. Since the angle of view is much wider than standard 35mm, the lenses must be roughly double the focal length in order to yield a similar field of view as standard spherical 35mm. Therefore, in anamorphic photography we find that wide-angle lenses span from around 35mm to 50mm, with medium focal lengths sweeping from 50mm all the way up to 200mm, and long focal length lenses, as one might imagine, are essentially of the telephoto variety. These generally range from 300mm and beyond, all the way up to 2000mm. On the whole when shooting anamorphic there is a reduced selection of lens focal lengths.

Most conventional prime lenses are limited to a close focus of two feet or more, although anamorphic lenses are usually in the three to five foot range, and no lens will produce the best quality image at such short focus distances. Macro lenses, as the name implies, are special lenses designed for extremely close focusing. They are available in a wide variety of focal lengths and are invaluable when the circumstance dictates their application. Exposure compensation must be made when using macro lenses due to the close proximity of the subject. Sometimes automatic exposure compensation is provided by the lens, but if one is left with the task of calculating the compensation a simple formula can be used based on the image size (the actual physical film frame dimension) divided by the object size in order to determine the magnification factor. We then add one to this magnification factor, and divide our measured f-stop by this value; in other words $f/(m + 1)$

or to combine all the variables into one formula $f/((I/O) + 1)$, where I equals image size and O equals object size. Moreover, lighting is typically a problem because of the close distances involved between the lens and the subject.

Zoom lenses are designed to have variable focal lengths only restricted by the range of the lens, i.e., the minimum and maximum focal length. Generally speaking a zoom lens is not as fast as a prime; whereas prime lenses frequently have maximum apertures of T-1.4 to T-1.9, most zoom lenses are limited to T-2.3, and long focal length zooms have maximum apertures not exceeding T-2.8 to T-4. Anamorphic lenses are even more limited with respect to maximum aperture.

Due to the greater loss of light from the added optical elements and the invariably lengthened barrel, it is important that a zoom lens is calibrated in T-stops as the use of f-stops may yield questionable exposure results, where the engraved aperture may not be accurate at long focal lengths. Telephoto lenses can have a similar problem regarding the accuracy of the aperture, but many of these have been converted for cinematographic purposes, so it can be assumed the recalibrated markings (T-stops) are correct. Like zoom lenses, telephoto lenses have a limited maximum aperture.

The minimum focus is typically less on zoom lenses, and depth of field is reduced in comparison to a prime lens of similar focal length. Notwithstanding these minor differences, a zoom lens is not considered to be a compromise, and in fact many directors of photography find them to be a convenient substitute for a set of primes. Qualitatively, the difference between the latest zoom lens and a prime lens is very negligible. The practical advantage of a zoom lens is that time can be saved by not having to change lenses as often. More importantly, a greater degree of control over framing is possible. The versatility comes at a price, however, and the obvious drawbacks to such a design are the physically larger lenses and the additional weight, both of which make hand-holding very questionable, and Steadicam usage even more so. Variable primes and lightweight zooms are most fitting for Steadicam or hand-held work, where the size of the lens is much reduced. Furthermore, additional support is always necessary when using a large zoom lens as more strain than usual will be placed on the lens mount, and this holds true for all telephoto lenses.

Most zoom lenses are fitted with an electric motor for smoother control over the rate of zoom, allowing more subtle changes in focal length. A straight zoom is currently uncommon in most films because of its unnatural effect: a sudden awareness of the camera which tends to detract from a scene. It is more frequent that zooming will be used in conjunction with a dolly shot, if at all. When zoom lenses were first introduced zooming was quite common, most likely because of the novelty.

In 16mm zoom lenses are by far the most common choice because both camera and lens are of a significantly reduced size, and the benefit of having variable focal lengths to choose from when composing a shot is of considerable importance for those who shoot documentaries or other projects under uncontrolled conditions; hence the zoom lens is ubiquitous on video cameras. Additionally, many of the latest 16mm zoom lenses will also cover the Super 16 format.

Positive supplemental lenses which decrease the focal length of a lens in terms of focus, but do not change the angle of view, are called diopters. The power of a diopter is the reciprocal of the focal length in meters, where 1/.250 (250mm) equals a $+4$ diopter. To determine the focal length of a diopter simply calculate the reciprocal of the diopter power, where $1/+4$ is 250mm. When a lens is focused at infinity with a diopter, one can ascertain the new focus distance by converting the focal length into inches, e.g., $1/+4$ (250mm), and multiplying the answer (250) by .0393; thus the new focus is 9.84 inches. Diopters are used to focus on close subjects or, in the case of split diopters, when it is necessary to hold two subjects in focus where depth of field is limited. Split diopters are usually aligned with a vertical or horizontal edge in a frame to reduce their visibility. The optical quality is questionable in higher power diopters, particularly anything over a $+2$, and it is not recommended that wide apertures be used. It is also better to use a single higher power diopter than combining two lower power diopters, as invariably more aberrations will be introduced. The convex side of the diopter should be pointed towards the scene and all focusing should be done by eye under these circumstances.

Extenders are negative lenses designed to increase the focal length of a lens. Unlike diopters, though, they are mounted on the rear of the lens. For example, a $2 \times$ extender on a 100mm lens will create the equivalent of a 200mm lens. Exposure compensation must be made when using extenders, and for the most common extenders, such as

1.4 × and 2 × , it is necessary to add 1 stop and 2 stops respectively. In many cases the image quality is not as good when using extenders, particularly at wide apertures, so they should not be used as a substitute for an available lens of similar focal length. Extenders find more frequent usage on long focal length lenses and telephoto lenses, where there is less choice in intermediate focal lengths.

The shift and tilt lens is a bellows-based system which is normally used with a variety of custom-designed prime lenses. By allowing movement of the lens via the bellows attachment, shifting and tilting are possible. The most common uses would be to modify the framing without moving the camera (very handy in cramped quarters) and changing the focus plane. Slant-focus lenses are similar to a shift and tilt system, but do not use a bellows attachment and only allow tilting. The slant-focus lens can be used much like a split diopter, where two different subjects can be held in focus at widely spaced distances by tilting the focus plane, solving the problem of limited depth of field caused by using wide apertures, long focal length lenses, or working very near to subjects.

Periscope and borescope (probe) lenses are commonly used where a traditional lens will not suffice, such as when shooting miniatures or low perspectives. A periscope is basically an optical relay tube connected to a 45 degree angle attachment (prism) which contains a prime lens, allowing extremely low-angle shots (mouse eye's view) and complex maneuvering between and around small objects where the physical size of the camera would normally be a problem, such as when following a mouse through a maze, or showing the rodent's point of view. The borescope essentially eliminates the angular attachment and instead adds an extension fitted with a lens, making it especially suitable for moving through small openings, an example being the narrow space between a partially opened door.

The assumed quality of a lens before any photographic testing is largely based on the reputation of the manufacturer. There are few companies producing lenses specifically for the motion picture industry, and the lenses manufactured by such companies are of extremely high quality. Photographic testing is usually a sufficient indicator of quality, particularly in the case of those who have used a wide variety of lenses and are therefore experienced enough to apply subjective evaluation, but modulation transfer function (MTF) charts may be consulted for more precise and objective analysis. The modulation transfer function is a means of indicating the resolution of a lens. A test object with a luminance that varies sinusoidally along its horizontal axis is imaged through a lens. By determining the object modulation and the image modulation, respectively $Mo = (Lmax-Lmin)/(Lmax + Lmin)$ and $Mi = (Lmax-Lmin)/(Lmax + Lmin)$, one can determine the modulation transfer factor: Mi/Mo. The modulation transfer factor decreases with increasing frequency (detail). By plotting the modulation transfer factors at a variety of spatial frequencies, a modulation transfer function curve is formed (see Figure 7.1).

The x-axis indicates the spatial frequency (line pairs/mm or cycles/mm) and the y-axis is the modulation transfer factor, which is indicated as a percentage. The less curvature in the plotted line, the more line pairs per millimeter that are resolved. Ideally, one would prefer a lens having the highest modulation transfer factor percentage throughout the range of useful frequencies, as this is indicative of a superior lens. It should be noted that considerably different results will be obtained if the lens is tested at different apertures, for reasons which will soon become apparent. In order to make valid comparisons between

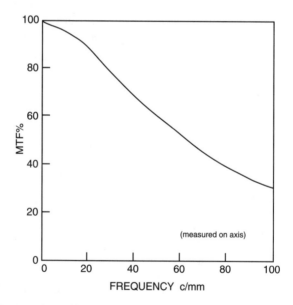

FIGURE 7.1 MTF of typical prime lens. Aperture at T-2.8.

different lenses, verification must be made regarding the aperture and focal length used for the test. The focus is normally set to infinity for testing.

Even given the quality of the latest computer-designed lenses, the fact still remains that an absolutely perfect lens does not exist. There are two reasons for this: aberrations and diffraction. Aberrations are optical defects, and diffraction (light rays bending) is a problem relative to the size of the aperture. Using two categories to broadly define aberrations, the terms monochromatic and polychromatic find frequent application.

Regarding the monochromatic, we have spherical aberration, coma, astigmatism, field curvature, and distortion. The first three affect sharpness, while the last two deal with poor focus and image warping respectively. When rays of light passing through the peripheral area of the lens do not focus at the same point as the parallel rays the lens is said to have spherical aberration. Therefore spherical aberration is more of a problem at wide apertures. Coma involves magnification differences in off-axis rays, and astigmatism causes images to form at two different focal planes. When the image is not sharply focused at the edges, due to off-axis rays falling short of the image plane, the aberration is noted as field curvature. Distortion is the most obvious of all aberrations, and causes vertical and horizontal lines to bend inwards (pin-cushion distortion) or outwards (barrel distortion).

In the polychromatic category, chromatic aberrations are caused by differences in the refractive properties (index of refraction) of the lens relative to wavelength. The speed of light is normally given as 3.00×10^8 m/sec, but this is only true in a vacuum. When light travels through materials of higher density, such as glass, the speed of light is lower, and this causes the light waves to bend or change direction (refract). By determining the ratio of the speed of light in a vacuum to the speed of light in the material, the index of refraction can be calculated. Unfortunately it is not quite this simple, as the index of refraction also varies with wavelength. Since the angle of refraction is based on this index, it cannot be expected that all the wavelengths will focus at the same point. Therefore a reduction in overall sharpness and a variety of color distortions (color fringing) occur. The use of low-dispersion glass can alleviate this problem, along with secondary corrective lens elements.

Glare (veiling and ghosting) is usually less problematic because all lenses minimize this by the use of various anti-reflective coatings, but all lenses will exhibit a certain degree of inherent flare. Older lenses exhibit more of a problem in this area due to inferior anti-reflective coatings. It is very important that the coatings are not ruined by solvents or overly abrasive cleaning as this will reduce the quality of the lens.

Diffraction is an unavoidable problem due to the aperture of the lens. When light passes through a small opening the rays are bent (diffracted). At wide apertures the diffraction is not severe enough to seriously affect the image, but at narrow apertures such as T-16 or T-22 the image can suffer a loss of sharpness. It is for this reason that most lenses will not provide the best performance at small apertures, while conversely at wider apertures aberrations are more problematic. Neither large apertures nor small apertures can produce the best image, which means one must use a mid-range T-stop for the best quality. Regardless of this technical fact, the use of wide apertures is very common due to the frequent use of low light levels. Whether the qualitative change is noticeable is relative, since most cinematographers aim for consistency through the use of a limited range of T-stops. When apertures are consistent, depth of field is consistent.

The term depth of field refers to an area of acceptable sharpness. In specifying depth of field one uses near and far distance measurements, the range of which indicates a zone of sharpness. In reality, there is only one plane of focus, but practical application proves otherwise. When viewing a projected image, or any photographic image for that matter, there is almost always an area of sharpness that exceeds the exact distance the lens was focused to; this is the so-called "depth of field." From a technical standpoint this can be explained by saying that even though there is only one point of convergence (where the sharpest image will be produced), objects that are behind or in front of the plane of focus that do not converge as a point at the film plane, but rather as a circle, will still appear as a point if the circle is less than a specific size. Therefore when calculating depth of field, a "circle of confusion" must be assigned. To a large extent this is a subjective matter.

Many factors contribute to depth of field: the focal length of the lens, the aperture, the distance of focus, and the resolution of the format. One can reasonably ascertain focus and depth of field if a bright viewfinder image is available (focus being the easier to gauge of the two), although this will be nearly impossible when a lens is stopped down. For greater precision, when possible, the focus distance is always determined with a tape measure and the lens set for this distance by the lens markings. Over very long distances this method does not apply. The constant measuring and placement of marks for subjects or camera movements are necessary in order to maintain control over follow-focus. Depth of field, in any case, is generally calculated rather than assumed by sight. For more rapid productions such as documentaries where one does not have the benefit of multiple camera assistants it is more common to focus by eye, as the unreeling of a tape measure when shooting is impractical. Auto-focus, a common feature on video cameras, is virtually nonexistent on film cameras.

Long focal length lenses produce less depth of field, wide apertures produce less depth of field, and short focus distances produce less depth of field. Conversely, wide-angle (short focal length) lenses produce greater depth of field, small apertures produce greater depth of field, and long focus distances produce greater depth of field. Lens quality and the intended final viewing conditions also greatly affect the perceived depth of field, as a higher resolution lens, a higher resolution image, and a larger screen produce the perception of a more limited depth of field. Lower resolution images and a smaller screen, such as provided by a television, perceptually create a greater depth of field. Of course, in high-definition television depth of field (or lack of it) is more noticeable.

Another factor that must be considered is the size of the image or optical squeeze of the image in the horizontal axis. Small image formats such as 16mm and 2/3-inch video require very wide angle lenses; therefore the depth of field is increased due to the short focal length lenses being utilized and, of course, in the case of video, the limited-resolution image provided by the monitor. When shooting in anamorphic or 65mm there is considerably less depth of field because both of these formats invariably cause one to use longer focal length lenses.

The hyper-focal distance is the distance at which the lens can be set in order to produce a sharp image from half that point of focus to infinity. Closing the aperture will bring the point of hyper-focal distance closer, while opening the aperture will move it farther away.

When examining a depth of field chart, with indicated hyper-focal distances, we are able to see this relationship very clearly. Hyper-focal distance is necessary in order to determine depth of field based on mathematical methods, but, for absolute accuracy, actual photographic testing of the lens is usually preferred. In the following formula L is the lens focal length and S is the stop.

Hyper-Focal Distance $(1/1000) = (L^2 \times .000129)/(.001 \times S)$

Depth of field can be defined mathematically by using three variables: the focus distance of the lens, the aperture, and the focal length of the lens. The circle of confusion is .001 (1/1000).

Scientific Calculator Program: Depth of Field

```
"35 Depth of Field":
"----------------":
"Lens"?→L:
"F Stop"?→S:
"Distance"?→D:
(L^2×.000129)/(.001×S)→H:
(H×D)/(H+D)→N:
(H×D)/(H-D)→F:
"-----Near-----":
"Feet":
Int N:
Int N→G▲
N-G→I:
"Inches":
I×12→J:J▲
"-----Far-----":
"Feet":
Int F:
Int F→P▲
F-P→Q:
"Inches":
Q×12→R:R↵
```

Scientific Calculator Programs: Diopters

Close focus with a diopter:

```
"Focus Distance"?→L:
"Diopter Power"?→D:
"New Focus (Feet)":L×.304800→Z:
Z/(D×Z+1)→A:
A×3.280833→F:
Int F→G▲
```

Diopter necessary to hold near focus:

```
"Far Distance"?→F:
"Near Distance"?→N:
"Diopter":
F×.304800→Z:
N×.304800→Y:
1/Z→A:
1/Y→B:
B-A→W▲
```

Hyp.	19		13		9		7		5		3		2		2		17
F Stop	2		2.8		4		5.65		8		11		16		22		mm
Dist.	Ft'	In"	Ft'	In"	Ft'	In"	Ft'	In"	Ft'	In"	Ft'	In"	Ft'	In"	Ft'	In"	.001 cc
2'	1	9.7	1	8.9	1	7.8	1	6.4	1	4.8	1	3.1	1	.9	0	11.0	Near
	2	2.9	2	4.2	2	6.6	2	10.4	3	6.0	4	10.6	14	1.4	INF	INF	Far
4'	3	3.5	3	.9	2	9.6	2	5.9	2	1.8	1	10.0	1	5.7	1	2.3	Near
	5	1.1	5	8.6	7	.1	10	1.9	28	2.9	INF	INF	INF	INF	INF	INF	Far
6'	4	6.5	4	1.6	3	7.8	3	1.7	2	7.5	2	2.0	1	8.1	1	3.9	Near
	8	10.2	10	11.1	16	10.1	66	1.9	INF	INF	INF	INF	INF	INF	INF	INF	Far
8'	5	7.2	4	12.0	4	3.7	3	7.4	2	11.3	2	4.6	1	9.7	1	4.8	Near
	14	.2	20	.5	56	5.7	INF	INF	INF	INF	INF	INF	INF	INF	INF	INF	Far
10'	6	6.1	5	8.5	4	9.9	3	11.7	3	2.1	2	6.4	1	10.7	1	5.4	Near
	21	6.9	40	2.0	INF	INF	INF	INF	INF	INF	INF	INF	INF	INF	INF	INF	Far
12'	7	3.6	6	3.7	5	3.0	4	3.1	3	4.3	2	7.7	1	11.4	1	5.8	Near
	33	8.2	121	6.4	INF	INF	INF	INF	INF	INF	INF	INF	INF	INF	INF	INF	Far
15'	8	3.7	7	.6	5	9.0	4	7.0	3	6.7	2	9.2	2	.2	1	6.3	Near
	76	9.7	INF	INF	INF	INF	INF	INF	INF	INF	INF	INF	INF	INF	INF	INF	Far
20'	9	7.8	7	11.9	6	4.3	4	11.5	3	9.4	2	10.8	2	1.0	1	6.7	Near
	INF	INF	INF	INF	INF	INF	INF	INF	INF	INF	INF	INF	INF	INF	INF	INF	Far
30'	11	6.0	9	2.7	7	1.3	5	4.9	4	.4	3	.5	2	1.9	1	7.2	Near
	INF	INF	INF	INF	INF	INF	INF	INF	INF	INF	INF	INF	INF	INF	INF	INF	Far
60'	14	2.7	10	10.8	8	.8	5	11.3	4	3.9	3	2.5	2	2.9	1	7.8	Near
	INF	INF	INF	INF	INF	INF	INF	INF	INF	INF	INF	INF	INF	INF	INF	INF	Far

Hyp.	47		34		24		17		12		9		6		4		27
F Stop	2		2.8		4		5.65		8		11		16		22		mm
Dist.	Ft'	In"	Ft'	In"	Ft'	In"	Ft'	In"	Ft'	In"	Ft'	In"	Ft'	In"	Ft'	In"	.001 cc
2'	1	11.0	1	10.7	1	10.1	1	9.4	1	8.5	1	7.4	1	5.9	1	4.4	Near
	2	1.1	2	1.5	2	2.2	2	3.3	2	4.9	2	7.3	3	.4	3	9.1	Far
4'	3	8.2	3	6.9	3	5.0	3	2.7	2	11.8	2	8.7	2	4.6	2	.8	Near
	4	4.5	4	6.5	4	9.8	5	3.2	6	.8	7	6.2	12	6.3	62	3.2	Far
6'	5	3.9	5	1.1	4	9.4	4	4.9	3	11.7	3	6.3	2	11.6	2	6.0	Near
	6	10.5	7	3.7	8	.7	9	4.6	12	3.1	20	1.5	INF	INF	INF	INF	Far
8'	6	10.0	6	5.5	5	11.6	5	4.8	4	9.1	4	1.6	3	4.7	2	9.4	Near
	9	7.7	10	6.0	12	1.5	15	4.8	25	.5	124	6.4	INF	INF	INF	INF	Far
10'	8	3.0	7	8.5	7	.2	6	3.0	5	4.8	4	7.3	3	8.4	2	11.9	Near
	12	8.4	14	2.9	17	4.8	25	.6	66	11.7	INF	INF	INF	INF	INF	INF	Far
12'	9	6.7	8	10.1	7	11.3	6	11.7	5	11.3	4	11.9	3	11.3	3	1.8	Near
	16	1.3	18	8.1	24	6.1	43	.1	INF	INF	INF	INF	INF	INF	INF	INF	Far
15'	11	4.5	10	4.4	9	1.9	7	10.7	6	7.1	5	5.3	4	2.7	3	3.9	Near
	22	.3	27	1.3	41	5.3	151	9.9	INF	INF	INF	INF	INF	INF	INF	INF	Far
20'	14	.4	12	6.4	10	9.7	9	1.0	7	4.8	5	11.9	4	6.5	3	6.3	Near
	34	9.6	49	5.3	133	11.4	INF	INF	INF	INF	INF	INF	INF	INF	INF	INF	Far
30'	18	3.8	15	10.2	13	2.2	10	8.5	8	5.3	6	7.8	4	11.0	3	8.9	Near
	82	10.5	280	11.7	INF	INF	INF	INF	INF	INF	INF	INF	INF	INF	INF	INF	Far
60'	26	4.3	21	6.4	16	10.7	13	.4	9	10.0	7	5.8	5	4.2	3	11.9	Near
	INF	INF	INF	INF	INF	INF	INF	INF	INF	INF	INF	INF	INF	INF	INF	INF	Far

Hyp.	103		74		52		37		26		19		13		9		40
F Stop	2		2.8		4		5.65		8		11		16		22		mm
Dist.	Ft'	In"	Ft'	In"	Ft'	In"	Ft'	In"	Ft'	In"	Ft'	In"	Ft'	In"	Ft'	In"	.001 cc
2'	1	11.5	1	11.4	1	11.1	1	10.8	1	10.3	1	9.7	1	8.8	1	7.8	Near
	2	.5	2	.7	2	1.0	2	1.4	2	2.0	2	2.9	2	4.4	2	6.5	Far
4'	3	10.2	3	9.5	3	8.5	3	7.3	3	5.6	3	3.6	3	.6	2	9.7	Near
	4	1.9	4	2.8	4	4.0	4	5.9	4	8.8	5	1.0	5	9.6	6	11.7	Far
6'	5	8.0	5	6.6	5	4.5	5	1.8	4	10.4	4	6.6	4	1.1	3	7.9	Near
	6	4.4	6	6.4	6	9.5	7	2.1	7	9.8	8	9.8	11	2.6	16	7.7	Far
8'	7	5.1	7	2.6	6	11.1	6	6.8	6	1.3	5	7.3	4	11.3	4	3.8	Near
	8	8.1	8	11.7	9	5.6	10	2.9	11	7.1	13	11.4	21	.7	54	3.8	Far
10'	9	1.4	8	9.7	8	4.5	7	10.2	7	2.5	6	6.3	5	7.6	4	10.1	Near
	11	.9	11	6.8	12	4.8	13	9.2	16	3.9	21	4.9	44	5.8	INF	INF	Far
12'	10	9.0	10	3.8	9	8.8	9	.4	8	2.3	7	3.8	6	2.6	5	3.2	Near
	13	6.9	14	4.0	15	7.6	17	10.4	22	5.2	33	3.5	172	0	INF	INF	Far
15'	13	1.2	12	5.6	11	7.5	10	7.6	9	5.8	8	4.0	6	11.2	5	9.3	Near
	17	6.6	18	10.0	21	1.8	25	5.4	35	10.0	74	9.4	INF	INF	INF	INF	Far
20'	16	9.0	15	8.8	14	5.0	12	11.1	11	3.2	9	8.2	7	10.1	6	4.6	Near
	24	9.7	27	5.4	32	7.9	44	2.4	88	11.6	INF	INF	INF	INF	INF	INF	Far
30'	23	2.9	21	3.9	18	11.6	16	5.7	13	10.5	11	6.5	9	.3	7	1.8	Near
	42	3.5	50	7.1	71	8.0	167	9.7	INF	INF	INF	INF	INF	INF	INF	INF	Far
60'	37	11.3	33	.9	27	8.9	22	8.5	18	.5	14	3.5	10	7.4	8	1.4	Near
	143	4.0	322	6.0	INF	INF	INF	INF	INF	INF	INF	INF	INF	INF	INF	INF	Far

Hyp.	363		259		181		128		91		66		45		33		75
F Stop	2		2.8		4		5.65		8		11		16		22		mm
Dist.	Ft'	In"	Ft'	In"	Ft'	In"	Ft'	In"	Ft'	In"	Ft'	In"	Ft'	In"	Ft'	In"	.001 cc
2'	1	11.9	1	11.8	1	11.7	1	11.6	1	11.5	1	11.3	1	11.0	1	10.6	Near
	2	.1	2	.2	2	.3	2	.4	2	.5	2	.8	2	1.1	2	1.5	Far
4'	3	11.5	3	11.3	3	11.0	3	10.6	3	10.0	3	9.3	3	8.1	3	6.8	Near
	4	.5	4	.8	4	1.1	4	1.5	4	2.2	4	3.1	4	4.6	4	6.6	Far
6'	5	10.8	5	10.4	5	9.7	5	8.8	5	7.5	5	6.0	5	3.6	5	.9	Near
	6	1.2	6	1.7	6	2.5	6	3.5	6	5.1	6	7.2	6	11.0	7	4.0	Far
8'	7	9.9	7	9.1	7	7.9	7	6.4	7	4.2	7	1.6	6	9.6	6	5.3	Near
	8	2.2	8	3.1	8	4.4	8	6.4	8	9.3	9	1.2	9	8.6	10	6.7	Far
10'	9	8.8	9	7.5	9	5.7	9	3.3	9	.1	8	8.2	8	2.3	7	8.1	Near
	10	3.4	10	4.8	10	7.0	10	10.1	11	2.9	11	9.4	12	9.9	14	4.2	Far
12'	11	7.4	11	5.6	11	3.1	10	11.7	10	7.2	10	1.8	9	5.9	8	9.6	Near
	12	4.9	12	7.0	12	10.2	13	2.8	13	10.0	14	8.0	16	3.8	18	10.4	Far
15'	14	4.9	14	2.2	13	10.3	13	5.2	12	10.5	12	2.7	11	3.3	10	3.7	Near
	15	7.8	15	11.1	16	4.2	16	11.8	17	11.7	19	5.0	22	5.0	27	6.1	Far
20'	18	11.5	18	6.8	18	.2	17	3.7	16	4.6	15	4.2	13	10.6	12	5.4	Near
	21	2.0	21	8.1	22	5.7	23	8.3	25	7.9	28	8.4	35	9.3	50	9.7	Far
30'	27	8.5	26	10.6	25	8.9	24	3.8	22	6.5	20	7.5	18	.7	15	8.5	Near
	32	8.5	33	11.1	35	11.3	39	1.7	44	9.9	55	.3	88	7.5	331	8.6	Far
60'	51	5.8	48	8.6	45	1.0	40	10.7	36	1.3	31	5.1	25	9.9	21	3.4	Near
	71	10.7	78	.9	89	7.8	112	7.3	177	3.0	663	5.1	INF	INF	INF	INF	Far

The selection of lenses for a production should also be color-matched, meaning that they can be used interchangeably with similar results. When using lenses that were designed as a series this is usually not a problem, but this is not the case when using special lenses, modified lenses, or those not part of a series. Color compensating filters can be used in severe cases of differing color reproduction between two lenses, but when it is inconvenient to do so, correction can be provided by the color timer or video colorist.

When renting lenses for a production it is important to examine each lens mechanically and optically before accepting it. The front and rear elements should be checked for scratches and pitting, while the internal components can be examined more carefully if a light is available to shine through the lens, which should reveal any fogging from moisture or dampness. Cleaning is required if any fingerprints are on the surface of the lens, while excessive dust can be removed with a camel's hair brush or by using compressed air. The focus ring should be checked for damage, as the follow-focus may not properly engage the geared ring. The iris ring should move smoothly throughout its range and the iris blades must not stick. Excessive wear on the outside of the barrel is a good indication of the degree of usage, and the more abused a lens appears, the more wary one must be. Focus scales should be checked against a suitable focus chart and, if necessary, film tests shot. With zoom lenses the focus should remain sharp throughout its range, and the crosshairs in the viewfinder should not shift during the zoom. It is also imperative when eye-focusing a zoom lens to always focus at the longest focal length and widest aperture, not only for test purposes, but also during production.

When splitting focus (as is commonly done with two-shots) the lens should be focused at the near focus point and then focused at one-third the distance to the far point of focus. Splitting focus equally between the two points is sometimes acceptable, but since depth to the far depth of field distance is usually greater, it makes sense to focus at one-third the distance, and allow the depth of field to hold the subject in the background in focus. Of course, as in all creative work, there may be artistic reasons for not following such basic principles.

8

Latent to Visible

THE LABORATORY

When any film production wraps for the day, the exposed film must be promptly sent to the laboratory for processing. Depending on the distance involved, this can be a ten minute drive or a trip halfway around the world. In any event, several precautionary measures must be taken, because at this stage the emulsion is most susceptible to the damaging effects of heat and humidity. The longer the delay between exposure and processing, the more likely a detrimental change will occur in the latent image, such as fogging, or contrast and color problems. While excessive temperatures and humidity are probably the most common problems a filmmaker has to contend with when shooting on location, damage from radiation must also be considered. Even if one has the benefit of rapid transport by air, special precautions must be followed to avoid X-ray machines. While many domestic airports do not use machines that are powerful enough to damage film (particularly slow-speed emulsions), it is a risk not worth taking when one considers the effort and expense involved in a film production. Unprocessed film should never be checked in as baggage for obvious reasons. Sending exposed film by courier service can also subject it to X-ray scanning devices, particularly if one is dealing with customs or foreign postal services at any stage in the shipment. The safest and most logical method of transporting film to a laboratory is usually dictated by the circumstances.

When a laboratory receives exposed film (which should have been placed back into the black plastic bag from whence it came, sealed in

115

the original can, and marked clearly with roll numbers) it is normally processed in the order it was received. Most laboratories run their processing machines almost twenty-four hours a day, so film that is brought in the night before can be processed, cleaned, and printed (or transferred to video) in order to provide dailies.

Negative processing, specified as ECN-2, is quite rapid. The prebath takes ten minutes and prepares the film for the remjet removal which follows. The film then plunges into the developer bath for exactly three minutes, at which point a stop bath is necessary for thirty seconds. A clean wash for two minutes prepares the film for a three minute bleach bath, which converts all the metallic silver back to silver halide. Another two minute wash and the film is on its way to a fixer bath for the same duration to remove all the silver halide content. A clean wash for three minutes is followed by a ten minute final rinse, and the film then moves onto the dryer. The whole process takes a little more than a quarter of an hour.

The print process (ECP-2B) is similar in most respects to the negative process, although the details are not quite the same. For example, the print process may involve a sound track developer (if final print for release). The latest print stocks have also eliminated the remjet backing and use antihalation dye layers instead, which are coated below the light-sensitive emulsion. Therefore the alkaline prebath is no longer necessary, and the antihalation dye layers are simply removed by the developer in a far more efficient one-step process.

When a print is desired for viewing purposes the negative is duplicated onto an appropriate print stock, which yields a positive image. Continuous-contact printers are used for typical printing, such as that required for dailies or when mass printing is necessary for release prints, although in the latter case they are operated at much higher speeds, sometimes as high as 960 feet per minute, while in the former case speeds rarely exceed 240 feet per minute. When the highest quality image is necessary, such as when producing intermediates, it is common to use a wet-gate process (also known as immersion printing). By coating the original film with a liquid of similar refractive index as the base, any scratches or abrasions on the negative will be masked in the duplicate.

Step optical printers, which essentially re-photograph the original image, are strictly used for a variety of effects (wipes, fades, dissolves, etc.), and for such specialized tasks as producing anamorphic prints from Super 35 or blow-ups from 16mm to 35mm. Because the negative and positive film are not in contact in an optical printer, but have completely separate paths, the original can be reproduced at different magnifications by changing the distance between the printer head and process camera. Step-contact prints can also be made on an optical printer if the negative and positive film are threaded through the same movement together. The printing speeds are substantially slower in optical printing, with 10 to 40 feet per minute being the most common.

Most laboratories (if no special printing requirements are indicated) will produce prints on a continuous-contact additive printer. In an additive printer the red, green, and blue printing lights are produced from a single 1000 watt tungsten light source split into its three primary colors through a series of dichroic mirrors. By controlling these three colors with individual light valves, the printer can automatically control the amount of red, green, and blue light which mixes to form the composite light that exposes the print stock after passing through the negative. Printing in such machines takes place with the negative in direct contact with the print stock—an emulsion to emulsion process—while running at a speed of 180 feet per minute or more. The positive stock is on the outside of the printing sprocket, while the negative is underneath, which is why the print stock has a longer pitch (KS-.1870 for 35/70mm and 1R/2R .3000 for 16mm) designation instead of that which is found on negative stocks (BH-.1866 for 35mm, KS-.1866 for 65mm, and 1R/2R .2994 for 16mm).

The processed negative, as we explained in Chapter 6, is made up of three dye layers: cyan, magenta, and yellow. These dye layers act as filters when the printing light passes through them, and each individual dye layer modifies the exposing light in a specific way, which is very much dependent on the color of the dye and its corresponding density.

As an example, in order to explain the interaction of the dye layers of the negative with the printer light, the corresponding dye formation on the print stock, and ultimately the result in projection, we will use a pure red subject which has been exposed on a color negative film. In doing so we avoid the complexity of dealing with an arbitrary color which is produced from a combination of dye layers and would, no doubt, lead to total confusion.

After processing, the red subject will appear as a cyan image on the negative for the obvious reason, as one may recall, that the red-sensitive layer of the negative forms a cyan dye after development. When the printer light passes through the negative image, the cyan dye that represents the red subject subtracts out the red wavelengths from the exposing light. The print stock receives this modified light precisely where the red subject's image will be formed, and exposes mostly the blue-sensitive and green-sensitive layers on the positive film, due to the fact that the red wavelength content has been mostly removed by the cyan dye in the negative. Furthermore, the density of the dye in the negative regulates the exposure of the print, where more density will produce a brighter print image and less density will produce a darker print image.

When the positive image is created during development, and the yellow, magenta, and cyan dyes are formed, the resulting area that represents the red object on the print will be composed of yellow and magenta dyes, with little or no cyan dye. When the print is projected in a theater, with a projector that uses as its light source a xenon lamp (5400K), the white light will be modified by the yellow and magenta layers of the positive image. Yellow, of course, is the opposite of blue, and therefore subtracts out the blue in the projector light, while magenta, the opposite of green, subtracts out the green light of the projector, so that the resulting color that reaches the screen in that specific object area will be red—the only wavelength which has passed through the print unhindered by a subtractive dye layer. Another way of explaining the end result is by simply stating that yellow and magenta dye layers, when combined, produce red.

Positive stocks have roughly the same spectral sensitivity as negative stocks, but several important differences are evident. First, they do not employ color masking and therefore have a clear base after processing. Second, the dye layers are not in the same order as negative stocks. In a color negative stock the yellow dye layer is on the top, the magenta dye layer is in the middle, and the cyan dye layer is on the bottom. In print stocks the magenta dye layer is on the top, the cyan dye layer is in the middle, and the yellow dye layer is on the bottom. This is done to counteract the effect of differing granularity levels in each dye layer. Since the magenta dye contributes the most to the perception of graininess in a projected image, it makes sense to place this layer on top, where the definition is always greatest. As the yellow layer, by its contribution to granularity, is the least offender, it is placed at the bottom. The cyan dye layer, then, is placed in the middle layer. By using such a method an improvement in the quality of the projected image can be attained.

Moving now to less scientific and more practical matters, the importance of understanding the process of color timing and the degree of control available in the printing process must be examined. Just as exposure and color balance are carefully determined during production when shooting the camera negative, this policy must be maintained when the printing stage is reached.

Most color timing is done using an electronic color analyzer and a Laboratory Aim Density (LAD) control film. A color analyzer is similar to a film to video transfer system (telecine) in that it allows the color timer to watch the negative film on a video monitor in a positive form in order to facilitate the color timing process. While the basic design has changed little since its introduction, new versions have increased functionality by the addition of a digital framestore, allowing comparisons to be made between shots. There is of course still a significant limitation placed on the system due to the fact that the picture provided is strictly video-based, meaning a certain degree of interpretation is required by the user when making changes. Unlike the film to video system where the final output is the same, the film color timer must color correct with a video system but must be able to visualize the result as it will appear on film. The color timer is faced with a far more intuitive task than a video colorist, who can simply rely on the image of the video monitor.

The purpose of the LAD film is to provide a means of calibrating a color analyzer in order to produce consistent printing results. The LAD control film, which is a processed negative film, contains a series of neutral patches, an abbreviated gray scale, and a woman's head as a fleshtone example. Color patches are also provided for subjective reference. The large white patch represents a scene tone of 90 percent reflectance, the large black patch a scene tone of 2.5 percent reflectance, while the LAD patch (a medium gray) is specified as having an original reflectance of 16 percent, almost the same as the 18 percent reflectance of a gray card. The LAD film is placed into the gate of the analyzer and the controls are set to produce a visual match of the LAD square on the film with a reference gray. The reference gray is normally obtained by using a neutral filter of approximately .70 visual density placed over a reference white generated on the monitor. The reference white is produced by the opaque frame area of the control film or by using a piece of black tape in the gate. In essence, if one can provide a reference gray on the monitor that produces the equivalent of 1.0 visual density on the print (as measured by a densitometer having a spectral response in close correlation with the eye), by matching the LAD square to this reference gray using the timing controls one can be assured that the density of the LAD patch when printed will be at the aim density: 1.0 equivalent neutral density (END) or Status A densities of R 1.09, G 1.06, and B 1.03. If the cinematographer provides a gray card or gray scale at the head of a shot, the color timer can use this in a similar manner as the LAD patch, thereby providing more precisely timed prints. A basic gray scale is also frequently utilized during production, and these can be fixed to the slate for convenience.

Laboratory aim density is also used for producing intermediates such as interpositives and internegatives, because it is imperative that the original negative is accurately reproduced. This can be done by using the LAD method outlined earlier, where the original negative tones will be centered on the linear portion of the D log H curve of the duplicating stock when correct procedures are followed. Densitometer measurements must be Status M when verifying the recommended densities on such intermediate films.

Ideally the one-light setting (which is derived from calibrating the color analyzer to produce the proper density on the print) is R 25-G 25-B 25, but these numbers are far from standardized as any pre-filtering may change these settings. Assuming the laboratory is using additive printing, these numbers represent the red, green, and blue light values that will be used by the printer. Most printers have a range of 1 to 50 printer points. As the print exposure is necessarily based upon the intensity of the printer's light and the density of the negative, one can determine the number of printer points necessary to produce a 1 stop exposure change if the gamma of the negative is known and, in addition, the log H equivalent of 1 printer point. Since 1 printer point equals .025 Log H (or 12 printer points per 1 stop change in exposure when using a film with unity gamma, e.g., intermediates), a negative with a gamma of .65 will require roughly 8 printer points to produce a 1 stop change in exposure, i.e., 12 × .65 = 7.8, as the density of the negative is not doubled for each stop of exposure as in the case of film stocks with a gamma of 1.

The underlying theory of LAD is that if the cinematographer uses the manufacturer's provided exposure index rating along with properly calibrated exposure meters and lenses, the negative should print close to this set of numbers, called printer points. In reality, of course, most laboratories do not have equal printer points, nor do they use the same equipment, lamps, voltage levels, filtering, etc., and this tends to create a very customized process, with noticeably different RGB values at each laboratory. Rarely will the negative print with equal lights, so a laboratory exposure report, which is based on these light values, will typically appear as Red 28, Green 32, and Blue 29, or any variety of combinations depending on the standard at that lab. Despite these inconsistencies, regular negatives should print reasonably close to the normal settings relative to *that* laboratory's set standard. If a gross error is found when dealing with exposure, and no lab explanation can be provided, it would be wise to check the calibration of your light meter.

Establishing a one-light standard for your own material is probably a good idea in order to obtain consistent results. The combination of camera(s), lenses, film stocks, and metering equipment can be factored into the initial printing, which should reduce the possibility of any surprises. Even if a personal one-light setting is determined with the assistance of a laboratory color timer for a specific production, taking the particular conditions into account, such as day or night, interior or exterior, etc., the cinematographer must still accept dailies for what they are: a method of assessing the previous day's work.

If the printer lights are lower than normal at a specific laboratory, one may assume that the negative was underexposed (a thin negative), while an overexposed negative (very dense) will print with higher lights. Essentially, the more dense the negative is the more intense the light must be to get through the film to properly expose the positive stock, while a thin negative needs less light to produce a comparable image because the film has an overall higher transmittance. A difference of 8 printer points represents 1 stop of camera exposure, so if the film prints 8 points lower than normal it would indicate that the negative is thin, or underexposed approximately 1 stop. Printing 8 points higher, of course, indicates just the opposite: a dense or 1 stop overexposed negative.

When particular scenes on the negative are not exposed properly, whether due to an error or the lack of enough light for the scene, we can use the printer to modify the exposure on the positive stock. Common terms refer to this process as printing up and printing down. When we print up we are printing at lower numbers (a brighter image overall), while printing down means to print at higher numbers (a darker image overall). The only drawback to this method is that if the negative was grossly under- or overexposed it may not be possible to salvage the image, or the results may not be acceptable when the shot is juxtaposed with other correctly exposed ones. A severely underexposed image (one that must be printed at a very low light setting in order to yield a normal print, due to the extreme lack of density of the negative) typically lacks contrast, which means the black level of the print is very poor. Because the black level of the print is a product of the printing lights, which are directly correlated to the original density of the negative, we can only produce a good black on a positive if we print mid-scale or higher on the printing lights. Usually an error of 1 stop in underexposure will not be significantly deleterious to the final print, but it is best not to push the limits because the original negative will be printed onto an interpositive (master positive) and internegative (color duplicate negative) before mass production of theatrical projection prints, and all of these copies can create a subtle loss of contrast.

Overexposure is far less of a problem than underexposure, because normally a proper black level can be maintained under these circumstances. When an overexposed negative is timed for the best results, the color timer will simply increase the printer points and print the scene down (darker), using more light. The only problem that may occur in some severe cases of overexposure is that the printer lights may reach a maximum number (which is normally 50) and at this point it will be impossible to produce a correctly exposed print. It will still look bright and overexposed because the negative is so dense that not enough light can be provided by the printer to pass through the negative and expose the print. If the mid-scale in the lab is around 25 or 27 an image could be as much as 2 1/2 stops overexposed and still produce an acceptable image when printed. Nonetheless, regardless of the corrective printing, a grossly overexposed negative will never produce the same print quality as a properly exposed negative, because the highlights will have considerably less detail.

If it is known that an entire roll is incorrectly exposed one may opt for a more complicated but generally accepted solution to improving the results, rather than relying on printing corrections alone. Based on the estimated exposure error, the time involved in the processing of the negative can be modified. This affects the contrast of the negative and can improve density levels when a film is exposed improperly. Since the speed at which the film moves through the continuous processor is the basis for controlling development, many laboratories offer push and pull processing as standard options. If the time it takes the negative to pass through the developer is longer than normal (extension of development) the film will be push processed, while conversely a pull process involves a more rapid transport speed, which reduces the time spent in the developer. Pull processing has less application for error-related exposure control because acceptable prints can be made from negatives that are several stops overexposed, but push processing is a common technique used when a film is known to be underexposed, either intentionally or unintentionally. Using this method will generally yield a superior print than if one relies on the printing process alone, as the invariably low density of the underexposed image is increased somewhat by the push processing. When the film is timed the printer points will be higher; thus the black level of the print will be superior to that obtained by simply adjusting the printer lights.

One should also remember that a purposefully over- or underexposed negative should not be printed at a higher or lower light level because the exposure effect will be canceled out. A correctly exposed negative can be printed darker or lighter just by changing the printing lights, which is the reason one must select a one-light print for dailies. If the image is modified by a color timer who may not know the intended effect, one cannot determine the accuracy of the initial exposure or its resulting print. This is of particular importance when dealing with color-related concerns, where an intended color bias from a filter may be removed by a color timer who is under the impression that the result was due to a color balance problem and was not intentional. Proper notes in lab reports can go a long way towards precluding such occurrences.

In comparison to a video colorist, the color timer has a very limited palette to work from, as the three color controls on the color analyzer (red, green, and blue) provide the means to change the color and contrast (density) of the resulting print. A problem in using RGB controls is that the result of modifying one of these color knobs does not produce the direct relationship one might automatically assume; that is, the color values are actually the printer lights, not the on-screen results. For example, if blue is increased on the electronic color analyzer, and the monitor is carefully examined during this process, the image will gradually turn more yellow. On the other hand, if blue is decreased the image will become less yellow. If green is increased, the resulting effect will be more magenta in the image. Increasing red, as we may have guessed, will invariably produce more cyan in the image. Essentially, the effect of changing these values is the opposite of what is expected because we are dealing with a negative image (Table 8.1).

LABORATORY PRINTING - ADDITIVE	
Printer Light	Effect on Print
+R	More Cyan
–R	Less Cyan
+G	More Magenta
–G	Less Magenta
+B	More Yellow
–B	Less Yellow
+BG	More Red
+RB	More Green
+GR	More Blue

TABLE 8.1 Printer light chart.

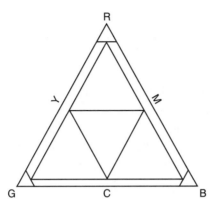

FIGURE 8.1 Color triangle: the combination of two primaries from one side of the triangle forms a secondary color, e.g., R + G = Y, while the color directly across from the primary is the complementary, e.g., blue and yellow. The combination of two secondary colors from one side of the interior triangle will yield the primary at the vertex of the larger triangle.

Therefore, when a change is required to produce more red, green, or blue in an image, two colors must be changed. For example, adding more blue and green will create an image with more red, adding more green and red will produce more blue in an image, and increasing red and blue will produce more green in an image. By decreasing two colors, for example, green and red, the image will now have less blue, and the same decreasing result applies to the color combinations enumerated earlier.

It may seem hopelessly confusing; however it is not as complicated as it appears because the color timer can view the effects of these changes on a color monitor. The real complexity of the process is maintaining the proper density when color changes are made, because when a light value is modified not only is a change in color balance taking place, but the exposure of the print will subsequently change. This makes the whole procedure much more involved. If one printing light is changed, more than likely a change will have to be made regarding the remaining lights in order to keep the density the same.

After the film has been edited, and the negative spliced into its proper order and printed, the cinematographer will normally consult with the color timer regarding the desired changes. It is at this point that scenes and shots will be matched as closely as possible and any obvious errors will be corrected. The color timer will save the data from each session, which will provide the basis for further changes, and the subsequent prints will be made using the modified data of the latest session, where the printer automatically controls the individual light valves based on this input. As each answer print is produced the results are carefully examined. This way, over a short period of time, the film can be fine-tuned.

After the last answer print has been approved by the cinematographer and the director, at which point the film may require hundreds if not thousands of copies to be produced for theatrical release, the laboratory will first make a correctly timed interpositive (color master positive) based on the saved printer light values from the final color timing. From this interpositive film an internegative (color duplicate negative) will be printed one-light, assuming that no changes were necessary on the interpositive. Interpositives are frequently made on triacetate stock, whereas the internegative is made on the much stronger Estar stock, as the latter is used to produce release prints. Depending upon the quantity of release prints needed, several internegatives can be made from the interpositive to reduce the inevitable wear on a single copy. These internegatives then provide a means of protecting the original negative, and simplify the printing process because all corrections have been made and the subsequent prints are struck one-light. The majority of release prints are now produced on Estar stocks, which have a durability exceeding the previously used triacetate stocks.

When optical printing is required (as in the case of reductions or blow-ups) it is important that the film is edited in its final form (keycode numbers do not print through unless a contact print is made) and an interpositive has been produced with the accepted timing. The interpositive can then be used in an optical printer to produce a one-light internegative in the correct format from which all subsequent prints can be made.

For example, one can use Super 35 as a substitute for anamorphic (a horizontally squeezed widescreen image) by shooting a full-frame negative and having the appropriate frame line markings in the camera for a widescreen extraction (2.35:1). It is then possible to extract this area from the timed interpositive when using an optical printer, producing an anamorphic internegative using an anamorphic lens in the optical printer. Subsequently, mass release prints can be made using standard high-speed contact printers. More internegatives can be provided by simply printing an interpositive from the internegative, from which further duplicate negatives are produced.

In the case of Super 16 it is more common to use the original negative for optical printing, thereby producing an interpositive blow-up to 35mm. This can then be contact printed to provide the internegative from which release prints can be struck. For color timing purposes a 16mm answer print is frequently still made.

When the priority turns to archival storage, RGB separations (three) can be made from the original negative onto panchromatic separation film (black and white), using an Estar stock with considerable longevity. Because there are no dyes to fade, a problem with all color materials, the image will last far longer. It is estimated that properly stored separations could last as long as five hundred years. The later addition of the appropriate filters as each separation is exposed onto a single piece of intermediate stock is all that is necessary in order to reproduce the original color image as an internegative. YCM separations are less frequently made, and these are produced from interpositives or prints. This process is common in the case of film restoration where the original negative may not exist due to damage or misplacement (see Figure 8.2).

As we have already discussed, pushing film is simply an extension of the development time, but now we will explore it as an intentional process, along with other modified processes all of which are used to achieve a particular effect. If it is known that a certain light level cannot be attained one can rate the stock at a higher exposure index. For example, an EI 200 film can be rated to EI 400 and the lab will push 1 stop in development to increase the density. Pushing more than 1 stop is extremely questionable and should be avoided for quality reasons. All pushing degrades the image in two ways: increasing the appearance of grain and creating more contrast. Severe push processing (in excess of 1 stop) may cause significant color imbalance due to the dye layers having different characteristic curves when developed, which may, in certain circumstances, preclude acceptable printing results. It is usually advisable to rate the film at a two-thirds higher exposure index when pushing 1 stop. For example, rate at 320 instead of 400 in the earlier case, which should improve density results at the lab.

Pulling film is the exact opposite of pushing film; the development is reduced by a specified time. The effect of pulling is a lower contrast negative with finer grain, and typically lower color saturation. If we want to pull an EI 200 film stock 1 stop, one would rate it at EI 100, thus overexposing it 1 stop, and then advise the lab to pull process 1 stop, which will yield a correct density negative. This technique is generally used when a certain effect is desired that can only be provided by such a process, or when a film stock has a particularly poor grain structure and the results of pull processing are desired to improve the overall image quality.

Flashing the negative is used to increase the lower densities of the negative. It brings out shadow detail otherwise not visible by adding density to the toe of the sensitometric curve, bringing the dark scene tones into the printing range without affecting the mid-scale or higher densities. Flashing can be done in-camera with the Panaflasher or Varicon (the latter does not operate the same as the former, as it fits into the filter slot of a 6.6×6.6 mattebox and adds to the existing light while the film is being exposed, allowing more subtle contrast control because the operator can view the effect through the viewfinder, while the Panaflasher is attached to the unused magazine port) or in the laboratory. In-camera flashing is usually defined by a percentage, unfortunately for which there is no set standard. It is advisable to do tests before actual production with different film stocks in order to determine the required amount of flashing necessary. Flashing in the lab might be preferred in some cases because the so-called "percentage" is more or less defined by more critical density measurements. A given percentage is really the additional density produced in the D-min of the stock, so if a 20 percent flashing is required on a negative film the lab will add .20 to the base measurement (D-min) of each layer. If filters are used during flashing the layers will produce different density results depending upon the color of the light. It should be remembered, though, that the color bias will only exist in the shadows when flashing a negative. Extensive testing is always necessary when flashing in-camera (or in the laboratory) to determine the desired effect. In addition, some laboratories may be wary of flashing an original negative because of the risk involved.

Flashing the print has the opposite effect of flashing the negative.

This procedure adds detail to low density areas on the positive, which means the highlights, not the shadows. Similar results can be obtained if the interpositive is flashed, which is more economical than flashing every print. Generally speaking, this technique is not used as often as flashing the negative because it has limited practical effect.

A special process which only applies to prints is the ENR process, where the color print is immersed in a black and white developer bath following normal color development, after the bleach step but before the fixer. Re-forming a percentage of metallic silver which is not removed by the subsequent fixer (only silver halide is removed by the fixer), the procedure adds density to the shadow areas, creating a deep black unattainable in a standard print. Color saturation is significantly reduced when higher levels are used and accordingly contrast increases. ENR is a more controlled process than extreme procedures such as bleach bypass because varying levels are possible, thus allowing more subtle control over the image. Like flashing, the degree of the effect is typically referred to as a percentage, although the laboratory actually uses more scientific methods to determine the amount of silver retained, i.e., densitometer measurements. The ENR process, like all custom processing that involves each and every print, is a very time-consuming and expensive proposition, making it somewhat impractical for use in wide-release films that may require three thousand or more prints. In many cases only a percentage of the release prints will be made as ENR prints.

The bleach bypass process is a technique that is used to leave the metallic silver formed from the reaction of the developer with the exposed silver halide crystals in the emulsion. In normally processed color negative material all of the silver content is removed, with the resulting three layers being only dye in composition. If the bleach process step is skipped when processing the negative, the subsequent prints will be quite contrasty (muddy) with very bright highlights. When the bleach step is skipped in a print made from a normally processed negative, the shadows are dark with muted colors. In many cases this will create unacceptable images, so a low-contrast negative will be necessary to begin with, which generally means some form of flashing, either in-camera or in the lab. It is usually recommended that the bleach bypass process be used on an intermediate so that the original negative is not subject to non-standard processing techniques, although different results should be expected when using an interpositive or internegative. In a laboratory that uses the persulfate bleach sequence instead of ferricyanide or UL bleach, the accelerator can be omitted from the process, yielding an image with a silver content of roughly 50 percent. The effect on a whole is less drastic when using such a method as versus a total bleach bypass.

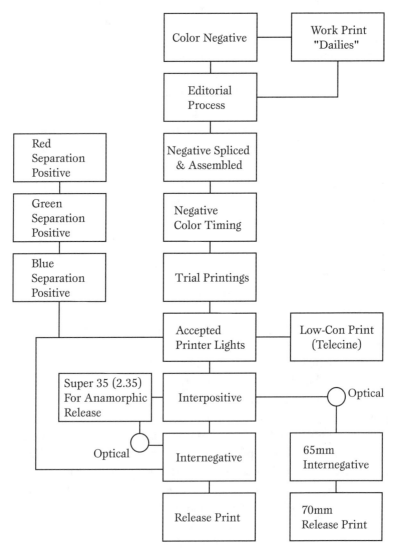

FIGURE 8.2 Laboratory process flowchart.

9

Lost Image Area

FORMATS AND THE THEATER

Historically speaking the formats available to the cinematographer have been quite varied. Since the early origins of film, whether still or motion picture, numerous combinations of aspect ratios and gauges have been proposed. Many where briefly implemented for varying periods of time, but as of today only four professional motion picture film gauges exist: 16mm, 35mm, 65mm, and 70mm. In production usage there are really only three gauges available as 70mm is strictly used for release prints.

A format is composed of a film gauge, such as 35mm or 16mm, a frame size within that gauge, and a feed technique based on the number of perforations per frame and the orientation of the film (vertical or horizontal). Due to the inconvenience of numerically specifying the frame size, typically a ratio is substituted instead. Because of the limited number of standardized formats and film sizes available, such a system allows easy understanding of the options a cinematographer may have before deciding on a film format. Currently there are only two aspect ratios in use in US theaters, these being 1.85:1 and 2.35:1, and in the few theaters so equipped, 2.2:1 70mm. The standard 1.33:1 aspect ratio of television has now been joined by its successor, 1.78:1 high-definition television, and for the time being both ratios coexist.

The 70mm proprietary formats are used to make special venue films for amusement parks and museums. Within this group we find Imax, yielding a very large negative due to its 15-perf horizontal feed. The Omnimax system uses the same perforation and feed combination, but is photographed with a special lens, allowing the image to be projected onto a concave screen. The Showscan format uses the same presentation as standard theatrical release 70mm, as it is also a 5-perf vertical-feed format, but operates at 60 frames per second in both camera and projector for the maximum temporal image rate. Various stereoscopic (3-D) processes are also in use in special venues. Few cinematographers will ever be called upon to shoot in these formats.

As we have already stated, in US theaters two 35mm formats are used: 1.85:1 (ratio of width to height) and 2.35:1. The latter is produced by the anamorphic optical process, yielding the 2.35 ratio, and is the format of choice for films that require a wide canvas for presentation. Very often it is called Cinemascope, or simply "scope." Both formats utilize the same vertically oriented feed and 4-perf pull-down.

The full frame size, or camera aperture, of a standard 35mm motion picture camera is defined as .980 × .735 inches, which creates a 1.33 image ratio contained within a 4-perf area. Although this is the maximum attainable image area on the negative, the entire frame can never be projected in a regular theater because a certain percentage is occupied by optical audio tracks. How long this situation will last remains to be seen, since two of the three digital audio formats found on theatrical prints do not utilize the optical track area. The details of this will be discussed later.

When sound became common the format known as Academy was introduced. It designated an aspect ratio of 1.37:1 with an imaging area of .864 × .630. If a comparison is made to the full frame area one can see exactly how the frame was reduced (all film frames are to scale). What is also obvious is the fact that the frame is no longer centered between the sprocket holes. The reduction in width has taken place on

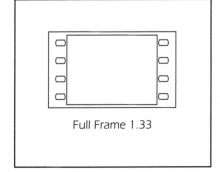

Full Frame 1.33

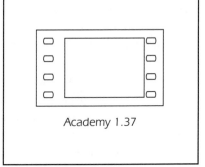

Academy 1.37

the left side only (when looking at a negative from the base side up) and a slight reduction has occurred in the height to create a 1.37 ratio. The Academy format reduced the overall image area but essentially maintained the aspect ratio. Later, after the introduction of the 1.85 ratio which created a widescreen picture, the image area was severely reduced through cropping of the top and bottom of the frame.

Today, because of the fact that 1.37 is not a standard anymore, all films shot on 35mm, and intended for theatrical release (assuming we are not using 2.35 anamorphic or Super 35) use 1.85 defined frame lines in the camera. The area is standardized as .825 × .446 and fits within the Academy frame described earlier. The flaw in this system (at least from the cinematographer's point of view) is that the final area to be projected is very much dependent on the accuracy of the projector pull-down and subsequent projector matte used to block out all areas that are outside of the original operator's frame lines. One

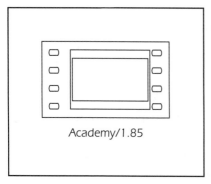

Academy/1.85

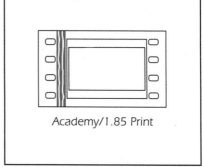

Academy/1.85 Print

can choose to employ a hard matte in the camera aperture matching the theatrical aspect ratio (instead of an Academy matte) to block out the rest of the frame, which will also serve the purpose of hindering any future attempts to use more picture area. A compromise would be the use of a camera matte with a marginally taller aspect ratio than 1.85, and as 1.78 television becomes more common, a matte of this ratio begins to make sense. Of course, 1.85 and 1.78 are similar enough ratios that there is only a minimal loss of picture area on the left and right edges when transferring a 1.85 theatrical framing to 1.78 television when the vertical height of the original is maintained.

When transferring 1.85-composed images to 1.33 television where a 1.85 matte was not used, we must compare the dimensions of the TV transmitted image area with the 1.85 area. If we protect for this extension above and below the normal 1.85 height (.594 versus the .446 of 1.85) the larger frame area can be extracted in a telecine process when the need arises for television presentation and home video.

The inherent problem in this method is that the original framing of the theatrical film is not used in the transfer of the film to video. While it may appear to be a logical solution to the undesirable problem of cropping the sides of the 1.85 area in order to fit the traditional 1.33 television standard, the utilization of the full height of the normal TV transmitted image area still does not give us the full width of the theater version, and the additional height only creates more headroom, which in most cases is undesirable. Another problem which only exacerbates this basic underlying flaw is that many transfers are done with improper framing. In other words, the telecine colorist will attempt to use as much picture area as is geometrically possible, which is, to say the least, a most shocking practice.

There are really only two alternatives when a film shot for 1.85 release must be made to fit the televised 1.33 ratio. The first is admitting the basic mathematical reality of placing a 1.85 image on a 1.33 screen, and simply maintaining the height of the original 1.85 frame while cropping the sides, or one could use a simple alternative: letterboxing. In the case of extracting for 1.78 high-definition television, the formats are so close in aspect ratios that matters are simplified, as the theatrical and television images will be almost identical. Additional vertical area can be extracted beyond the 1.85 height, or if one wishes, slightly less horizontal area.

The benefit of letter-boxing is that the aspect ratio of the original film is maintained. This process creates black bars above and below the image on the television screen, which are the blank image areas formed after the full width of the 1.85 framing is placed within the 1.33 aspect ratio of a television. Even though letter-boxing is now common in home video release, it is rarely seen in broadcast television.

The 2.35 anamorphic format presents an even greater challenge when transferred to 1.33 television. This is the widest projection image available in 35mm, even wider than 2.2:1 70mm. The process by which a regular motion picture camera can obtain images suitable for this type of projection involves the use of special lenses on both the camera and the projector, along with a viewfinder that can unsqueeze the image for the operator during the filming. As implied by this statement, the anamorphic lens produces an image on film that is squeezed two times in the horizontal dimension. The frames when viewed by eye will reveal a very noticeable vertical stretching of recorded objects. In its direct form the image is distorted beyond any practical use, but by the introduction of an anamorphic projector lens at the presentation stage, the image is unsqueezed to its intended widescreen ratio.

The dimensions of the anamorphic frame are .864 × .732, which indicates greater height than the Academy frame but the same width and offset. The projection aperture is slightly smaller at .838 × .700 (matching the viewfinder lines). Most will use an anamorphic matte in the camera, with the .864 × .732 dimensions enumerated earlier.

Anamorphic photography presents a unique situation for the cinematographer; therefore, before deciding to use this format many factors

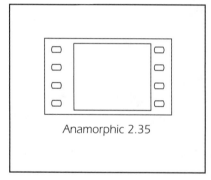

Anamorphic 2.35

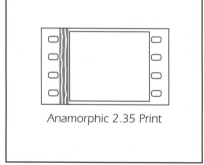

Anamorphic 2.35 Print

must be clearly understood. From a technical standpoint the two advantages are the wider aspect ratio and the improved resolution in the theater. It is obvious that the negative is sizably larger than standard 1.85, although the advantage in this respect is limited by the quality of the camera lenses, the anamorphic projection lens, and the design of the theater. Obviously a large multiplex theater should be capable of presenting these films in a reasonable fashion, while the smaller outlets can be severely hampered by the excessive horizontal area, which commonly causes the picture to project beyond the screen area. There are also some production disadvantages to using the anamorphic format.

Due to the fact that the anamorphic process yields a much greater horizontal dimension versus 1.85, a 50mm anamorphic lens will produce results very similar to a 25mm lens in 1.85. Longer focal length lenses are necessary (roughly double for the same field of view as 1.85) because of this extreme width. A normal lens in anamorphic photography will be 100mm, a focal length with severely restricted depth of field. When the director calls for a close-up and it is necessary to use a lens that might be in excess of 150mm, the depth of field becomes so tight that it will be nearly impossible to split focus without a split diopter, or hold a background in any definable state of clarity.

A solution to the lack of depth of field is to use higher T-stops (smaller apertures), although this has the disadvantage of requiring much higher light levels. With high-speed film stocks this not as difficult as it once was, but it still presents some restrictions for those who wish to have good depth of field. Higher light levels and wide focal length lenses create greater depth of field, meaning that anamorphic is more suitable for panoramic productions primarily taking place outdoors. Despite the fact that it would appear to be unwise to shoot a film that takes place in cramped quarters with the anamorphic process, this is not to say that it has not been done, as it is quite frequently employed nonetheless. It is commonly assumed that anamorphic cinematography is more expensive than regular spherical photography, but in reality the only additional cost is a slight increase in the rental rate of lenses, which is insignificant when viewed in relation to the overall cost of a 35mm film production. Of practical concern is the inherently large size of the lenses, although in most circumstances this is not particularly relevant. Also, anamorphic lens availability is somewhat limited.

The problem that a 2.35 ratio presents in the telecine transfer is quite substantial. With standard television providing only a 1.33 image, extreme cropping of the left and right must occur during the process. As with 1.85 images presented on television, a significant modification to the original framing must be made, but with the even wider aspect ratio of 2.35 the loss is more than just boundary areas on the sides of the frame. Due to the unacceptable cropping of the original frame area (areas that may contain crucial image information or even actors) a more complex method must be employed to counteract this phenomenon.

The solution is "pan and scan." It is a somewhat crude process that leaves, in a sense, the directing up to the colorist. While this may seem like a rash statement, it is in fact quite true. By panning the frame in-shot during the transfer in scenes that have important image information at the furthest horizontal periphery, the telecine operator has now been given the task of re-directing the film. Static shots from the original picture are now transformed through this method into static pans between frame-left to frame-right, or vice versa.

Again, a preferred option is letter-boxing. When the film is presented with the full width on the television screen and the correct aspect ratio is maintained, the viewer will see the film as it was intended—at least within the limitations of television. Understandably, because of the rather wide dimensions of a 2.35 image, the screen will present especially large black areas above and below the picture. Resolution on the television screen will be reduced substantially by this technique, but the improvement over pan and scan seems more than enough to justify its application. In the case of 1.78 high-definition television, of course, the image could be presented without letter-boxing with reasonably acceptable losses on the left and right sides of the frame, or again could be letter-boxed.

An alternative to producing a film with the anamorphic process for 2.35 presentation is the use of Super 35. This format provides another method of attaining a 2.35:1 aspect ratio image, and because it uses regular spherical lenses, the most common drawbacks of anamorphic production are eliminated. Super 35 reverses the situation inherited by the use of offset framing when sound was coupled with the picture. The full frame aperture is always utilized, with a horizontal dimension of .980, a vertical dimension of .735, and an image centered with respect to the sprocket holes. When forming a 2.35 image area (.945 × .394) on a full-frame negative with an aspect ratio of 1.33, cropping must, as usual, occur. Two choices exist. One can simply center the 2.35 image area vertically within the camera aperture (symmetrical) or one can choose a common top line, which means the 2.35/1.85/1.33 extraction all have the same top frame line. Due to the obvious fact that a 1.33 TV transmitted frame has the largest vertical dimension, essentially the 2.35 and 1.85 frame lines are raised to the height of the 1.33 TV transmitted top line. The advantage, as one might have suspected, is that the same top framing for all three formats can be extracted from this negative, with the option of creating an enormous number of aspect ratios from the original. Unfortunately, shooting three different aspect ratios at the same time is difficult at best, but it is theoretically possible with adroit camera operation, though some or all of the aspect ratios must in the end be compromises.

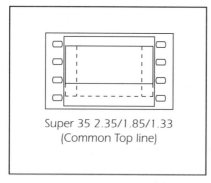

Super 35 2.35/1.85/1.33
(Common Top line)

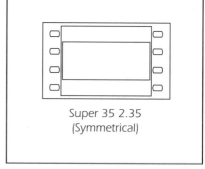

Super 35 2.35
(Symmetrical)

A downside to the Super 35 format for 2.35 presentation is that the original image cannot be projected in a standard theater; therefore an optical step is introduced in order to create an anamorphic print. While it may seem rather absurd to go through the whole Super 35 process and just end with the same anamorphic print for projection, there are obvious advantages. The cinematographer can concentrate on getting the film done using typical lenses and techniques without depth of field limitations. The only real disadvantage is the additional expense of optical work in post production, but this cost is relatively nominal. Far more important is the *quality* of the color timed interpositive, and the subsequent internegative produced on an optical printer, at which stage the anamorphic process is accomplished.

Relative to television the Super 35 2.35 image, which is a full frame, allows the telecine operator more choices during the transfer. If the producer uses a common top line during production the bottom of the frame can be protected. When the time comes for the video version, the colorist can simply line up the common top line on the negative, extracting the 1.33 horizontal area, which includes the protected frame bottom, and create the necessary 1.33 aspect ratio of current television. This method is an improvement over the panning and scanning of an anamorphic print, though the full width of the 2.35 frame is not quite utilized, and it still produces an unquestionably annoying situation—the original framing is not maintained and now we have added substantial image area at the bottom of the frame.

In the case of symmetrical Super 35 2.35 generally a common top line is not used, meaning that the larger vertically dimensioned television aspect ratio can be extracted by using additional image area from both the top and the bottom of the frame, or one can choose to simply crop the sides and maintain the original top and bottom lines. For 1.78 high-definition television a production shot in 2.35 Super 35 can be transferred with the original framing reasonably intact, or again, like anamorphic, the left and right can be cropped or it can be letter-boxed. Super 35 gives us the most framing options no matter what the desired ratio.

The vexing matter of framing is one which can best be controlled through the use of a camera matte, and if one does not wish to leave much room for modification of the framing, then a camera matte can be made use of in Super 35 just as we might employ one in shooting offset (Academy) 1.85. This hard camera matte could be 2.35 if we want to preserve top and bottom lines exactly, but it might also be 1.85, 1.78, or theoretically anything we choose, provided a matte can be found or manufactured. In special effects work, particularly of the digital variety, deciding what the maximum frame area can be for video transfer is of some importance, and we will examine this further in Chapter 12.

The added benefit of using Super 35 for television is also obvious. Since television production does not require the use of an Academy matte and an offset for the sound tracks, we are always shooting full-frame anyway. Once it is accepted that we are using the full aperture area of the camera, the offset is pointless. The use of Super 35 for television allows the operator to use markings that conform to the HDTV 1.78 standard ($.945 \times .531$) and also frame for 1.33 TV transmitted within this ratio ($.706 \times .531$). The vertical dimension is identical for both video extractions. This greatly simplifies television productions which may be presented in either 1.33 or 1.78 ratios. In the current 1.33 version the left and right of the frame will be omitted in the transfer or video down-conversion from 1.78 high definition.

The TV transmitted 1.33 Super 35 extraction from within the 1.78 TV transmitted area uses a smaller negative area than regular TV transmitted ($.792 \times .594$ versus $.706 \times .531$), but in terms of NTSC resolution

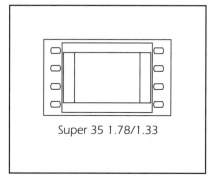

Super 35 1.78/1.33

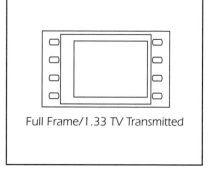

Full Frame/1.33 TV Transmitted

it is not deleterious. The TV safe extraction in current NTSC 1.33 is .713 × .535 and in the Super 35 version of 1.33 TV safe it is .636 × .478. When 1.78 becomes widespread the smaller 1.33 area will be irrelevant, the salient fact being that the proper 1.78 ratio is using the largest possible negative area.

When a production is strictly intended for NTSC television and Super 35 is not employed, the cinematographer will typically still shoot a full frame area on the negative (as protecting for the sound track is not necessary) and utilize camera frame lines that conform to the TV transmitted standard. The actual dimensions are .792 × .594 and, like the 1.85 format, are within the offset Academy frame, even if no such matte is being employed. When the time comes to transfer the negative on a telecine the colorist can simply extract the TV transmitted area, the result hopefully matching the frame lines of the camera. TV safe action (.713 × .535), the common name for the receiver image area, can also be marked on the camera ground glass within the TV transmitted frame lines.

When using Super 35 for television production another option is available: 3-perf. By using a three-perforation pull-down instead of the usual four, a 33 percent increase in the running time of a magazine is realized. This format is very useful for sitcoms where maximum shooting times can be attained from 2000-foot magazines and cameras fitted with 3-perf movements. Some reduction in image size does occur, but it is negligible as far as picture quality is concerned (4-perf 1.78 is .945 × .531 whereas 3-perf is .910 × .511).

With three-perforation television formats in use, one might ponder the possibility of using a similar technique for 2.35 theatrical purposes. If we are only interested in producing a 2.35 frame for the

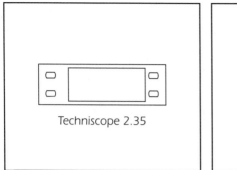

Techniscope 2.35

Super 35 3-perf 1.78/1.33

subsequent optical work, the perforations above and below this inherently narrow vertical image area are essentially unused, thus allowing the possibility of a two-perforation pull-down. Such a widescreen format actually predates Super 35.

Techniscope, as the 2-perf format is known, has been around for quite some time, and even had a strong following among certain producers. By employing a two-perforation pull-down the running time of the film rolls is exactly doubled. The drawback (and it is a serious one) is that image quality suffers with such a small negative within the offset, 2-perf Techniscope area. The dimensions are only .839 × .355 for optical extraction, where the reduced vertical height causes a similar reduction in width in order to yield the 2.35 negative area. In the end this negative must be optically manipulated to produce anamorphic prints in exactly the same fashion as Super 35. Despite its cost-saving aspects, Techniscope has essentially been supplanted by Super 35, which provides superior image quality and more versatility.

While on the topic of cost savings, naturally one must bring up the topic of 16mm. The standard 16mm frame is defined as .404 × .295 (1.37:1) and is placed vertically between two sprocket holes, yielding an image area only 22 percent the size of a 35mm Academy frame. The substantially lower resolution of 16mm images in both projected form and when transferred to video is clearly a result of this glum fact.

Because 16mm is rarely projected in professional applications, typically most users will opt for Super 16 which, like Super 35, exposes the image into the area normally reserved for the soundtrack, thus providing the largest negative possible in this format. The specific dimensions of a Super 16 frame are .486 × .295, ultimately producing an aspect ratio of 1.66 and an image area 21 percent larger than a regular (1.37)

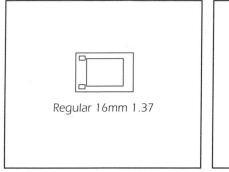

Regular 16mm 1.37

Super 16mm 1.66

16mm frame. For projection purposes, as in a Super 16 blow-up to 35mm, when a producer finds it desirable to present a film in a normal 35mm-equipped theater, the 16mm frame is optically enlarged and cropped at the top and bottom in order to produce a standard 1.85 35mm frame. In European markets, where the 1.66 ratio is found in theaters projecting 35mm, the original Super 16 frame can be blown up without cropping. Obviously the results fall far short of 35mm-originated material, and there is also the added cost of optical lab work to consider. More often Super 16 is transferred to video (particularly in documentaries) where the 1.66 ratio can be maintained in a letter-box format and maximum negative resolution is utilized. If the image is cropped for 1.33 TV there is essentially little benefit in using Super 16 versus regular 16mm because the extraction area is essentially the same. When shooting in the 16mm gauge for 1.78 high-definition television Super 16 is essential to minimize the loss of negative area.

For maximum image quality one might choose to shoot 65mm. Using a 5-perf pull-down, 65mm yields a dimension of 2.072 × .906 for the camera aperture, and a projector aperture of 1.912 × .870 with an aspect ratio of 2.2:1. Because added width is required for multiple magnetic audio tracks, the release print is 5mm wider than the camera negative, creating the 70mm we are all so familiar with. Some confusion is apparent when confronted with a format which appears to have different camera and projector gauges, but what is not so obvious is the fact that the actual distance between the sprocket holes is identical. The extended dimension is strictly outside the sprocket hole area (on both sides), so the 65mm negative can be printed onto 70mm positive stock through the normal contact process. Since relatively few pictures have been shot in 65mm, the majority of 70mm prints viewed

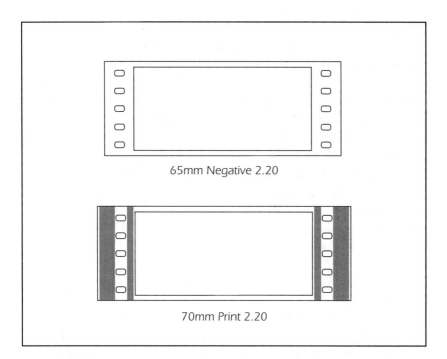

65mm Negative 2.20

70mm Print 2.20

in theaters are, of course, optical enlargements from 35mm. Anamorphic 2.35, Super 35 2.35, and regular 1.85 can all be used to produce a 70mm print. If created from 1.85 the original aspect ratio is maintained, but the 2.35 format can either have a small amount cropped from the sides to fit 2.2:1, or the top and bottom of the 2.2:1 area can be slightly reduced to maintain 2.35. In the case of a direct enlargement from Super 35, more image area can be used at the top, bottom, or both.

The magnetic audio tracks on 70mm prints are far superior to the optical tracks found on 35mm prints, and this means that 70mm has traditionally been associated with, in addition to better image quality on a larger screen, better sound. The arrival of digital audio on 35mm prints eliminated this advantage, and when combined with the limited number of 70mm-capable theaters, the result is that 65mm is primarily used for shooting optical effects, where the large negative is advantageous when going through multiple generations to accomplish these special effects.

Another format used for such work is VistaVision, which began life as both a camera and projector format, but was in fact only rarely projected in its native format. It is an 8-perf horizontal-feed 35mm system and contains the largest frame area of any 35mm format. In current usage VistaVision is strictly in-camera, and is employed for special effects work as an alternative to 65mm.

The proliferation of digitally generated special effects, film scanners, and film recorders has reduced the overall necessity of shooting both 65mm and VistaVision, as the creation of these effects shifts more and more into the purely digital realm. Nevertheless, under circumstances where high-speed film stocks will be used, a larger negative is still preferable for scanning purposes in order to obtain a fine-grain image.

Based on the reality that all film formats came about through a process of evolution, it seems very apparent that a change may be arriving soon. With the advent of 1.78 HDTV, and the now wasteful use of image area for printing obsolete optical soundtracks, theatrical projection of Super 35 might be in order. Since all digital soundtracks are placed either between the sprocket holes (Dolby Digital) or outside the perforations (SDDS), with the exception of DTS, which does not even use film-based soundtracks (it is on separate media entirely) but does use the area inside the optical track for synchronization purposes, a format that utilizes the full width of the aperture would be the most logical progression. With a corresponding modification (centering) of theater projectors, this full-width frame could be directly projected without resorting to optical printing. The Academy format was a necessity at one time, but given that the practice of placing optical tracks directly onto film is virtually obsolete, it is imperative the lost negative area be reclaimed.

Currently the use of Super 1.85 (which has a substantially larger negative area than standard 1.85) serves little practical purpose, as an optical reduction to fit within the Academy 35mm frame (or enlargement to 70mm) must be made for release to standard theaters. The theatrical projection of Super 35 would allow the direct (with no optical printer stage) use of Super 1.85, and also 2.35 Super 35. Logically, it would likewise make sense to create an additional ratio of 2:1, combining a reasonably large negative area (though still smaller than Super 1.85) with a wider screen ratio than 1.85.

Another advantage of Super 35 for projection would be that in large multiplex theaters outfitted with 1.85 ratio screens which are widened by blocking the top for projection of 2.35 anamorphic prints,

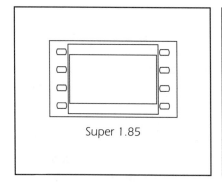

Super 1.85

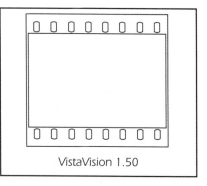

VistaVision 1.50

the increase in the size of the screen and the magnification of the image would be matched by a corresponding increase in the image area being projected. Overall, Super 1.85 would then come at least reasonably close to anamorphic 2.35 in quality as a 35mm projection format. Also, in theory Super 35 projection allows any aspect ratio from 1.85 to 2.35 (anything wider than 2.35 would use too small an image area) to be used if the appropriate projector matte exists, but for standardization purposes the simple addition of a 2:1 ratio makes the most sense.

It is now incumbent upon us to discuss theater projection practices and the impairment of quality that can occur if certain standards are not acknowledged. First and foremost is cleanliness of the projector aperture and associated parts; secondly, proper registration, and thirdly, a quality projection lens of the correct focal length for the projection distance and screen size. These are basic standards that must be met if a system is to mechanically and optically perform correctly.

On a more complex level, the screen luminance and color temperature must be ascertained for proper brightness and color. The projector's xenon arc light provides the illumination, and though it is a set standard for most professional systems, it is still necessary to determine if the screen conforms to the 16 foot lambert luminance requirement and a correlated color temperature of 5400K.

When measuring the screen brightness it is absolutely necessary to run the projector without film in the gate, and measure the screen from the center. Inevitably light fall-off will occur at the edges, so it must be accepted that measurements taken from the extreme peripheral area of the screen will not yield similar or consistent results. When measuring color temperature, distance and location are less important, but readings taken from the center of the screen (facing the projector) will allow for the most accurate evaluation.

Due to the lack of spot meters that measure luminance as candelas per meter squared or foot lamberts, a conversion must be possible for those who own a more typical device indicating only f-stops. The equivalent to 16 foot lamberts is as follows: a spot meter set on 100 ISO/ASA, at 24 fps (1/50th exposure) should produce, when measuring screen center, an f-stop of 3.2 (2.8 1/3).

As far as the proper procedure for screen aspect ratio usage goes, it seems some theaters are equipped with 2.35 aspect ratio screens and follow the rule that the height should always remain the same, and when projecting a film that requires a wider horizontal area, such as anamorphic, the side curtains will be opened from 1.85 to adapt the theater screen for the wider format. Depending on the theater and its design, however, the screen may be of the 1.85 aspect ratio, so that for projection of a 2.35 picture the screen height will be reduced to accommodate the wider aspect ratio. This practice is very disappointing to the producer of a 2.35 film, as the picture will be projected onto a smaller overall screen area than a 1.85 ratio picture would be in that particular theater. In a large theater using this latter presentation system (where the projection distance is long) the 1.85 image is arguably overmagnified.

One must have spent time in a projection booth to realize the somewhat outlandish practices that are frequently employed, such as utilizing the central incisors on occasion as a crude substitute for scissors to initiate a splice, and acknowledging that "scope" is a nuisance format for the size-compromised theater. There is little that can be done about the latter, but the former practice has been mitigated by the widespread use of the much tougher Estar stocks.

10

Voltage as Pictures

UNDERSTANDING VIDEO

The television monitor is the basic component that allows us to view the video image, so how the image is formed on the screen should be explained in detail. The color video monitor uses three electron guns housed in a cathode ray tube (CRT) which produce the appropriate scanning beams necessary to activate the red, green, and blue screen phosphors. Correct placement (fall) of the beams is expedited by using a series of vertical slits or holes behind the screen itself, thereby only allowing the correct scanning beam to activate its respective phosphor dot or stripe. A shadow mask tube uses holes and phosphor dots, while the Trinitron uses vertical slits and phosphor stripes. Deflection coils (both vertical and horizontal) around the neck of the tube force the electron beams to scan across the screen from left to right. As each horizontal line is scanned the beam is terminated and retraced to the next line. When the scanning beam reaches the bottom of the screen it is retraced back to the top and the process is repeated. When every line is scanned in succession to complete one frame it is called progressive scanning, whereas skipping every other line produces interlaced scanning. If the frequency of this scanning is sufficiently high enough (at least 50Hz) the eye will perceive the image as a whole.

Whereas color film operates on the subtractive principle, using cyan, magenta, and yellow dyes, color television uses an additive system. In the additive system of color reproduction red, green, and blue are mixed to form a wide range of colors. By placing the red, green, and blue phosphors in close proximity on the screen, so that to the eye they are

147

indistinguishable as separate colors (forming a pixel or picture element), the perceived color and brightness are functions of the individual voltages applied to the three electron guns which are targeted onto the phosphors. For example, if equal voltage is applied to all three guns, where the intensity of all three phosphors will be the same, the eye will perceive this pixel as white. Black, of course, cannot be produced with additive color, so this amounts to zero or near zero voltage; in NTSC this is actually 7.5 IRE, not 0 IRE. Yellow can be produced by activating the red and green phosphors of a pixel, a pale blue if only blue and green are activated, and so on. By this method a wide range of colors can be reproduced on the video monitor.

To determine the actual range of colors a monitor can display one requires the chromaticities of the three phosphors. By plotting these coordinates on a chromaticity chart (x,y) a color gamut can be formed, where the interior of the triangle will indicate the color reproduction that is possible (see Figure 10.1). The CIE chromaticity chart is a subset of the CIE color specification system, which is an objective method of converting a spectral power distribution to tristimulus values. Using this system of colorimetry, colors can be defined using psycho-

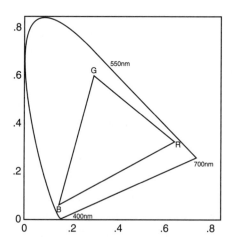

FIGURE 10.1 ITU-R 709 color gamut as defined by the chromaticities of the RGB phosphors.

physical methods based on the trichromatic nature of human vision. The actual process of producing tristimulus values from a spectral power distribution involves the use of standardized CIE color matching functions, generated using trichromatic matching experiments with human observers. The result is a quantifiable means of defining color. Film has the ability to capture and display far more colors than video, and though it cannot encompass the whole visual gamut (as defined by the full boundary used in the chromaticity chart), it exceeds the total number of colors produced using screen phosphors.

White, as reproduced on the monitor, can be specified by a correlated color temperature or by the chromaticity coordinates of a standard illuminant. Most monitors approximate daylight, meaning they have correlated color temperatures of 6500K. For this reason it should be noted that if one is filming a television monitor using tungsten-balanced film, filtering will be necessary to correct the excessive blue. Other considerations regarding this topic were discussed in Chapter 2.

In order to understand gamma as it applies to video it must be understood that a cathode ray tube has an output (intensity) that is not proportional with respect to applied voltage. The intensity will typically be the voltage raised to the power of 2.5 (intensity = voltage$^\gamma$). In other words, at least in this example, the monitor will be stated to have a gamma of 2.5. This has implications for video cameras and telecine systems, which must apply gamma correction to compensate for this effect, and if left uncorrected results in poor tone and color reproduction. Gamma correction can be determined by calculating the reciprocal of the monitor gamma. By this corrective measure the system gamma will then be 1. For example, an uncorrected voltage input of .2^2.5 will yield .017888 (nonlinear), whereas .2^.4 (gamma corrected) will produce .52530, which when raised to the power of gamma (2.5) equals .2, and thus a linear relationship is formed.

Generally, most video cameras use .45 for gamma correction, which would indicate a slightly more contrasty image than that provided by unity gamma (2.5/2.222 = 1.125). In the sensitometry chapter we noted a similar (but more pronounced) process in the case of 35mm motion picture prints, where such a system gamma can be in the range of 1.85 to 1.95. This is necessary due to perceptual problems involving the dark adaptation of the eye. In fact, one can test this phenomenon using a television, where the contrast will appear higher if some ambient light is provided by daylight or lights (as long as they do not produce screen flare), whereas viewing a television in a totally dark room will perceptually produce the least contrast because the black in the image will deteriorate to gray. While under ideal viewing conditions a monitor with a properly set black level may achieve a contrast range of over 50:1, the viewing environment of typical display devices will only allow a range of 30:1 or less.

In the US, the television standard referred to as NTSC (National Television Standards Committee) has been employed (though its phasing out has been scheduled to coincide with full-scale digital broadcasting). The NTSC image is formed using 525 scan lines, a 2:1 interlacing architecture, and a frame rate of 29.97. These are fixed parameters, as they, along with the color coding scheme which is particular to this system, essentially define the basic attributes. Due to the interlaced scanning a video frame must be constructed as two fields. One field contains all the odd lines while the other, normally referred to as field two, contains all even lines. Each field produces 262 1/2 scan lines, for a total of 525. The first field is scanned across the screen, activating the phosphors. Then a period known as the vertical blanking interval occurs, sending the beam back to the top of the screen to scan the next field. The blanking intervals are contained on the horizontal axis of each line (horizontal blanking) and the vertical axis of the screen (vertical blanking). Sync pulses are activated during these intervals for timing. The PAL system, in use throughout many parts of the world, is similar in basic operation, but is based on a 50Hz (25 frames per second interlaced) system, with a total of 625 scan lines.

While computers use progressive scanning as opposed to interlaced scanning, in broadcast systems considerations must be made regarding bandwidth. Since 29.97 frames per second cannot be used in an analog video system in which the frame rate and screen refresh rate are linked without detrimental flicker (film projection can use 24 frames per second only because the flicker rate is increased by the use of a multi-bladed shutter), increased frame rates are necessary in video applications. 60 frames per second would solve the problem, but at the expense of double the bandwidth, which was not viewed as a viable solution in the early days of television. The compromise was to use interlaced scanning, where odd and even lines are contained within separate fields. These fields, by their 2:1 interlaced architecture, effectively double the frame rate (i.e., 59.94Hz), resulting in an image presentation which is flickerless. Interlacing, although an efficient method, reduces vertical resolution and creates spurious patterns when an image contains closely spaced horizontal lines, such as window blinds or fences. Progressive scanning is a superior method when compared to interlacing, and the 1280 × 720 (1.78:1 ratio, or in video parlance, 16:9) high-definition digital television format is based on the progressive-scan architecture. The flicker problem in digital systems with appropriate monitors is not dependent on frame rate, since the monitor refresh rate is the determining factor in this matter. Even if our source material is 12 frames per second, the monitor will still refresh the image at its usual refresh rate, say 75Hz. The 720p system, which will be examined more closely in the latter part of the chapter, can operate at different frame rates, ranging from 24 to 60. Those in the computer industry encourage progressive-scan video systems for compatibility with computers.

As bandwidth is the key to both the resolution of a television system and the number of broadcast stations possible, where one affects the other—i.e., one must choose between either a limited number of stations with higher bandwidth (better resolution) or more numerous stations with lower bandwidth (reduced resolution). The NTSC television system uses an encoding method (a compositing, or combining of information) specifically designed to limit its total bandwidth (including audio) to a 6MHz channel, being assisted in this task by the implementation of interlaced scanning. Concerns for reducing the broadcast bandwidth are more prevalent than ever (due to higher resolutions), having now taken a more sophisticated path involving complex digital compression schemes which we will delve into later.

In electronic imaging the picture is recorded using a charge-coupled device (CCD), which is a matrix array that can contain a million or more light-sensitive elements, where each sensor is comparable to a pixel. The number of elements on a single chip determines to a large degree the resolution of the camera. Most professional cameras employ a 2/3-inch frame interline chip (FIT) used in a group of three— one for each color channel. These are precisely registered and fused to a dichroic prism block. By this process, the light entering through the lens is directed onto the three separate CCDs, therein generating the necessary red, green, and blue signals.

In a charge-coupled device each element produces an electrical charge relative to the intensity of the exposing light and the duration of the exposure. Once the CCD has been exposed it must transfer the acquired charges into a temporary storage area (registers) for subsequent processing, and then ultimately into a suitable signal for recording onto magnetic videotape. In the latest video cameras digital signal processing (DSP) is utilized, and the signals are recorded in either a composite or component digital format, although DSP does not preclude the use of analog recording formats as long as the appropriate output is provided. Elucidation of these topics will follow shortly.

Video cameras produce linear red, green, and blue components by process of their three CCDs, and nonlinear values after the appropriate gamma correction has been applied, but it is impractical to record these signals individually because of the excessive bandwidth needed. Instead, a luminance signal (Y) is derived from the gamma corrected RGB values, which is representative of the monochrome signal used by black and white televisions. The formula for calculating luminance from RGB is $Y = .299R + .587G + .114B$. In other words, luminance is formed by taking specific percentages from the three CCDs. The color information (chroma) is then created by producing color difference signals (R–Y) and (B–Y). These color difference signals are then adjusted to form a subset of two components (UV or IQ) and reduced by filtering so that the bandwidth is limited to roughly one-third or less in comparison to the luminance signal. While this may seem like a rather severe reduction in resolution, it works because the eye mainly perceives detail based on varying luminance levels within a scene.

This is not the end of the encoding process though, as the two color components are combined in a process called quadrature modulation. The subsequent composite signal is then produced by combining both luminance and chroma through frequency interleaving. Decoding of this composite signal takes place at the monitor, where it is converted back into the appropriate signals, thus actuating the three electron guns respectively. In broadcast applications, where a television is receiving a transmitted signal that is RF-modulated (radio frequency), the signal must also be demodulated. This whole process, as one might expect, is far from perfect because both luminance and chroma cannot be perfectly separated during the decoding and thus contaminate each other to varying degrees. Also, any post production encoding activity on a composite signal, such as color correction or re-framing, is impossible without decoding and encoding again; therefore generation errors and quality impairments occur. Although composite signals (and their associated problems) are ultimately necessary for current broadcasting, most high-end professional video post production is based on component signal processing, in either an analog or a digital form.

Having established the basics of the NTSC system, we must now delve into the question of resolution. Video resolution is defined by the bandwidth of the system (i.e., the luminance signal) and the visible scan lines. Bandwidth in the video domain is essentially a measurement of cycles, such as the number of times a signal can go from 0 percent voltage to 100 percent voltage. Naturally, we measure these cycles in hertz, a unit that defines cycles per second, i.e., Hz. The number of scan lines that contain picture information can be determined by the number of lines lost during the vertical blanking period. Since 21 lines are lost during the time it takes the electron beam to retrace to the top of the screen for the start of each field scan, a total of 42 lines must be subtracted from the original 525. This will produce 241.5 lines per field, or a total of 483 scan lines per frame.

Due to the fact that the vertical resolution is fixed at 483 lines, the horizontal resolution is the only parameter which can be improved with increased bandwidth. By utilizing a simple mathematical formula one can determine the maximum theoretical resolution of any video system based on its bandwidth. First, however, we need to define the term resolution as it applies to video. Vertical resolution is the number of horizontal lines resolvable in an area equal to picture height, which is abbreviated TVL/PH. As we stated earlier, there are 483 scan lines available for picture information out of a total of 525, but because an interlacing system is employed, a Kell Factor of 2/3 (.7) is typically multiplied by the 483 scan lines, which yields a more realistic answer of 338 TVL/PH. This is the limit of vertical resolution in the NTSC system, and always remains a fixed value.

Horizontal resolution, on the other hand, is defined as the number of vertical lines which can be discerned in an area equal to the picture height, also abbreviated TVL/PH. In order to perform the necessary calculations, we must first collect data on the system in question.

Frame rate is the first variable, which for NTSC is 29.97. The second is the total number of scan lines, i.e., 525. By multiplying these two variables together, we can determine the line rate in Hz—15734.25 to be exact. Now, by dividing one million by the line rate we can convert our previous answer into microseconds (μsec). The result will be, in this example, 63.56 μsec. Due to the horizontal blanking period between each line (the time it takes for the beam to retrace to the start of the next line), which takes up approximately 10.7 μsec, we can reduce our original result to an active line rate. In this case it would be 52.86 μsec. With our active line time determined, we can now simply plug in our luminance bandwidth (MHz) into the equation below.

$$\frac{(\mu sec) \text{ active line rate} \times 2 \times \text{bandwidth (MHz)}}{4/3 \text{ (aspect ratio)}} = TVL/PH$$

In the case of broadcast NTSC television, the image-related bandwidth obtainable within the 6MHz channel allocation is only 4.2MHz. As we can see by the example below, the maximum horizontal resolution possible in broadcast is 333 TVL/PH.

$$\frac{52.86 \text{ }\mu sec \times 2 \times 4.2 \text{ (MHz)}}{4/3 \text{ (aspect ratio)}} = 333 \text{ } TVL/PH$$

Due to the fact that we are dividing our answer by the aspect ratio (4/3) the result is strictly TVL/PH, which as we know is imposing the limiting factor of picture height—in effect assuming a square screen. While this method of measurement may still be the most common in video engineering, it is misleading to those who are more familiar with computer resolutions, which are often quoted as the number of pixels per picture width by the number of pixels per picture height; hence common resolutions, such as SVGA, termed 800 × 600. If we were to expunge the aspect ratio from our equation, we would find the actual viewable horizontal resolution of NTSC to be 444 lines. In computer terms we could describe NTSC as having a resolution of 444 × 483, though as it is an analog interlaced scanning system, the Kell factor must be taken into account, so the effective resolution could (depending on how we define resolution) be described as 444 × 338.

Now, after a rather technical overview, we must explain the characteristics and limitations of video imaging. From a cinematographer's point of view, the current video camera has two serious problems in comparison to film. First we must accept a camera with limited exposure range, which invariably produces contrasty pictures when the exposure range of the scene exceeds that of the camera, and likewise a lack of subtlety in tone reproduction. The latest video cameras have less severe clipping of excessive exposure through the incorporation of signal compression circuits (knee correction), but the transition from a detailed white to a no-detail white is still quite abrupt and is far less pleasing than the gradual loss of detail in film until D-max is reached. In addition, the color quality is compromised by the lack of full-bandwidth color after processing, although a positive side, which should not be overlooked, is the ability to white balance the camera to a wide variety of sources (such as fluorescent) without resorting to filters. Normally this process is performed with an automatic switch and a white card properly situated in the primary illumination. Undoubtedly this is advantageous, particularly given the rapid setups required in electronic news gathering (ENG) operations or in industrial video applications where specialized lighting fixtures are normally in limited quantity and existing lighting is used more often. For convenience many video cameras will have several filters built in which can be selected with a knob. These normally include neutral density filters and the basic correction filters.

Resolution is also of concern when a high-quality image is to be obtained, and all video falls far short of film resolution. In color, exposure range, tonal quality, and resolution, the video camera is still inferior when compared to film. It does, however, have the obvious advantage in the ability to acquire an instantly viewable image, a primary failing of film. When using film a delay must be incurred for the subsequent processing, printing, or transfer steps necessary, and the results cannot be judged until these have taken place. A video camera feeding a properly calibrated monitor in effect provides instant dailies. This does not imply that a knowledge of lighting and exposure is irrelevant when using this medium, but it does make the video operator's task far simpler. The expense of shooting video is naturally far less than shooting film. For these reasons, video has entirely superseded film for news gathering.

Exposure in the video camera is based on the exposure time and the sensitivity of the camera. The exposure time is more or less a fixed parameter, and will be the same as the field rate, i.e., 1/60th of a second, unless a special electronic shutter, e.g., Sony's "clear scan," is utilized (this will in effect decrease the sensitivity of the CCD). Moreover, the sensitivity of the camera is only fixed when set to zero gain, and can be increased by changing this parameter, which is expressed in decibels, e.g., 0db, 9db, 18db, and finds application when lighting conditions are insufficient for proper exposure.

Waveform monitors, it should be noted, display video signal levels. These range (at least in the NTSC system) from 7.5 IRE to 100 IRE, the latter being the brightest acceptable elements and the former the darkest. Waveform monitors can be used to determine the levels in a video image, and thus to a certain degree allow exposure decisions to be made from their output. A properly calibrated monitor can serve a similar function, but is limited in critical applications.

Many video cameras are simply used in the automatic exposure mode, particularly for less precise news gathering work, or the operator can manually set the exposure based on the "zebra" level indicator in the viewfinder. Most of these are set to 70 IRE, which corresponds well with properly exposed flesh tones. Using a waveform monitor for exposure control during production is usually restricted to studio work.

From an optical standpoint video lenses are inferior to those used in film production because of the inherently limited resolution of the medium, and the only factor worth noting is the enhanced depth of field due to the small size of the imaging area. It is also standard practice to fit video cameras with zoom lenses, and most are generally variable between 10mm and 110mm. Wide-angle lenses in video are 10mm, 14mm, etc., which if we remember the basic rules of depth of field, are indicative of vast areas both in front of and behind the plane of focus that will appear acceptably sharp. If one is attempting to get a more cinematic look from a video camera, longer focal lengths must be chosen or wider apertures must be used.

The aspect ratio is limited by the television receiver used for display (unless we wish to letter-box the video frame). Some regular NTSC cameras have switchable aspect ratios which allow the use of 1.78 instead of 1.33, but the resolution of the CCD is not high enough in the horizontal dimension to make good use of this technique; moreover, the lack of widescreen NTSC televisions would appear to dictate its limited practical application. High-definition cameras are another matter, as they are designed for the 1.78 ratio.

A myriad of NTSC video formats are currently in use, and it seems appropriate that a thorough explanation of the choices is in order. Originally (and this was not long ago) the producer using video was very limited in videotape formats, and composite analog recording was the only choice. Formats such as 1-inch Type C, and 3/4-inch or 3/4-inch SP are representative of this era. The picture quality of equipment of this kind, even though it is still in use, is quite poor when compared to the latest videotape formats.

Component analog is the successor to composite analog video. The component system keeps the luminance (commonly referred to as luma, the symbol being Y) and color difference signals separate. It is referred to as YPbPr, and Sony and Panasonic have developed component analog videotape formats. Sony's version is Betacam SP, a format which uses two tracks, one for luminance and one for the color difference components (R–Y) (B–Y) with a luminance bandwidth of roughly 4.5MHz. MII, the Panasonic component analog product, utilizes a similar recording scheme and has the same luminance bandwidth. The Betacam SP format has almost entirely superseded all analog formats when high-quality analog video is required, although certain facilities use MII instead.

Having reached the discussion of such formats as D-1 and D-2, it is probably best that an explanation of digital video is provided. Digitization is a process that requires both sampling and quantization. Still derived from an analog source, whether a CCD or a microphone (as both are inherently analog), the digitization of a signal creates the ability to produce a consistently higher quality recording with virtually zero generation loss when duplications are made. All digital recordings are inherently less detailed than the original analog signal, as the process of digitization involves sampling the analog signal, not necessarily duplicating the original, but this does not indicate a loss of quality because if the sampling rate is sufficiently high the image or sound will perceptually appear to be unchanged by the process. In fact, a digital signal is superior to an analog signal for processing, recording, and transmitting, because the wide variability in voltage levels has been eliminated.

It is common practice to sample an analog signal at double its highest frequency. In other words, the highest frequency of the sampled signal must be one-half or less the sampling frequency itself in order to avoid aliasing; this is referred to as the Nyquist rule. For example, an analog audio signal that contains frequencies up to 20KHz will require a sampling frequency of at least 40KHz. In fact, it is for this very reason that CDs are sampled at 44.1KHz and DAT (Digital Audio Tape) is sampled at 48KHz. Sampling is performed by an A-D (analog-digital) converter, and is subsequently quantized.

Quantization is the assigning of a specified number of bits in order to define a particular signal level at that sampling moment. The number of individual values possible is therefore based upon the number of bits used in the quantization. Given the binary nature of digital processing (i.e., 0 and 1) the formula 2^x (where x equals the number of bits) will reveal how many values are possible. If we assume for the moment that the image being digitized is black and white, and is quantized at 8 bits, it is apparent that 256 levels of gray will be possible, i.e., 2^8. Because the bit rate is exponential, an increase from 8 to 10 bit quantization produces 1024 shades of gray. The use of more bits improves the signal to noise ratio (SNR) and produces better tone reproduction in images.

Digitization of a composite analog video signal is defined, as one might expect, as composite digital. This involves the sampling of a composite NTSC signal at 14.32MHz. This was derived from the frequency of the color subcarrier (3.58), and therefore it is commonly referred to as $4 f_{sc}$. The signal is quantized using 8 bits. Using the total line rate of 15734.25Hz (525×29.97) of NTSC and the sampling rate, we can determine the total number of samples per line, e.g., $14.32/15734.25 = 910$. Due to the time lost in the horizontal blanking (electron beam retrace) the active samples per line is 768. D-2 is the most common NTSC composite digital videotape format, and has a data rate (video) of approximately 114Mbits/s, derived from 8 bits (per pixel) × (H) 910 × (V) 525 × 29.97 (fps) = 14.3Mbytes/s, where the megabits can be derived from the megabytes by simply multiplying 14.3×8 (8 bits to a byte). D-3 is another composite digital videotape format, and is virtually identical to D-2 in all regards, although D-2 cassettes are 19mm and D-3 cassettes are 1/2 inch. While D-2 and D-3 are substantially superior to any composite analog format, such as 1-inch Type C (hence their widespread usage in broadcast operations), D-2 and D-3 are still limited by their composite encoding structure. In post production, component digital is preferred.

Component digital uses a sampling frequency of 13.5MHz for the luminance signal Y (which is quantized at either 8 or 10 bits) and 6.75 MHz for the color difference components, Cb and Cr, which are subsets of the (B–Y) (R–Y) color difference signals; commonly written as YCbCr. Thus it is frequently noted as a ratio, i.e., 4:2:2, representing the fact that the luminance component is sampled at double the frequency of the chroma components. The eye will accept an image readily with half-resolution color as long as the luminance (Y) component remains at full resolution. This method is also employed—but with greater severity—in composite signal encoding by using bandwidth-limited UV and IQ signals.

ITU-R 601 (formerly CCIR-601) is the internationally agreed upon standard which defines the existing 4:2:2 component digital video formats. This sampling rate produces 858 total samples per line, or 720 active samples per line. D-1 and D-5 are the component digital videotape formats which correspond to this sampling structure, the former using 8 bit quantization, the latter 10 bit. D-1 uses a 19mm cassette and D-5 uses a 1/2-inch cassette. With a total of 16 bits per pixel, the data rate (video only) of D-1 is 27Mbytes/s or 216Mbits/s; that is, $16 \times 858 \times 525 \times 29.97 = 27\text{Mbytes/s} \times 8 = 216\text{Mbits/s}$.

In a system which uses 13.5MHz sampling of both luminance and chrominance components (noted as 4:4:4, which can be either YCbCr or RGB) the number of bits per pixel will be increased to 24. As one might imagine, the data rate is prohibitively high. This sampling structure would no doubt provide the best quality, since the color components are full bandwidth and are not horizontally subsampled as in the 4:2:2 system.

4:1:1 uses a 13.5MHz sampling rate of the luminance signal and 3.375MHz for the Cb and Cr components, which is only one-quarter the bandwidth (resolution) of the luminance signal. 4:2:0 uses the same 13.5MHz sampling rate as 4:1:1, but subsamples the chroma not only horizontally but vertically as well.

Even given the obvious benefits of digital video, the fact remains that the data rates and storage capacities necessary for many of these formats is excessive. It is also impractical to transmit uncompressed digital video, as the bandwidth required for such a task is inordinately high for existing systems. Interest in reducing the associated high bit rates of digital video provided the impetus in developing video compression schemes.

While the first real widespread use of compression was limited to computer-based nonlinear editing systems, where storage and transfer rates were insufficient for the data rates of uncompressed video, such coding methods on the whole have now been widely accepted. M-JPEG, a variant of the ubiquitous JPEG compression used for static images, has become the common compression method upon which such nonlinear editing systems rely.

Due to its obvious benefit, compression has now moved into the production and transmission end of the industry, the latter spurred on by the exorbitant data rate of high-definition television (where the question of storage and transmission is more pressing than ever), and the former brought about by an interest in providing professional digital camcorders which are physically smaller, use less power, and allow smaller tape sizes, along with more cost-effective digital VTRs for the post production facility. Formats such as Digital Betacam, Ampex DCT, DVCPRO, DVCPRO50, Digital-S, Betacam SX, HDCAM, and other compressed tape formats on the drawing board indicate an industry-wide trend. In addition, MPEG-2 compression has found widespread acceptance in digital satellite delivery systems, the DVD video format, and the transmission of high-definition television.

Compression has its flaws, though, and most notably this takes the form of visible artifacts and distortions in the image. The degree of impairment is usually based on the coding scheme utilized and the level of compression. Severely reduced data rates, which are indicative of high compression ratios, will most likely produce spurious or consistently poor results. Video compression is not a lossless procedure because it must necessarily discard data. For this reason it is important to understand the process of compression and what it entails.

The coding methods commonly used include MPEG-2 (this comprises a set of so-called profiles and levels), DV, and partially proprietary methods such as those employed in Digital Betacam and Ampex's DCT. Compression of images involves removing spatial redundancy and temporal redundancy, known as intraframe and interframe processing respectively. If interframe processing is utilized lower bit rates are possible, but at the expense of creating a very complex bitstream; that is, the Group of Pictures structure (GOP). Intraframe processing will yield an overall higher bit rate, but allows the frames and fields to remain largely intact, which makes it more suitable for tasks such as editing. The sampling structure used can be either 4:2:2, 4:1:1, or 4:2:0, indicating component digital systems with either half, quarter, or half vertical and horizontal subsampling of the color difference components. Choosing a method with fewer color difference samples per line will produce fewer bits but at the expense of reduced color quality.

The root of all of these enumerated compression schemes lies in the discrete cosine transform. DCT coding, in its most basic sense, involves dividing an image into blocks of 8 × 8 pixels and then transforming from each block the existing values into frequency coefficients. If during quantization the high-frequency coefficients are quantized at fewer bits per pixel, the total bit rate is reduced. Therefore, the quantization is responsible for producing the actual compression. Subsequent to this process, variable-length coding techniques are used (sometimes referred to as Huffman coding). This is an effectual method of compression because it employs a perception-based coding methodology, i.e., the reduced sensitivity of the eye to high-frequency areas. With the exception of Betacam SX, which is based on a subset of MPEG-2 4:2:2 P@ML, all of the previously noted formats use intraframe (or intrafield in the case of Digital Betacam and DCT) processing only.

MPEG-2 lessens the bit rate by including interframe processing in addition to the standard intraframe processing already employed. This allows temporal redundancy to be dealt with effectively by using motion estimation and compensation techniques; this is facilitated by creating one macroblock for every four DCT blocks. The basis for such a method is grounded in the fact that the image content from frame to frame does not change frequently unless a cut occurs or the camera and scenery are rapidly moving. Motion prediction, then, is possible by using a Group of Pictures. These GOPs consist of I frames (intraframes), P frames (predicted), and B frames (bidirectional). I frames are self-contained, P frames are (as the name implies) predicted from earlier I or P frames, and B frames are predicted from prior or upcoming I or P frames. Since the I frame starts the sequence in the Group of Pictures, the number of frames between each intraframe (I) determines the length of a GOP. Commonly this varies from as many as 15 frames to as few as 2 frames. A typical 15 frame GOP would be IBBPBBPBBPBBPBBI, although any order or length is possible depend-

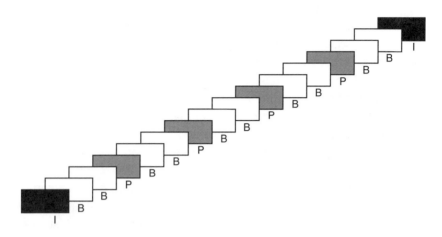

FIGURE 10.2 MPEG-2 15 frame Group of Pictures.

ing upon the application (see Figure 10.2). Due to the complexity of the coding process, particularly in the case of MPEG-2, the compression hardware is more expensive to implement than a DV-based system.

Digital Betacam is a component digital format (4:2:2) employing a modest amount of compression (DCT field-based), roughly 2.3:1, a 13.5MHz sampling rate with 10 bit quantization, and utilizes a 1/2-inch cassette for recording. The data rate (video only) is in the order of 90 Mbits/sec. This is a popular alternative to using uncompressed component digital formats (such as D-1 and D-5) in post production, and Sony's line of Digital Betacam camcorders allows this format to be used in the field for news acquisition and high-end video productions, where a digital component recording is desired.

Ampex's DCT format uses 2:1 compression based on the discrete cosine transform (field-based), a 4:2:2 component digital sampling structure and 8 bit quantization. The data rate (video only) is similar to Digital Betacam, and it records onto a 19mm cassette.

DVCPRO is a component digital format which uses a 13.5MHz sampling rate for the luminance and 3.375MHz for the color difference components, i.e., 4:1:1, and 8 bit quantization. The compression is 5:1 DV/DCT-based, and a data rate of 25Mbits/s is obtained. The physically small size of the cameras, the accompanying reduced weight, and the extremely compact cassettes (the tape is only 6.35mm wide) have made this format ideal for electronic news gathering and situations where a larger camera is not practical. The lower cost is also a benefit for producers who prefer a component digital format without the high price normally associated with equipment of this kind. It has been designated as D-7.

DVCPRO50 is a 50Mbit/s version of DVCPRO, and utilizes the same sampling frequency of 13.5MHz for the luminance, but samples the color difference components at 6.75MHz instead of 3.375MHz, thus providing superior chrominance resolution. The compression is 3.3:1 and is also, like its 25Mbit/s predecessor, DV/DCT-based. This format has all the benefits of DVCPRO but with improved picture quality. DVCPRO and DVCPRO50 are ideal video formats for those who need compact equipment.

Digital-S, marketed and developed by JVC, is a 4:2:2 component digital format, quantized at 8 bits and recorded on 1/2-inch cassette-based media. The compression is 3.3:1 (DCT-based), which makes it similar to DVCPRO50, and the data rate (video only) is 50Mbits/s. As an additional benefit, some Digital-S decks can play back S-VHS cassettes because of the similarity of the tape housing design. It has been designated as D-9.

Betacam SX uses MPEG-2 4:2:2 P@ML compression for significantly reduced bit rates, down to 18Mbits/s for the video content, a 4:2:2 sampling structure as indicated, and a two frame Group of Pictures, which consists of an I frame and a B frame. The compression ratio is approximately 10:1, and it records onto a 1/2-inch cassette. Also, some Betacam SX decks can play back Betacam SP tapes.

DVD video is a disc-based consumer video format that uses the same size disc as current CDs (5 inches), but increases capacity with a smaller track pitch, and allows increased data transfer speeds due to its higher rotational velocity. The compression is a variant of MPEG-2 MP@ML (Main Profile at Main Level), using a 4:2:0 sampling structure and variable bit rate encoding (VBR). By allowing VBR encoding, the compressionist can choose the bit rate depending upon the scene content. In other words, complex images can be encoded with more bits to improve the picture, while less complex images can use comparatively lower bit rates. The maximum bit rate is 9.8Mbits/s, and the average varies from 3 to 5Mbits per second. Compression is in the range of 40:1 from the source material (frequently 216Mbit/s D-1), and the maximum resolution is 720 × 480 in its current form.

The data storage possible on a DVD is based on two factors: the number of sides and the number of layers. A single-sided single-layer disc will hold 4.7GB and a single-sided double-layer disc will hold 8.5GB, whereas a double-sided single-layer disc will hold 9.4GB and a double-sided double-layer disc expands this to 17GB. The quality is considerably superior to VHS, but because the format comprises complex encoding procedures that involve human judgment (the compressionist), this format is really not suitable for dub-level usage, as in dailies and viewing copies. As an editing format it also has less functionality because the bitstream is comprised of GOP sequences, though editing systems based on the MPEG-2 studio profile are apparently now workable.

In the high-definition realm there is HDCAM, a format which uses 7:1 DCT-based compression, a sampling rate of 74.25MHz, with each color difference component sampled at half that frequency, 10 bit quantization, and records onto a 1/2-inch cassette. The recording data rate is 180Mbits/s, which is roughly 22.5 megabytes per second. For field-based work, Sony's HDCAM camcorder allows high-definition recording in a compact one-piece package.

Current studio formats for high definition are now becoming more commonplace. A variant of D-5 exists that uses compression to record high-definition signals on a standard 1/2-inch D-5 tape. Both 1080 interlaced and 720 progressive formats are supported, and further down-conversions are possible to other television standards.

D-6, a component digital high-definition format, is available for those who want to avoid using compression in order to maintain the highest possible image quality. This format uses 19mm cassettes, similar to D-1, and records up to 1.2 gigabits of data per second, although naturally this limits the tape recording times; the maximum is only 64 minutes. A fundamental difference between D-6 and other current formats is the fact that it is not strictly a videotape format but a data storage device, which makes it far more practical, particularly given the fact that DTV standards include a variety of frame rates and scanning methods. Philips has recently introduced the VooDoo media recorder, which essentially puts D-6 into actual application in the post production arena.

With a growing interest in high-definition television, which is not all that surprising considering the limited image quality currently provided on a typical home receiver, and the even further compromised VHS format, it seems a brief but detailed account of digital television (DTV) is in order.

The current digital television standard (compression formats) allows four resolutions, six possible frame rates, and two scanning methods. Furthermore, both 1.33 and 1.78 aspect ratios are supported, although the former is only used in standard-definition (SDTV) television (see Table 10.1). The two primary high-definition broadcast formats (or data structures, we might say) are commonly referred to as 1080i and 720p, indicating the number of active scan lines and the scanning structure utilized. The input formats have also been standardized. They are SMPTE 274M, which uses 1920 active samples per line and 1080 active lines, SMPTE 296M, defined as 1280 × 720, and 720 × 483 (ITU-RBT 601-4).

HORIZ. × VERT.	ASPECT RATIO	PROGRESSIVE (Frame Rate)	INTERLACED (Frame Rate)
1920 × 1080	1.78 (square samples)	23.976, 24, 29.97, 30.	29.97, 30.
1280 × 720	1.78 (square samples)	23.976, 24, 29.97, 30, 59.94, 60.	Not Supported
704 × 480	1.33 or 1.78	23.976, 24, 29.97, 30, 59.94, 60.	29.97, 30.
640 × 480	1.33 (square samples)	23.976, 24, 29.97, 30, 59.94, 60.	29.97, 30.

Table 10.1 ATSC digital television compression formats.

While it may appear odd that no single standard seems to exist, one must remember that we are ultimately dealing with compressed video and, to a certain specified degree, an open-architecture system. The basis for the ability to implement such a system lies in the fact that displays must be compatible with such stated standards; thus "DTV-ready" televisions will receive and display a variety of formats.

Transmission of HDTV requires substantial bit rate reduction in order to utilize a 6MHz channel for terrestrial broadcasting, as this format needs roughly 1Gbit/s (125 megabytes per second) of data flow for uncompressed transmission. Therefore a form of MPEG-2 MP@HL (Main Profile at High Level) is used with a 4:2:0 sampling structure. By this method it is possible to use 50:1 compression and send a 19.4Mbits/s (approximately 2.5 megabytes per second) data stream instead (with audio), which is the practical bandwidth limit of a 6MHz channel. If proper encoding is performed on the source material, the subjectively viewed picture can be acceptable.

Since the bit rates are necessarily tied to the resolution and scanning architecture, it is possible to use a lower quality input into the compression system (such as 720 × 483) and provide multiple programs within the allocated channel while still maintaining the same bit rate as noted earlier. This would allow a broadcaster to expand program services without using additional bandwidth. Although the quality of such a technique leaves much to be desired, and in principle defies the original intent of the FCC, one must admit that DVDs can produce an acceptable image with an average of 3 to 4Mbits per second, almost half of the 8Mbits/s that could be used in a multiple SDTV service. While the use of standard-definition digital, particularly in a progressive system, does offer an improvement over analog NTSC, the high-definition variants of DTV are of the greatest interest to the cinematographer.

As we have mentioned, there are two basic high-definition resolutions (both 1.78 aspect ratio): 1920 × 1080 and 1280 × 720. The 1080 format as it is currently being broadcast is interlaced, and the 720 format is progressive. Obviously a television monitor must be either interlaced or progressive, meaning one of these incoming data streams cannot be viewed in its native format and must be converted for display. Currently, most high-definition consumer televisions are 1080 interlaced displays, and so must convert the progressive 720 data. If a monitor with a 1.33 aspect ratio is called a "digital television," it most likely is a progressive-scan unit, but is designed to display the SDTV 720 × 483 picture, though when used in combination with a receiver capable of decoding all high-definition formats, it could display all of these, albeit at 720 × 483 progressive.

In the US, some of the major broadcast networks have selected interlaced 1080, while others have chosen to implement the progressive 720 high-definition format instead. From an initial glance, one might conclude 1920 × 1080 to be superior, but the fact that 1280 × 720 is a progressive system makes this point debatable. 1280 × 720 progressive viewed on a display in its native format, not converted for display on a 1920 × 1080 interlaced monitor, is at least comparable to a 1920 × 1080 interlaced picture. Presumably such displays will be available to consumers at a reasonable cost at some point in the future, and it is conceivable (and in the long run, even likely) that high-definition displays will eventually all be progressive 1920 × 1080.

The fact that there is no single digital television or high-definition format has brought the 1920 × 1080 progressive 24 frames per second system to the forefront. By utilizing progressive scan at the 1920 × 1080 resolution, we are getting the highest quality image possible within the bounds of the DTV standards (which allows for 1080 progressive), while at the same time matching the frame rate of film. This eliminates the problem of converting 24 fps film to a different video frame rate (the presently employed solution will be discussed in the following chapter). In addition, any form of a whole frame rate system eradicates the NTSC drop-frame time code matter created by the fact that NTSC video time code assumes 30 frames per second, while NTSC video in fact cycles at 29.97 frames per second, an unhappy result of the introduction of color into the previously monochrome signal.

The 29.97 fps actual frame rate used with time code based on 30 fps creates a disparity between real time and time code time. The disparity is small, but it is important in broadcast operations, where the time code on VTRs is utilized for critical accuracy. Time code lags behind real time (it is slow), meaning that the duration of a program is in real time longer than is indicated by the time code clock. The error is roughly 1.8 seconds per 30 minutes.

When preparing NTSC video for broadcast, this necessitates the use of drop-frame time code, where a certain specified number of time code "frames" are "dropped"—not actual video frames—in order to bring the time code into sync with real time. The duration in real time of a program, whether the master tape was edited drop-frame or non-drop-frame, is exactly the same. In drop-frame time code, numbers are skipped to bring the time code into synchronization with actual time, so the system could more accurately be described as "skip-number" time code.

The 1920 × 1080 progressively scanned 24 frames per second format is gaining acceptance as the film-originated mastering format for high-definition video, and its use will eliminate such concerns during post production. From it one may derive all possible DTV formats.

An interesting aside is the fact that a high-definition 24 frames per second progressive video camera is being tested for feature motion picture use, an enterprise of Lucasfilm, Sony, and Panavision. The plan is to employ a 24 progressive-scan high-definition video camera to shoot feature films, transferring the picture data onto film for release to theaters until the electronic alternative to a film print is in widespread use in theaters, developments one can only assume the gnomes toiling away in Rochester must be watching closely.

If such a device can produce an image rivaling (or at least approaching) film, there seems little doubt it will gain a rapid foothold. Gone would be the loading of magazines, the threading of the camera, the unloading of magazines, and the interminable wait to view the dailies and assess the day's work when the day is no more.

11

Image Conversion

FILM TO VIDEO

While the fact remains that film still provides the highest quality image and is by far the most desirable mastering format currently available, most film is ultimately destined to be viewed electronically, the vast majority never being projected as a print. For this reason it is of primary interest to understand the procedures involved in film to video transfers and, one might add, the inherent limitations regarding image quality, a particular concern for the director of photography. Before delving into the specific issues regarding these matters, a brief account of the telecine itself is the logical place to begin.

Telecines can be categorized as two basic types: the flying spot scanner and the charge-coupled device (CCD)-based system. Both of these systems use a continuous-motion film transport instead of the intermittent movement found in optical printers and cameras; thus all film (particularly negative) can be transferred without fear of damage caused by equipment malfunction or improper loading procedures. This method also provides a significant advantage in that different gauge films can be accommodated by simply switching gates, and higher speeds do not increase the chances of damage occurring as would be the case with an intermittent movement.

The imaging system of the flying spot scanner is based on a high-intensity cathode ray tube which produces a very narrow beam of white light that scans the film image. The beam which is emitted from the face of the CRT is focused onto the film by an appropriate lens, and provides—by its single-line scan—the horizontal information of the image (the equivalent of one television scan line). Color modulation of the light beam is produced by the film's dye layers in the region (line) being scanned after passing through the emulsion, and this single beam is further separated by beam-splitting optics into three color components which are directed into photomultiplier tubes. Line by line scanning is facilitated by the movement of the film through the gate. In this manner the film image is converted into a raster format by progressive scanning. Interlaced signals and the 3:2 pull-down are created in a digital framestore which provides the necessary frame rate conversion (for NTSC).

In a CCD telecine the film is "projected" onto a line-array of discrete sensors by using light provided by a high-wattage halogen lamp. Focusing of the light is expedited by using a lens in the film gate in a fashion similar to a flying spot system. The CCD chips are based on the same design as those which are used in professional video cameras, but use only one line-array per device, not a matrix—meaning both axes cannot be sampled without the film physically moving across the array. The light, after passing through the film, is separated into its respective color components by a prism block and then received by three separate (permanently bonded and registered) line-arrays in the same fashion as a three chip video camera. The line by line scanning, as implied earlier, is provided by the same continuous motion of the film through the gate as that employed by the flying spot scanner. Likewise, interlaced signals and the appropriate frame rate conversion are produced by a digital framestore device.

Most current standard telecines are designed to be used for either 525 or 625 work, i.e., NTSC or PAL, and output component digital signals, i.e., 4:2:2. In the latest systems 4:4:4 is an output option, which allows for full-bandwidth color, although this sampling structure cannot be directly recorded using existing videotape formats and is only practical as an input for graphics or compositing workstations. While the output can obviously be converted to any format, such as component analog, composite analog, and composite digital by using an appropriate encoder, it is preferable to use a component digital format if available.

Choosing a good quality video format is important. Analog video should be avoided for the obvious reasons, but if digital video cannot be used for budgetary reasons, then a professional component analog system should be used, for example Betacam SP. In the ideal situation, where cost is not a factor, D-1, Digital Betacam, or D-5 should be used. Dubbing is less of a concern when using digital video, as the quality is not degraded with each successive generation. In the composite digital realm, formats such as D-3 and D-2 can yield an image which almost rivals component digital, but with reduced user cost in terms of the entire post production process. Whether D-2 is more economical than Digital Betacam depends on several factors. The primary cost increase with component digital is the component digital on-line assembly. In many cases Digital Betacam is actually less expensive in the film transfer stage, which is one reason it has become the ubiquitous video mastering format for high-end filmed television.

The use of digital tape formats is more crucial if it is decided that the final color correction is going to be performed tape to tape. During this process another generation is created from the edited master, which means the program producer must invariably choose a digital format for the reasons outlined above. While this does not hinder the use of composite digital formats, there is a practical advantage to be gained by using component digital VTRs. Color correcting machines typically utilize component inputs and outputs, and the ability to have the color signals separated during processing yields considerably superior results. For this reason D-1, D-5, and Digital Betacam are frequent choices as mastering formats in telecine.

It is also possible to transfer footage directly to a hard drive from a telecine machine, a system devised to provide instantly editable dailies. This can be of particular advantage when component digital VTRs are not available in the edit suite, and a high-quality input format is desired for a low compression rate edit, which might be considered acceptable for creating a master direct from the nonlinear editor. Unfortunately, the advantages of using such a system for any reason are limited due to reliability problems and the added complexity during the transfer, and when one considers the expense involved in any film to video transfer, particularly when paying by the hour, it makes more sense to digitize dailies for nonlinear editing systems in a less expensive environment. Not surprisingly, this process is rarely available outside of a few select facilities. The basic premise, though, is a valid one and will likely become more common in the near future when linear videotape formats give way to nonlinear data storage devices, something which is more realistically attainable with compressed video formats.

The latest telecines cross the line that once existed between traditional film to video transfer systems and true film scanners by their drastically enhanced resolution and direct data output capability. The only criterion that appears to still divide the two is the intended application, where film scanners are only used for the express purpose of acquiring an image that will be recorded back onto film. Pin registration and steadiness are also technical factors one must consider if such machines are to be used for both telecine and film scanning. While the most recently introduced telecines are capable of standard-definition transfers (and are used for this purpose when the highest obtainable NTSC or PAL image quality is desired), the real impetus behind the development process is the inevitability of high-definition television in the marketplace, where such a video system necessitates a superior film transfer device that can support the increased resolution of this format.

As in existing telecines, both flying spot and linear array CCD systems are employed, the former utilizing a smaller scanning spot, while the latter has an increased pixel count CCD and high-intensity xenon light source. By this method some of these systems can output resolutions as high as 2048 × 1832. Of course, in all other respects these machines have significantly improved transfer characteristics by using vastly improved components throughout their design. Superior color and dynamic range along with a total lack of noise are primarily of interest to those who want the best electronic image possible, and for the producer who may need to provide several different formats in the future, these systems are multi-format: both standard-definition, i.e., 10 bit 4:2:2 and 4:4:4 (full-bandwidth color), and high-definition (1920 × 1080 or in some cases 1280 × 720) formats are supported. Furthermore, it is now possible to directly output data in the standardized DPX format on some of these systems for further image processing using computer workstations, where recording back to film is the intended end result.

The technical complication involved in a film transfer to NTSC is caused by the inherent disparity between film and video regarding frame rate, something alluded to in the preceding chapter. Film is captured at 24 frames per second and video, at least in the NTSC system, operates at 29.97 frames per second. Furthermore, the video frame is not complete, but rather it is the product of two fields created by the interlaced architecture employed in the video system. The field rate, then, is exactly half the frame rate, i.e., 59.94Hz. This has created a somewhat complicated procedure because naturally one cannot simply increase the film speed during the transfer without introducing obvious and unacceptable modifications, nor can additional video frames be generated in succession without detrimental image redundancy. Repetition is unavoidable, as we will soon see, but a workable method is employed to limit our awareness of its use.

In order to provide an appropriate conversion, and thus create an electronic image from film that is compatible with television, two methods are employed. First, the film travels through the telecine at an exact speed of 23.976 (a .1 percent slowdown from the camera rate of 24 frames per second), a necessity because the video frame rate is not an even integer, and therefore a precise six frame difference relationship is made. Second, after suitably reducing the film frame rate, six additional frames must be added in order to create the required frame rate of 29.97. This is done through a process known as 3:2 pull-down, which creates two fields from film frame 1 and three fields from film frame 2. Basic math will reveal that ten fields of video are created for every four film frames. In other words, we are creating five frames of video for every four frames of film or, during every one second interval, a total of six frames of video are added, therein establishing the correct frame rate of 29.97 (see Figure 11.1).

While this process is undoubtedly acceptable enough from a visual perspective, and has proven to be a reasonable solution, it does have serious drawbacks. Primarily speaking, the main problem is field repetition, which is caused by utilizing film frame 2 to generate three video fields. One can see that these fields subsequently produce video frame 2 and part of 3. Duplicity is an unavoidable fact of film to video transfers; however, due to the nature of the video image (its low resolution), one is not readily aware of these inconsistencies. The 3:2 pull-down process is always necessary in countries that use the NTSC system, while PAL (625/50), a common interlaced video format in Europe and the rest of the world, does not require such methods because it is based on 25 frames per second, i.e., a 50Hz field rate. Therefore film shot at 25 fps can simply be transferred 1:1, or 24 fps source ma-

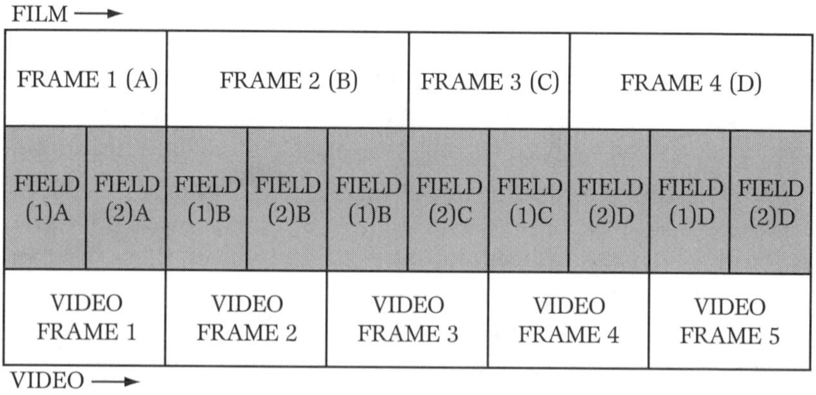

FILM ⟶

FRAME 1 (A)	FRAME 2 (B)		FRAME 3 (C)	FRAME 4 (D)	
FIELD (1)A	FIELD (2)A	FIELD (1)B	FIELD (2)B	FIELD (1)B	FIELD (2)C	FIELD (1)C	FIELD (2)D	FIELD (1)D	FIELD (2)D
VIDEO FRAME 1	VIDEO FRAME 2		VIDEO FRAME 3	VIDEO FRAME 4	VIDEO FRAME 5

VIDEO ⟶

FIGURE 11.1 NTSC 3:2 pull-down sequence.

terial can be increased to 25 fps during telecine with little visible difference. Of course in the NTSC system one always has the alternative of shooting 30 fps film to eliminate the 3:2 pull-down, but this option is very infrequently exercised.

All telecines are capable of transferring both negative and positive film material. The determining factor for film choice in a transfer will largely be dictated by the production. In the case of television commercials it is common to simply transfer an uncut original negative, and this also applies to many television productions which will finish on video. Whether the negative for a television project will ever in fact be cut and spliced together to form a film master depends on the production. The popularity of this practice varies, but in a world of multiple, ever-changing video formats and standards, accompanied by the emergence of high-definition television, one may find a cut negative to be the best choice, reducing costs in the long run if the program requires a re-transfer. Feature films are commonly transferred from a timed interpositive. Prints are less frequently used, as the invariably high gamma values of these stocks do not provide the same transfer characteristics as a negative or interpositive film. The very high density range of the positive stock reduces the ability of the telecine system to provide a wide tonal range, and the result is usually excessively dark shadows. The latest telecines have improved print transfer capability, and good results can now be obtained in many cases. For those who prefer a print for transfer (prints still have a different look from that obtained by using a negative), but prefer transfer characteristics more suitable for a telecine, special low-contrast print stocks are available. The additional cost of making this special print is not usually of serious concern, but when one considers that it is useless for projection, meaning it has a very limited and singular purpose, most will opt to use the original negative for both convenience and cost.

A negative film will provide the best image quality possible on any telecine system due to its inherently low gamma (which means there is less density range), and of course the fact that it is the original also contributes to its superior transfer characteristics. Further advantages are gained by not only avoiding additional printing costs, but knowing that by using the original camera negative any spurious printing errors are entirely eradicated—a not uncommon problem on rapidly produced contact prints. Increased color saturation and more open shadows, and therefore more choices in the reproduced tonal range, are the primary benefits of using a negative film. The full range of the negative, however, is impossible to reproduce, so all film transfers are still a compromise when compared to the image quality obtainable by direct projection of a contact print.

In a typical transfer, any image on the negative that was exposed 4 stops below mid-scale gray will appear as black on the television monitor. At the opposite end of the scale, the highlights, video fares even worse. The gradual curve, or compression, that occurs in the shoulder region of film, which allows an emulsion to record substantial overexposure, becomes far more abrupt when transferred to video. A 90 percent reflectance white card will be well into the 90 IRE range, and in some cases, can easily exceed 100 IRE. As one might suspect, the tonal range is roughly 4 stops below mid-scale gray and maybe, at best, 2 1/2 stops above 18 percent gray. In comparison to the 10 or more stop range that the latest negative film stock allows, it is easy to understand the limitations of a telecine.

The fact remains that current video has a limited contrast range when compared to film, and this is of primary concern for those who must make decisions regarding tone reproduction in a film to video transfer. In addition, the color reproduction of a film image on a television monitor is a mere fraction of that captured by the original negative film. Resolution is also drastically reduced by this process. As telecine systems improve it is becoming easier to record the nuances of the film image, but until high-definition transfers become commonplace, the image will always suffer from the shortcomings of existing television standards.

Before a film is transferred it is common practice to clean and prepare the film for telecine. The laboratory will do this as a matter of course if it is known that the film is intended for transfer. In addition it is important that a framing chart be provided at the head of the roll to expedite proper extraction, which should coincide with the ground glass frame lines used in the camera. A chart such as SMPTE RP-40 will work fine, and can provide very accurate width and height measurements for video extraction. Shooting a custom chart with the actual production camera can also be useful, but if the exact measurements are known for the ground glass in use, then little is to be gained by going to the added expense and trouble of creating your own, since the laboratory can splice a standard framing chart onto the head of the lab rolls before cleaning the film for transfer. Obviously in the case of widescreen formats, such as 1.85 or 2.35, the intended aspect ratio and correct framing cannot be used unless the film is letter-boxed. In the case of anamorphic, pan and scan is the only viable solution if letter-boxing is not an option.

If the film was shot for television, then it will almost certainly have been framed with either 1.33 television transmitted markings on the ground glass (in offset Academy 35 or Super 35), or in the case of Super 35, with 1.78 markings, 1.33 markings, or a combination of both. Many colorists attempt to use the largest negative area possible, and this haphazard method almost never matches the finder markings. Most television productions do not utilize a hard matte, which means there is a full frame exposed, and despite the seemingly small difference between the television transmitted area and the usable remaining area, there is sufficient negative available outside the television transmitted region to alter the intended framing to a noticeable degree when the image is viewed on a television screen. The 1.33/1.78 common top and bottom line markings of Super 35 exacerbate the problem when an attempt to transfer the most negative area possible is made and the transfer is intended for 1.33. Never assume a colorist will somehow know what the framing should be without instructions.

All telecine systems have very accurate x and y zoom controls for framing, which can be of much use when re-framing a shot is necessary for creative or other purposes. Programmable zooms and pans can also be done within a shot, and if done correctly, are little noticed. In fact it is preferable to do any re-framing within the telecine itself, as re-framing in video during editing will seriously impair the quality of an image.

The logging of data during the telecine transfer is absolutely necessary if the negative is to be conformed to a video edit, and even if one does not plan on doing so, it is still recommended in the event a re-transfer is necessary. Logging is normally done automatically with special film readers and the appropriate computer software in order to create a database that can be output in a number of industry-standard formats. These systems will log keycode, time code, audio time code, footage count, camera number, date, production name, transfer speed, film type, lab roll, pull-down sequence, etc., and drastically simplify editorial concerns by creating a link between the post production processes.

It is also common practice to punch or tag the first frame in a transfer for physical identification and negative match-back purposes, and in the case of cut negatives which do not have continuous keycode, a punch or tag should be provided after each splice. Normally this is done on a zero-frame reference mark.

When film to video transfers are done for features cutting on a nonlinear editing system it is usually more practical and economical to splice out the "print" takes from the camera rolls and assemble lab rolls based on these takes. It is also possible to simply indicate which shots to transfer (if proper slating procedures were followed and the scene numbers and takes are readable) and keep the original camera rolls intact, but it is not as foolproof as the former system. Videotapes with time code and keycode "burn-in" should also be available to the editor if necessary.

Though the details of the transfer process can vary depending upon the intended purpose, the first step in almost all productions are the video dailies, since editing is generally done in the nonlinear com-

puter-based environment for both features and productions that originated on film but will finish on video, e.g., commercials, television
productions, etc. There are two common methods used in film transfers and both present unique problems for the cinematographer. In the
case of short form work, such as commercials, it is typical to scene to
scene color correct during the initial transfer. This will undoubtedly
provide the best quality image, but invariably requires a supervised
transfer by those concerned, i.e., the director of photography and various bottled-water-swilling agency types. Long form work can also be
transferred in this manner, but it is more common now to provide
"best light" video dailies, where scene to scene color correction is
omitted, and the colorist essentially transfers the film with minimal
changes from the basic setup, although what exactly this setup is appears to be in practice highly subjective. What this implies is that the
skill and preferences of the colorist have a considerable effect on the
outcome. In this scenario, tape to tape color correction is normally
employed after the on-line to provide scene by scene correction.

The concern for the cinematographer is that dailies should represent within the confines of the video format what was exposed on
film. In conventional film dailies, of course, this is easier to accomplish, and while the results may not be flawless, at least they are usually
indicative of the previous day's work. In the realm of film to video
transfers, where one is already dealing with a limited-output medium
(video), acceptable dailies are more difficult to attain. The problem is
compounded by the fact that subjective judgment on the part of the
colorist may not coincide with the cinematographer's intent, which is
why detailed information regarding this matter should be included with
all film that is to be transferred (instructions regarding the desired
"look"), and furthermore the technical issues concerning established
practices with respect to transfers that will be subsequently modified
in a tape to tape color correction process leave much to be desired.

The importance of video dailies is less significant if the film is
destined for the theater, as in this case they are strictly supplied for
nonlinear computer-based editing purposes and print dailies will still
be supplied. Of course, if there are no print dailies for budgetary or
other reasons, but the picture is intended to be theatrically released,
the task of evaluating such material is nearly impossible unless a reasonably accurate transfer is done. For this reason it can be best to color

time such material using traditional techniques and determine the exposure from the Hazeltine timing lights. One is not obligated to print this material, and some (or at least a few) laboratories will perform this task for a nominal fee.

It is also now possible to produce similar exposure reports during the telecine transfer by using a telecine calibration film designed for this purpose and the appropriate look-up tables (LUT) for each film stock. Kodak's telecine exposure calibration film (TEC) is an example of such a system, and provides a means of correlating video voltage (by using a waveform monitor) to RGB printer (transfer) points from an 18 percent gray card included in the scene. It is also necessary to have a "gray-finder" system installed for this to work properly. Unfortunately, the impracticality of shooting a gray card at the head of every shot, including the limitations of such a method in the first place, along with the time taken for the colorist to perform this additional task during the transfer, makes it less practical than it might at first appear.

Unsupervised video dailies are an unfortunate reality of most productions, unless one happens to be shooting a mile from the transfer facility or can stay awake twenty-four hours a day. The procedure makes sense for the producer, who is concerned with cost, and the transfer facility, which needs to keep the service rapid and continuous (many transfers occur at the wee hours of the morning in order to provide such "dailies"), but the director of photography is left with the task of evaluating material that in many cases will not be representative of the obtainable image quality. Furthermore, image evaluation is made far more difficult when non-broadcast tape formats are used, i.e., VHS, which are typically supplied because of their convenience (bad dubs can exacerbate the problem). There are several steps that one can take to improve unsupervised film to video transfers, although at times none may accomplish the goal.

In the ideal situation the director of photography would be present at the transfer, providing valuable input for the colorist, thereby producing dailies that require very little further correction. In many cases, though, it is impossible and impractical to do this, so a compromise must be made. As has been noted, the director of photography can supply the colorist with very detailed information regarding the desired "look," from which the colorist can make decisions, or one can use a variety of so-called "calibration systems" which rely on gray scales and specially prepared and exposed film designed to help the colorist set up the telecine to produce a one-light result. In the former case there are a variety of ways of doing this, but generally any report might work that is sufficiently understandable, provided the colorist receives the report along with the film. In this way the cinematographer can expect better dailies than would be provided if the decisions are entirely left to the colorist. In the latter case, when calibration charts are shot, one must carefully follow outlined procedures in both production and post production in order to get the desired results, but the results are sometimes worth the effort.

As an aid for the transfer, some cinematographers may opt to shoot a gray card at the head of the roll. If a reference white and black are included with the gray card, the colorist can fine-tune the transfer characteristics for your specific roll, and use the gray card as a means of determining how well the film is exposed. The idea is that if one wishes to see exactly what was shot, without corrections of any kind, as with a one-light print, a gray card with black and white patches can be used to set up the telecine and then everything will be transferred with fixed settings.

An additional complication in getting representative image quality from video dailies has now been introduced by a growing trend to provide conservative transfers for further tape to tape color correction, meaning the contrast is particularly low and only minimal color correction has been applied. This method makes assessing work very difficult, because a kind of video intermediate is being created which does not accurately show what the photographic intentions were, but also does not represent the finished product.

Tape to tape color correction is in many cases preferred because it allows the final correction to be done using the same color correction equipment that would be utilized in a telecine room, but without actually using the telecine machine, which generally means a faster and less costly process. The edited master is used as the source tape and changes are made to produce better matched shots (scene to scene correction), something which is more difficult to do with unedited material in the dailies stage. This is the most common method of color correction on long form material, and while it has its obvious merits, the degree of correction possible is not as vast as that which can be accomplished in a film to video transfer.

The colorist has the option of modifying the image in many ways to get the best possible quality. Typically this would be image enhancement and noise reduction for a cleaner and sharper image (the latter much needed for 16mm), or working with a variety of color correcting controls. The degree of noise in a video image is dependent to a large extent on how well the negative was exposed. Underexposed 16mm would present the worst-case scenario. In matters of color, primary correction provides gain, gamma, and lift control in each color component. If the image has poor black levels, a simple modification of the lift can rectify the problem. Or if a change in the gamma is necessary, then the gamma control can be utilized to shift the gray scale, thus affecting the image contrast. Overall correction of underexposed or overexposed images can be improved with the master gain.

On a more complex level, one may work with a six-vector secondary color correction unit, which allows modification of red, green, blue, cyan, magenta, and yellow. Within a single channel one may choose to increase the saturation, change the hue, or increase or decrease luminance. This allows for a very wide range of color-related choices, many of which can be used for artistic effect as easily as for corrective purposes. The latest color correctors allow isolation of frame areas for precise color and tone changes which will only affect the specified area, i.e., "power windows," and the ability to target an existing color for modification without affecting other colors in the scene. Color can also be completely removed from a scene if one desires black and white images.

It is obvious that an incredible range of control is available during a color correction session, and this is largely responsible for the latest trends in such fare as music videos, which invariably require a distinct look, and eye-catching television commercials, where presenting an idealized image is of primary concern. For the feature cinematographer the goal is to produce a representative video version of the film within the confines of the color, contrast, and resolution-limited electronic medium. The irony of this situation is emphasized by the fact that color correction is far more advanced in the telecine suite than is possible using conventional film color timing and additive printing. This has no doubt sparked an interest in producing so-called "electronic intermediates" as a substitute for traditional film intermediates. Such a system would allow an unprecedented degree of image control for the cinematographer by scanning the negative into digital image data which could then be modified in ways that are impossible with traditional photographic methods. While the additional costs are not inconsequential, considering an entire film must be scanned, stored electronically, and then recorded back onto an intermediate stock, the benefit of using such a system would be improved quality without the inherent generation loss currently incurred by the intermediate film elements, although this necessarily assumes that the scanning and recording resolution is sufficiently high as to not produce degradation of the image itself; probably at least 12 bits per pixel at 4K × 3K. As film scanning and recording systems become faster, less proprietary, and less expensive, this technique could become a viable option.

The future of telecine is high-resolution scanning and data output for the multi-format world of digital television, where one master format can provide the basis for extracting all other formats. Given sufficient resolution and proper framing, it would be possible to create different aspect ratios, in varying resolutions, without having to re-transfer the original film. Furthermore, conversions between television standards could be simplified by choosing a mastering format that eliminates the 3:2 pull-down of current film transfers, therein allowing digital storage in originating frame rates. Thus there is a growing interest in mastering film in a 24 fps environment in order to provide one video format from which all others can be obtained. An additional benefit is that film material can be scanned and digitized in its native frame rate for nonlinear editing systems, which will create a simplified post process, without the complexities introduced by the pull-down of the telecine. This is advantageous both for productions that will finish on film and need to create frame-accurate cut lists for the negative, something which is the source of much doubt using current systems, and film productions finishing on video where a conformed negative is deemed necessary. For the compressionist, 24 fps source material for MPEG-2 encoding will eliminate the inherent redundancy that exists in all conventional (3:2 pull-down) film to video transfers, a not inconsiderable detriment to the entire encoding process. In the long run 24 fps will produce more efficient compression, a matter of growing importance in the compressed digital environment.

12

Dye Layers and Data

DIGITAL SCANNERS AND FILM RECORDERS

Film scanners and recorders merge the assets of traditional film technology with the power of digital image processing. Film is an ideal medium for producing compelling and superb imagery, but it lacks the versatility of a digital imaging system. In a sense, the film image is locked in time by its physical dyes and layers and cannot be significantly changed without direct manipulation or additional film elements. This concrete nature of film creates inherent limitations. Any modification of the film image directly necessitates the use of optical printers and other complex and generally imperfect photo-mechanical methods. Digital images are quite the antithesis, allowing countless changes and modifications without any degradation or damage to the original, and zero generation loss.

Creativity is expanded when working with digital images because one is not hindered by the mechanical and optical limitations of film technology, although naturally the digital system has its own set of particular problems. The digitization of film images provides the basis for combining the best that film has to offer with the obvious benefits of the latest digital imaging technology, and the film scanner is the key component in this input process. The film recorder, which provides the output, performs the much-needed task of getting the raster format image back onto film, where one can expect a seamless integration with existing footage if all goes well.

In concert with discussing the many ways in which digital film systems are implemented, an account of the basic tools of the trade must be provided. It seems only logical to deal with the scanner first, the image processing second (which involves a combination of computer hardware and software), and the film recorder third.

Film scanners are not all exactly alike in specification and performance, but mechanically they must be extremely accurate. Pin-registration for precise frame positioning is absolutely crucial for proper operation, and they must provide a zero-fault transport system. The sensors must also be of sufficient resolution to capture the full detail of a film frame so as not to introduce a reduction in quality, and the full density range of the film must be acquired if the tonal qualities of the original negative are to be maintained. A film scanner must necessarily also produce accurate color reproduction with sufficient color depth in order for integrated footage to appear identical to that which has not been scanned and recorded. This is not an easy task, and any errors regarding these matters can negate the efforts of all involved.

Film scanners use line-array CCDs to capture film images in a similar method as that utilized by charge-coupled device telecines, although in this case the focusing optics are not in the film gate but in front of the sensors. A diffuse light source produced by a high-intensity tungsten halogen or xenon light illuminates the negative or intermediate film which is optically projected onto three line-array CCDs. In many cases the magnification of the image is fixed by the lens, and the line-array is designed so as to image an area equal to the width of a full 35mm frame (.980). Vertical movement of the film past the lens yields the vertical (y-axis) dimension of the film frame.

In order to provide the necessary resolution and color reproduction the three line-arrays must contain in excess of 4000 discrete elements (usually 4096), and must be filtered respectively with red, green, and blue filters in order to provide a color image. The spectral sensitivity of the scanner must also match that of the subsequent print stock if accurate color results are to be obtained.

Quantization of the analog signal is usually 12 or 14 bits. This provides, in the case of the former, 4096 levels per color channel, or in the latter 16,384. The total number of colors captured would then necessarily be 4096^3 or $16,384^3$, but file formats are usually only 10 bits or even 8 in some cases. Images are also typically stored as logarithmic data, such as Cineon 10 bit log, as it correlates to the logarithmic density measurement of film, allowing a specific density to be matched with a respective code level. For example, a 10 bit log format will allow 2^{10} or 1024 levels for gray scale, or 1024^3 (1,073,741,824) possible colors at 30 bits per pixel. 8 and 16 bit linear image formats are possible when using TIFF or SGI, but only 256 gray levels and 16.7 million colors are produced (24 bits per pixel) with 8 bit files, and this does not provide the necessary image quality for film output, but is more suited for digital video applications. Of course, the greater the number of bits per pixel the larger the image file, yielding a superior image but causing a reduction in processing speed.

It should be noted that 24 bit "true color" is standard on most computer systems, and many 8 bit linear files can be used with conventional off-the-shelf (and therefore less costly) software, which admittedly adds a degree of versatility to the process. In some cases 8 bit video files converted from 10 bit log files may be used for this reason, although as stated before, 10 bit log files are preferred for film recording (output). For compatibility and exchange between computer systems the Digital Moving Picture Exchange (DPX) file format was created.

Negative, interpositive, and internegative films are all acceptable for scanning. Print films are not normally used. Given the fact that the original negative is the most desirable for scanning, one should make protective elements (interpositives) before the scan process in the event the originals are damaged. Some facilities may even require this to be done or a waiver must be signed. Of course original negatives are transferred in telecine with few if any problems ever occurring, so the risk is not really any greater, and in fact it is probably significantly less. It is also recommended that one use a DPX leader consisting of special purpose test patterns and images. These should be spliced onto the head of all film rolls in order to ascertain such matters as color reproduction, gray scale reproduction, digital aim density (similar to LAD), aspect ratio, steadiness, focus and resolution, etc., in the evaluation and calibration of digital film scanners. A leader can also be used for the same purpose when images are output to a film recorder if it is available in a digital form.

The scanning resolution chosen is normally dependent upon the film format used during production, although for lower resolution work a film frame can be scanned at one-quarter, one-half, or three-quarters of the frame's resolution. 35mm full aperture, Academy, anamorphic,

35mm FORMAT (Scan Area)	RESOLUTION (x,y)		
	FULL	HALF	QUARTER
Full Aperture (.980 × .735)	4096 × 3112	2048 × 1556	1024 × 778
Academy (.864 × .630)	3656 × 2664	1828 × 1332	914 × 666
Cinemascope (.864 × .735)	3656 × 3112	1828 × 1556	914 × 778
Vistavision (.980 × 1.470)	4096 × 6144	2048 × 3072	1024 × 1536

TABLE 12.1 Common digital film scanner resolutions.

and VistaVision are supported by all motion picture film scanners, and a few scanners are even capable of scanning 65mm, including 15-perforation Imax.

Film scanners which have variable optical magnification can offer higher resolutions (more pixels) across the width of a smaller frame, while a scanner with a fixed magnification must invariably cause a reduction in the resolution (fewer pixels per width) when the frame area to be extracted is physically smaller. See Table 12.1 for typical resolutions used in the scanning of various 35mm film formats.

Even though the x-axis resolution never exceeds 4096—and initially this may seem to present a problem with VistaVision's large 8-perforation horizontally oriented frame area—one must remember that the scanning takes place with the film in a vertical configuration. Therefore in the case of VistaVision the x-axis resolution is the height of this format (.980) while the y-axis resolution is the width (1.470). As the y-axis resolution is not fixed by the elements in the CCD line-array, but is in fact determined by the vertical movement of the film, 6144 pixels can be captured for this format. Anamorphic (2:1 squeezed) can be scanned just as easily as regular spherical formats, and then simply unsqueezed using the appropriate software when a 2.35 aspect ratio image is necessary for further image processing.

In fact, when a Super 35 image is scanned, where the intention is to output an anamorphic internegative for subsequent contact printing (in order to provide theaters with an anamorphic print for 2.35 projection), one can produce the necessary squeeze through software-based methods. The digitally squeezed image can then be exposed back onto film using a film recorder without the inherent loss of contrast (flare) which must be dealt with when conventional optical printing methods are employed. For those attempting to obtain the best possible quality from a Super 35 negative, this method would appear to be an interesting route to follow, although the process of film scanning and recording is naturally going to cost more than optical printing. However, it could be justified if large portions of the film were already scanned for special effects work.

Determining the frame area to scan in the case of anamorphic is not much in question, since obviously the entire anamorphic frame must be scanned, but 1.85 and Super 35 (if a hard matte was not used in production) allow for framing options. The decision depends upon whether the television version will be extracted from within the theatrical framing or will include additional picture area. If the scanning and subsequent digital work are only within the 1.85 or 2.35 framing, then a hard matte might as well have been used in the camera (at least for these shots), since any extra picture area cannot be transferred for television. In these formats the framing for scanning varies from project to project, the decision based upon the television extraction choice. Here it might also be noted that if the 1.85 aspect ratio is being used, and most or all of the finished footage is to be scanned, the somewhat unusual Super 1.85 format might be a viable option, the reduction to regular 1.85 being accomplished through software, without the limitations of the optical reduction process.

Due to the extremely high resolutions captured and the subsequent data processing necessary, film scanners cannot work in real time. It normally takes several seconds per frame to scan a film image at full resolution. The actual speed, of course, will vary depending upon the manufacturer, and some scanners are faster than others. Because of the high volume of data involved it is also conventional to use linear high-capacity storage devices, e.g., DST, Metrum, or DLT.

The storage necessary is determined by the scanning resolution and the bit depth chosen for the files. For example, a single scanned frame of Academy format 35mm film can easily require 36.5Mbytes of storage ($3656 \times 2664 \times 30/8 = 36.5$Mbytes) when 30 bits per pixel are used—10 bit log image files—which means 24 frames of film (one second of actual running time) can take up almost one full gigabyte (actually 876Mbytes) of storage. Based on this fact, roughly 19 minutes of film scanned at this resolution will require one terabyte of storage, i.e., one thousand gigabytes.

When actually working with such files on a computer workstation, normally nonlinear disk-based systems, e.g., RAID arrays, are used for temporary storage during the duration of the project. By using systems with high-speed throughput (fiber-optic), or as a minimum SCSI, the transfer and access time is decreased, bottlenecks are reduced, and work can be done far more efficiently than with tape-based storage. Furthermore, by implementing large scale network storage systems with several terabytes of capacity it is possible to have over an hour of material on-line and also allow multiple users to access the same data from different workstations.

In addition, once film has been scanned and stored in the appropriate file format, this data can be sent across the country (or the globe for that matter) using high-speed fiber-optic lines in order to provide digital film media to other post houses that may be involved in the production. While this involves a cost all its own, it does avoid the danger of sending actual film materials, where physical damage or loss of camera originals will likely be catastrophic. For the producer this also allows shot and scene previews from different facilities without the travel expenses involved because a site can be chosen that has such a "link" and all material can be screened at this one common location. This also cuts down on the seemingly endless collection of media formats (videotapes, data tapes, etc.) that are normally sent back and forth during post production.

Once scanning is complete and digital files are available a vast array of options becomes possible. Opportunities exist for color correction (digital film timing), painting (rig, wire, scratch, and object removal), compositing, titles, and film restoration and preservation. What was once the domain of the optical printer is now fast becoming the realm of digital scanners, recorders, and software in the hands of skilled operators. There are few limitations in the digital world, and the only burden is the creative mind of the user.

Probably the most basic (but nonetheless the most interesting to the cinematographer) aspect of this technology is the ability to digitally color correct a scene or sequence, or a whole film for that matter, without the limitations of conventional color timing and printing. The power of digital film technology is therefore available for both creative and corrective purposes, and can be applied to either end. Admittedly, digital color correction for film output has yet to gain widespread acceptance because of the expense involved. One can only assume that in the future this will become a common step in the post production process.

Rig and wire removal is another major task that is handled with precision on the computer workstation. As it is common in many films (particularly action films) to employ harnesses and cables for a wide variety of stunts and effects, these specific shots can be scanned and then the wires and rigs painted out frame by frame using software designed for this task. This involves a combination of duplicating areas of the frame that are adjacent to the wire as replacement pixels, and digitally painting over certain areas in order to get shadows and colors to match precisely so that the audience will be completely unaware of the process. If one has shot clean background plates (devoid of wires, related objects, or humans) this task is made even easier. Such paint tools are also used extensively for creating realistic textures on computer-generated objects after rendering. Other common applications for painting include the removal of modern objects in period films, and in the worst of circumstances, the elimination of scratches from original negatives by cloning adjacent pixels.

Compositing is considerably faster and simpler with computers, and eliminates the complex and tedious printing processes which are not only prone to error, but reduce quality with each successive generation. Foremost in this latest technology is the ability to use computer-generated images (CGI) composited with live-action footage, providing believable renderings of such things as aliens, dragons, and dinosaurs, seamlessly integrated into films. There are also fewer restrictions when using front and rear lit blue screens and green screens in both the studio and on location, because there is less concern for slight variations in screen intensity due to the ease of correctability during the digital compositing stage, and rigs used in conjunction with blue screen shots can be removed faster by using digital painting techniques. The quality of a composite can also be easily ascertained by simply examining the effect on the computer monitor, and combinations of compositing techniques (with virtually unlimited layers) such as rotoscoping may be used for greater effect.

Although film titles can still be produced using conventional methods, the ability to create such sequences using computer software allows an unprecedented degree of artistic manipulation. Three-dimensional letters and complex movement can be created, and sequences can be modified endlessly until the desired version is produced.

Film restoration and preservation in the past were normally limited to purely photo-mechanical means, and while these methods are still frequently used today, the digital environment expands the possibilities for rejuvenating damaged or faded film. Scratches and blotches can be removed using digital paint restoration techniques, and given the wide range of color correction possible with digital film systems, something of primary importance when dealing with original negative or intermediate elements that have faded dye layers and can no longer produce balanced prints with any degree of printer light manipulation (and this generally includes poor contrast reproduction), a digital intermediate can be made which corrects all color and contrast problems. Film that is physically warped or torn will still need to be duplicated using conventional methods because there is no point in trying to scan such materials, but once a duplicate is available scanning can be done as with any other film.

The final stage, after the image has been modified and processed through the appropriate software, is the output. The film recorder handles the chore of exposing the raw stock with either a CRT or lasers, using rasterized digital image data from the computer workstation. The link between the recorder and the computer is normally also either of the fiber-optic variety or SCSI for the maximum transfer rate, although, of course, neither type of film recorder can work in real time.

Film recorders used for motion picture film exposure can be broken down into the aforementioned categories: CRT or laser recording devices. Regardless of which design is actually used, both must have absolutely precise mechanical registration if acceptable images are to be produced.

In CRT-based film recorders a magnetically deflected electron beam scans across the back of a phosphor-embedded screen, creating a spot of light for every pixel value stored on the host computer. The voltage of the electron beam controls the intensity of the corresponding spot. Between the light beam and the film there is a focusing lens, and a filter wheel fitted with red, green, and blue filters, providing sequential exposure for each film layer in synchronization with each scan. The main concern in CRT-based recorders is spot uniformity and maintaining proper focus across the full width of the tube. It is also imperative that the phosphors are properly placed or film images will suffer from brightness fluctuations. Assuming these concerns have been properly addressed, which will be the case with all high-end film recorders, the only limitation of CRT recorders until recently was the inability to expose intermediate (slow-speed) film stocks, and thus one had little choice but to use higher speed negative camera films. The latest film recorders can now expose these stocks by using higher intensity CRTs, although recording times are still considerably slower than a laser recorder.

The laser-based film recorder eliminates many of the concerns associated with CRT devices by using three lasers to directly record onto film stock. Red, green, and blue lasers are mixed to form a co-linear beam in order to produce a point or spot. Exposure of the film in all three layers is created by modulating the intensity of the three lasers based on the rasterized image data. This co-linear laser beam is then moved across the film frame by a rotating mirror assembly. Focusing of the beam is further expedited by a precisely aligned optical system. Furthermore, the wavelengths of the three lasers are matched to the peak sensitivity of the emulsion layers in current intermediate film stocks. For example, Kodak's Cineon recorder uses 633nm (red), 543nm (green), and 458nm (blue) lasers.

The main advantage of laser film recorders is the ability to expose very slow-speed intermediate stocks, for example 5244, and provide faster recording times per frame when compared to CRT-based film recorders. This is most notable when using intermediate stocks with CRT film recorders, when recording times can be in excess of two minutes per frame, whereas a typical laser film recorder can expose a full resolution intermediate stock film frame in under fifteen seconds due to its considerably higher intensity.

Film recorders can expose all standard 35mm formats, including VistaVision, and some recorders can expose 65mm 5-perf, 8-perf, and 15-perf (Imax) film. Resolutions vary in each device, with some CRT film recorders indicated to have a maximum resolution of 8K. All are capable of at least 4096 pixels per line. Color depth is usually either 36 bits per pixel or 42 bits per pixel, depending upon whether 12 bit or 14 bit linear data is used.

An area which may soon see further expansion is the transfer of high-definition video to film using laser or CRT film recorders. While this has been done in the past using standard 30 fps or 25 fps sources at relatively low resolutions, one may expect enhanced results through the use of 24 fps high-resolution progressive sources. No doubt this would be the most practical current application of high-definition video camera technology in the existing world of theatrical film production and distribution. In time, it is certain that the gap between the electronic world and the film world will be breached.

There is little doubt that film scanners and recorders have expanded the creative possibilities for all concerned. The many special effects laden films of the past few years which utilized such scanning, image processing, and recording technology attest to that fact. It is hard to imagine anything but an increase in the use of digital film systems in the future as they redefine what is achievable, taking on more of the tasks once the exclusive domain of the laboratory.

13

0010100101001

THE DIGITAL IMAGE AND THE COMPUTER

As we have observed in the preceding three chapters, both video and film are now immersed to one degree or another in the digital realm of computer hardware and software, as a means of editing, storing, modifying, or displaying moving pictures and their associated data. The term data is used frequently now in reference to both film and video, because this is what both are converted to for processing by computer systems. Of course, sometimes the picture data is not imported into the computer, but created as a digital image, and it may or may not be combined with live-action photography. In this way imagery generated with computers is not used to supplement standard production methods, but to almost entirely replace it. How practical computer-generated imagery is depends on the processing power of computers and the relative costs associated with digital technology when compared to photographic and optical processes.

In contrast to a dedicated hardware system such as a digital VTR, computers have limitations based on the ability of the various components to transfer and process the image data. The first extensively applied use of computers to display and process video was in the form of the nonlinear editing system. While the pictures produced by the early versions were unusable for anything but basic off-line editing, it did not take long before processor speed, storage capacity, and interface speeds of desktop computers progressed to a level where the nonlinear editor gradually became a viable alternative as not only a means of producing a video edit decision list or a film negative cut list (the reliability of these is beyond the scope of our discussion, though the majority of negative cutters never work strictly from a software-generated negative cut list if it can be avoided), but also as a means of finishing a project to video. Very low compression M-JPEG rates were made possible by the speed improvements in computer hardware, and it is now possible to digitize, process, and output uncompressed NTSC video from a desktop-based system with the addition of a specialized video card, a large amount of memory, and a fast hard drive (or preferably several of them). Purpose-built computer systems were the first to offer uncompressed video input, processing, and output, and while there are some advantages to such dedicated hardware and software combinations, the versatile desktop computer, based on mass-manufactured processors and common operating systems, is reasonably comparable when properly configured, though this last statement is commonly disputed by various operating system factions.

Nonetheless, finishing post production entirely within the computer realm has become a reality, as hard drive storage capacities seem to rise almost geometrically, while on a cost to capacity basis the hard drive is becoming relatively inexpensive. The fact that fifteen minutes of uncompressed ITU-R 601 video takes up about 20 gigabytes of storage space was at one time considered to be an impractical demand, but these storage limitations were overcome by the introduction of the ability to edit at a high compression rate and then re-digitize at a lower compression rate to obtain an acceptable picture for final output. Those not requiring uncompressed video were the first to begin mastering on computers, and this method has been popular with video-originated, non-major network television programs for quite some time.

Our primary interest is how the expanded use of computers to finish productions has affected the cinematographer. When a computer-based nonlinear editing system is considered suitable for mastering, the control of the final product's images is in the hands of the editor and whoever else may be in the editing room (producers, etc.). Whether or not the editor or attending personnel are capable of completing the job the director of photography began is sometimes questionable, usually debatable, and almost always unknown. Most nonlinear editing programs have reasonably extensive image-modifying capabilities, and in some cases these software controls closely resemble conventional video tools found in a traditional edit bay. Dailies digitized and stored on the hard drives of a computer can be completely modified before being output as a video master, so even if a cinematographer shooting film manages to get good video dailies, there is every possibility that the editorial process may change the images to a lesser or greater degree, going beyond the simple matter of if and how much compression is used in the digitization process.

While this may seem a grim view of the bounties of the computer industry, it is only one view. The fact must be considered that if the cinematographer can exercise direct influence (i.e., get behind the keyboard and mouse), previously improbable or impossible benefits may be gained. The most important advantage of the desktop-based post production method is that it offers control, and places that control in the hands of one person. Instead of an arcane collection of proprietary hardware, incomprehensible instructional notes taped to desks, control panels, and VTRs, and custom setups which vary from post house to post house (or even room to room in the same facility), familiarity with a few of the popular software packages opens up the entire realm of post production image processing.

The use of desktop computers to finish a project also offers another advantage: compatibility. The cinematographer with a personal computer can run most of the same software used in post production, including image processing software which, while being essentially designed for still image work, is frequently used in television and film post production. Capable image processing software is by no means inexpensive as compared to most consumer software, but it offers interesting creative possibilities to the director of photography, not only through its ability to import and export virtually all industry-standard file types, but also as a device to communicate more clearly with others through actual pictures (and the precise information relating to them) what a shot will look like, should look like, or could have looked like.

Since throughout this text details on the technicalities of the various image recording, processing, and display systems have been to a lesser or greater degree explored, the technical details of computers will now be examined, with the primary focus being the desktop workstation and personal computer, the differences between the two having become something of a question of terminology.

In general, computers optimized for processing video and graphics have the fastest processors, ample random access memory, fast trans-fer buses and hard drives (and controllers which can handle large arrays of drives), and graphics accelerators with substantial on-board memory. A high-end personal computer which one might use in the home or office is generally comparable to an entry-level workstation. When-ever one takes up the topic of computer technology there is always the almost certain fact that what sounds like a powerful computer con-figuration today will seem hopelessly slow and outmoded in a year or two, so reference to direct performance figures will be avoided.

Naturally the processor speed (clock rate) in megahertz is a major factor in determining how well a computer can run a specific software application and how efficiently it can work with video information. As in frame rates and video refresh rates, hertz refers to cycles per second, although in the case of computer processors we are speaking in terms of millions of cycles per second. The processor, however, is only one component (albeit an important one), and other factors are equally critical, if not more so, which is exemplified by the fact that certain graphics workstations have processors with slower clock speeds than many home computers. Obviously the architecture of these sys-tems is designed for high data rate transfers between components, multiple processors, and other enhancements, making them superior in many respects than a typical desktop computer with a faster proces-sor.

Memory can dramatically influence computing performance. Soft-ware performance is enhanced when a system can store substantial data in RAM. The hard drive will not have to be accessed as frequently to store and then retrieve information. In the case of rendering video effects or 3D or 2D graphics the amount of memory available is in some ways as or more important than the processor clock speed. Given a choice between a 10 percent or 15 percent processor speed increase or doubling the amount of RAM, the latter improvement will increase the performance of a system more than the former, and is generally more cost-effective.

When playing back video, the hard drive and hard drive interface are critical in determining to what extent the image data must be com-pressed. The manufacturers of video software and related specialty hardware generally specify both the hard drive interface type required and the exact specifications of the drives relating to seek times, read and write times, and spindle rpms. The hard drive interface and hard drives must be capable of sustaining specified data transfer rates, depending on what level of compression (if any) will be used. The advertising material for hard drives more commonly refers to a transfer rate which is in fact the maximum burst transfer rate, not the sustained transfer rate. For practical purposes the sustained transfer rate is the significant figure.

The M-JPEG board is the controlling factor in the digital video editing system. It is with this component that video is digitized, played back, and output. As mentioned in the discussion of video compression in Chapter 10, the M-JPEG compression scheme keeps the individual frame information intact, and is therefore not as efficient as MPEG-2. While MPEG-2 editing systems do exist, for the time being M-JPEG is still the preferred editing compression scheme. For off-line editing, compression levels between 50:1 and 20:1 are common, but for finishing quality (in NTSC or PAL frequently referred to as "Betacam" quality) compression ratios ranging from approximately 5:1 to 2:1 are necessary. There are also video input/output boards capable of processing uncompressed ITU-R 601 video. The most useful of these have component digital serial interfaces, whereas less expensive cards have, at best, component analog interfaces for the input and output of video.

The graphics accelerator, secondary in video editing, is an important component when creating computer-generated imagery. The graphics accelerator determines how quickly images can be processed and rendered, and how the computer's display operates in terms of its resolution and ability to produce colors. The graphics accelerator also controls the refresh rate of the monitor, and a better accelerator can display full color (24 bit, or 32 bit with alpha channel) and high resolutions at rapid refresh rates. Absent a dedicated decoder card, the graphics accelerator may also have to process and decode DVD video data if the computer is equipped with a DVD-ROM drive, though for post production purposes the DVD, as we have mentioned earlier, is of very limited use at present.

Another matter of interest is whether the implementation of digital television will make the use of relatively low-cost desktop editing and finishing systems viable only when standard definition is desired. High-definition image processing places far greater demands on all the components we have discussed. It is only reasonable to assume that computer technology will meet the challenge of high definition, and that the move from tape-based linear editing and finishing solutions to computer-based, disk-based, nonlinear editing and finishing systems will continue. Whether compression of high-definition video in the post production stage will be acceptable for most productions is a major factor in determining how rapidly low-cost software and hardware configurations adapt to the demands. Presumably producers do not mind the compression of Digital Betacam for NTSC use, and most of the emerging high-definition formats utilize even higher compression rates. Initially, uncompressed high definition will require dedicated hardware.

Of course, not only are there digital editing systems capable of color correction, creating slow motion through frame interpolation, and the simulation of various traditional optical and printing effects, but there are also numerous software packages which provide some or all of the capabilities required to build and generate computer images. While the actual use of computers to generate effects, specifically in features, has been at times exaggerated, the traditional optical and mechanical methods being ignored as if every frame was computer-generated, there is no doubt that CGI has dramatically changed the thought process and approach to producing for both film and television, with the resulting technical matters at times falling squarely on the shoulders of the director of photography.

Rather remarkable digital images can be created on a computer with any number of software packages, but it is by no means simple (as the budgets associated with features and television commercials festooned with effects can attest). Completely computer-generated features, with photo-realistic, three-dimensional characters and settings, output to film at essentially film resolution, and projected in theaters, have obviously been successful enterprises, though production of such a film is a long and tedious process. The CGI television commercial, with dancing products flying about or cats talking, is (comparatively) simplified due to its short length and lower resolution. The software and methods used are the same in either case, commercials requiring fewer computers and a correspondingly smaller number of graphics and animation personnel.

Not unlike typical production, the realm of CGI and computer animation requires a combination of technical and creative skills. The terminology and tools of CGI software are taken largely from live-action production. Imaginary lights are used, and an imaginary camera with a fictitious lens of a specified imaginary focal length is employed to photograph the scene, but unlike standard production, the colors of a set can be changed with a few or many clicks of the mouse button, and the problem of lens flare is simply a question of whether lens flare is desired or not desired. The addition of fog and other diffusion into the atmosphere is likewise only a few mouse clicks away, though viewing the end result may take several seconds, minutes, hours, or sometimes days.

Much of the basic terminology may be analogous to the usual photographic and lighting phrases, but what is actually being created exists in an imaginary three-dimensional world, where everything is based on mathematical calculations which attempt to simulate reality—i.e., how light is reflected or how the intensity of a particular light source changes with distance. As we have discussed earlier, such matters do have certain mathematical rules associated with them, so the basis for this artificial world is in a sense the real world, at least to the degree the software programmers wish to follow it and the user of the software attempts to mimic it.

The question faced in planning a production is whether a shot requires CGI or can be accomplished in front of the camera. A traditional optical process might also be the best solution. If computer-generated imagery is being considered, one may be bombarded with references to splines, nurbs, polygons, surface-texturing, ray-tracing, render resolutions, render times, input file formats, output file formats, wireframe compatibility, and whether several plug-ins might have to be located, acquired, or possibly custom coded.

The basics of CGI are not overly complex, and while it takes considerable practice before any particular program can be used efficiently, most of the software works along similar lines, although the interfaces can vary and the command terminology is not always consistent. Most importantly, standardized file formats provide a high degree of compatibility between most CGI software. How well certain programs work together is also variable.

The CGI program is generally comprised of the modeling component, a renderer, and if part of its capability, an animator. From a cinematography standpoint, the renderer and animator are of prime interest, but this is not to say that the creation of models is not linked to the other two.

The modeler is where the wireframes are constructed, and in CGI, everything must be a wireframe at one point or another, whether the model is fabricated within the software environment or is digitized from some other source. These sources might be actual constructed models which are then converted into a 3D wireframe through the use of a mechanical, laser, or light scanner. Photographs might also provide the basis for the 3D data.

3D scanners take detailed measurements from the actual object. The mechanical method employs an arm which can trace three-dimensional objects, limiting the size of the object which can be scanned, whereas laser and light scanners measure distances through reflectance. The photographic method uses photographs taken from specific angles and distances. The photograph is scanned and digitized (unless a digital camera was used) and a program designed for such purposes calculates the various 3D properties based on this information. This is a much less precise method of acquiring 3D data than a mechanical, light, or laser scanner, but it is useful for large objects. Some laser scanners, however, can scan an entire house.

The creation of the wireframe allows the object to be worked on within the digital 3D environment. There are two basic types of wireframes: polygons and nurbs (or NURBS, non-uniform rational B-spline). The nurbs modeler uses far fewer lines to represent objects, and these lines do not form the numerous triangles associated with polygon modeling (Figure 13.1). Because of the fewer number of lines needed to represent an object or surface, nurbs-based modeling is faster in terms of working with the wireframe. It also provides a smoother render without having to use special rendering methods to hide the polygon intersections, which can never actually be smooth due to their basic geometry. At one time nurbs modeling was confined to a few very high-end packages, but it has now been implemented in numerous software CGI products to varying degrees.

The renderer is where the wireframe information is used to create the finished image (Figure 13.2). Obviously the wireframe will be rendered frequently as work progresses, although once complex lighting or textures are incorporated into the work, render times will be much

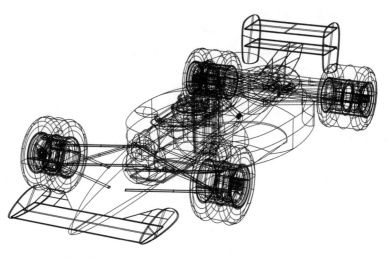

FIGURE 13.1 Nurbs wireframe model.

FIGURE 13.2 Rendered model.

longer than when rendering a non-textured object or scene with simple lighting. A cinematographer may have little interest in wireframes or how they are created, but if an object or entire scene will be composited or intercut with live-action photography, the use of lighting within the 3D modeler is of at least some concern, as are the colors, textures, and reflectance characteristics of the rendered items.

While the rendering of surface textures and objects and surfaces themselves is a mathematically complex operation, the lighting calculations add even more complexity, and this task becomes quite demanding on computer processing power. A detailed, complex object with many textures, situated in a multiple light-path scene, will sometimes require a surprisingly long amount of time to render one frame. Naturally, the rendering is done at lower resolutions until the work is finalized.

The final element in the illusion is the animation of the objects, and the possible use of simulated camera movement. In terms of the imaginary camera, there are unlimited focal length lenses available, and these operate more or less like real lenses, with depth of field being part of the effect. The rendering of an animation is, of course, a matter of rendering one frame at a time, which can (particularly at film resolutions) be a tedious process to say the least. The rendering of completed shots is frequently processed overnight, and the creators do not know if an error exists until they stumble in the following morning, only to find that the required texture was not applied to the port side of the spacecraft, and that the shot is not completed at all.

How long it takes to create a particular shot or element of a shot using computer-generated imagery depends on the type of shot, the duration of the shot, what resolution is required, and finally, how photorealistic the shot must be. An example of a difficult CGI shot would be one in which an organic object must be animated for an extended duration and composited with live-action photography where the camera moves and the lighting is complex.

In something of a paradox, the use of digital methods, while frequently taking much of the control of a shot away from the director of photography, provides far more possibilities in terms of production lighting and camera use than when traditional optical techniques are relied upon to create a certain effect. In any event, CGI is a useful method of accomplishing shots which could not feasibly be completed any other way, but it is an expensive and time-consuming method of creating images even when compared to the costs of studio or location production.

While the features, television productions, and commercials with obvious computer-generated images are the most talked about aspect of this field, the mundane tasks enumerated in the preceding chapter, such as removing rigging wires, erasing television antennae out of a shot from a period piece, or repairing a scratched or otherwise damaged section of negative containing an important shot which exists nowhere else, are just as important. These have an added level of difficulty in that the work must not leave any tell-tale traces which viewers might detect. The application of digital solutions is not always planned, particularly if the problem was not (and could not possibly have been) foreseen. It is generally preferable that the use of these expensive technologies be part of a calculated plan. No matter how capable digital systems may appear to be, the assumption that everything can be improved or repaired in post production is a costly one.

Overall, the digitization of image footage, be it film, film-originated video, or video, permits drastic changes to be made to the acquired pictures, some of which may be desirable, others not, depending on one's point of view. The changes might be the result of color or contrast work performed with a digital nonlinear editor or compositing program, or video effects where a shot or scene is imported into a graphics program and more dramatic changes are wrought. At the same time the basic color and contrast range (or even the lighting) might also be modified within the CGI realm.

This brings us to the subject of the "digital backlot." The concept is to produce projects using digital imagery and compositing to minimize the expenses and delays associated with field production, not strictly to create the imaginary, but to recreate or simulate something which would not normally be considered difficult to accomplish with a camera. Instead of constructing a vast or detailed set, we might instead opt to build in the digital world only, or construct only a simple set, not adding the details until later. Weather delays and construction problems could be avoided, and the limitations of time made less of a factor in terms of shooting scenes since we can always return to the location—the sets are never actually destroyed to make way for new ones.

A common protest against the further intrusion of digital imagery and digital technology into the filmmaking process is that the digitally created image is not *real*. One must consider the fact that no film or video image is real, and that the entire end product, no matter what the precise nature of the technology, is illusory. Computer-generated imagery is simply another method of accomplishing this task. The extent and quantity of CGI in any given production is dictated by the requirements of the script or storyboards and the cost factors associated with every known or devised production method.

There is yet another use for digital image creation, and that is as a means to plan a production. While there are no direct substitutes for diagrams and storyboards, computer-generated imagery can assist in the visualization of a production at an early stage, providing for a higher degree of understanding for all involved. Some rendering software has lighting based on data from actual lights, including professional studio fixtures. In a theoretical but visual way the cinematographer can experiment with illuminant types and placements, along with camera angles, before anything has been built or a final location determined.

Obviously there is a limit to the complexity of these renderings before they become productions unto themselves, but the basic structures of most sets or locations are not overly taxing to create, and if no textures or details must be rendered, even animations showing camera movements as they would appear on-screen can be accomplished given suitable software and a computer with sufficient processor speed and memory. Using such software directly allows one to realize that it is sometimes possible to accomplish seemingly complicated modeling, rendering, animation, or effects, while a simpler creation may become frustratingly difficult to complete—leading to a direct understanding of how computer-generated imagery works and when it should be called upon.

14

Popcorn and Pixels

DIGITAL CINEMA

Recent application of electronic cinema technology has prompted the addition of this last chapter. While far from ubiquitous at this time, the further development of so-called "digital cinema" has far-reaching implications for those involved in film production and distribution, and regardless of whether one approves or disapproves, it remains an intriguing and undoubtedly practical concept, particularly for those who have a financial interest in reducing the vast expenditures now allocated to cover the cost of producing film prints for thousands of theaters.

The basic premise of electronic cinema is to eliminate film altogether from the presentation process. While film remains the standard by which all other imaging mediums are judged, and clearly provides the best picture quality currently available, it does have its intrinsic physical limitations. For those concerned with the on-screen image, though, replacing the conventional film projector with a high-resolution electronic projector, and replacing film with a digitally stored duplicate may appear to be a highly questionable endeavor at best, even given the typically spurious quality obtained in high-speed release printing and the image degradation caused by repeated film projection. It is not the intent to debate the future of digital cinema, nor extol the virtues of such a system, but rather to simply explain how this concept can be achieved with existing technology.

At present there are two workable projectors which have been recently put to practical use: the Hughes-JVC image light amplifier (ILA) projector, and the Texas Instruments digital light processing (DLP) system, the latter employing the digital micromirror device (DMD).

The ILA projector uses three projection CRTs, a xenon arc lamp, and three image light amplifier modulators, a specific type of liquid crystal light valve. In the most basic description possible (and this will take some effort), each CRT is reproducing one of three signals; that is, red, green, or blue. Each CRT image is focused onto an ILA which is constructed of a photosensitive layer and a liquid crystal layer. Between the photosensitive layer and the liquid crystal layer is a reflecting mirror and light blocking layer, which provide the necessary separation between the CRT light and the xenon light. The CRT provides the input in the form of a rasterizing light beam which scans across the photosensitive layer, where the beam intensity is modulated by the signal input. The light beam produces a lowered resistance in the photosensitive layer which, in turn, causes a rotational change in the liquid crystal cells by increasing voltage.

The rotation of the liquid crystal cells can be made to cause xenon light that has been polarized by a beam splitter to reflect from the mirror side of the ILA either back into the light source (unchanged polarization), or towards the screen (changed polarization). As the degree of polarization determines the ability of the reflected light to travel back through the beam splitter and into the projection lens, varying light intensities can be produced on-screen which are representative of the original signal through the polarizing (rotational) action of the liquid crystal, which is ultimately controlled by the light produced by the CRT. Color pictures can be observed by separating the high-intensity xenon light into its RGB components with dichroic mirrors, directing these beams at their respective ILAs (after the appropriate polarization by the beam splitters), and overlapping the projected images on the screen, thus employing an additive method of color reproduction.

The DLP projector system takes a different and undoubtedly unique approach by directly modulating light with a digital micromirror device (DMD). Although difficult to grasp at first, the DMD is simply an electromechanical array of mirrors that can be tilted in one of two directions by electrostatic control. Beneath each mirror is a memory cell which receives the input data. In this way a single mirror is analogous to a pixel in a conventional display, although only simple bi-level images can be reproduced, as 1 and 0 (in a binary representation) are respectively on or off, i.e., + 10 degree tilt and –10 degree tilt. It should be noted that each mirror is only 16μm square, and a 1280 × 1024 array contains 1,310,720 of these micromirrors in an area only 1.1 inches diagonal.

Because the mirrors are either reflecting or not reflecting light, the intensity cannot be varied. However, the eye will perceive a short burst of light as low-intensity, and a long burst of light as high-intensity. In order to produce gray scale images from one DMD, the time duration of the light is controlled by each bit in the digital word; this is known as binary pulsewidth modulation (PWM). For example, in an 8 bit digital word, 00000000 is black and 11111111 is peak white. Intermediate levels of "intensity" are created by all possible combinations of bits in the digital word (2^8) or 256 gray levels. Therefore a pulse of long duration will produce a brighter tone, while a pulse of short duration will produce a darker tone.

In a color projector three DMD arrays are used, one for each color channel. By using a high-intensity xenon lamp and a special prism assembly, the light source is split into its RGB components and then directed at the appropriate DMD. By controlling the individual micromirrors in each array with the appropriate input data, the micromirrors can be made to reflect the projector light source (xenon lamp) by the tilting action of each. Thus, light can be directed (pixel by pixel) into the single projection lens or away from the lens by each array. As the three separated light beams are recombined for projection, this system also uses an additive color process. If 8 bits are used—given three arrays—a total of 16.7 million colors is possible (24 bits total). In a 10 bit system, 1024 gray levels can be produced by each array for a total of over 1 billion colors (30 bits total).

The novel feature of both of these projectors is that a video source is used to provide the input to either the CRT, as in the ILA system, or the DMD, as in the DLP system, but the output is similar to that of projected film. In other words, both projectors are simply modulating a high-intensity xenon light source, albeit in a far more complex method than that provided by the three dye layers of a positive film.

Because both systems are inherently video projectors by input, the aspect ratios (as fixed by physical design) are similar to that of standard television, though in the case of the most recently demonstrated version of the Texas Instruments DLP the aspect ratio is identical to that of high-definition television, and that is in fact the resolution of the latest version: 1920 × 1080. The DLP system utilizing a 1280 × 1024 array has a 1.25 aspect ratio, whereas the Hughes-JVC projector uses a 51mm × 38mm ILA, yielding an aspect ratio of roughly 1.33. It should be noted that the resolution of the image light amplifier cannot be defined in conventional "pixel" terms because there are no pixels to speak of, although the resolution of the accompanying CRT is clearly a primary determining factor. The resolution capability of the ILA is 2500 TV lines across the horizontal axis, but in practice (with a CRT input) the resolution is closer to 2000 TV lines.

Both systems handle the problem of presenting widescreen images differently. The DLP 1280x1024 system uses two different anamorphic lenses, one for 1.85 images (1.5 ×) and one for 2.35 images (1.9 ×). This would seem to imply that an unsqueezed anamorphic print or interpositive (roughly 1.19:1) could be transferred to video and projected with the appropriate lens with minimal scaling applied, or that a 1.85 image must be "squeezed/scaled" for presentation on a system which necessarily relies on anamorphic optics for both formats. The 1920 × 1080 DLP would require a less extreme squeeze to fit the 2.35 widescreen image within its bounds, or in the case of 1.85, possibly none.

The Hughes-JVC ILA projector takes a different approach to the same problem by electronically modifying how the image is rasterized onto the ILA. Through this method, for example, a 2.35 format film can be transferred to high-definition (1.78) videotape in a partially squeezed form, and then unsqueezed electronically by the CRT. Thus the ILA is essentially receiving a letter-boxed image in any format other than 1.33. Resolution is not reduced by any practical amount because the ILA easily exceeds the resolution of the current high-definition input format, but loss of light is a drawback when the total surface area of the ILA is not completely utilized. Light control will be improved in actual production models to maintain a brighter image when the entire ILA is not used. Unlike the DLP projector which must use anamorphic lenses for all widescreen formats (at least in its current application), only regular spherical projection lenses are used with the Hughes-JVC ILA projector.

The input format presently employed with digital cinema projection technology is a conventional video source derived from a film to video transfer. In the case of the DLP projector, if a 30 fps source is used, in order to obtain 24 frames per second for presentation from essentially a 30 frames per second video source, inverse telecine is employed. In effect, this eliminates the added video fields created during the 3:2 pull-down process, and presents the film image in its native frame rate. The first ILA theatrical projection systems have used interlaced 30 frames per second video, maintaining the 3:2 pull-down, but production models will utilize the 24 frames per second progressive architecture. Here is another instance where a high-definition 24 fps progressive video source as a film transfer mastering format is advantageous.

In addition, by using progressively scanned input formats, the required progressive-scan conversion from interlaced sources need not be applied in the case of the DLP system. Whether 24 fps progressive high-definition video can indeed replace film altogether remains unclear. If high-definition video images were transferred to film using a film recorder (producing a film intermediate), and then scanned back to video using an appropriate telecine, this would likely be a viable method of obtaining a film-like quality from a video source, if in fact a film-like image is a requirement. Software processing is a another way in which the qualities of film might be obtained from a digital video source, although without a substantially higher resolution video camera than is currently available, the ability to entirely mimic 35mm film through electronic means is uncertain.

Leaving that issue aside, to date high-definition film transfers onto D-5 HD employing M-JPEG 4:1 compression have been used. Material was then transferred onto a disk-based digital video recorder for theatrical presentation. In the future it may be possible to implement a distribution method similar to that which is used by broadcast television networks, where digital data can be relayed to satellites and then transmitted to individual theaters for temporary disk-based storage during the duration of the showing. For those who propose such a method, the advantages are deemed to be twofold. The material is non-physical, which means film prints do not have to be shipped to the theaters, and when the film reaches the end of its run, there are no prints to destroy or ship back to the distributor. The success or failure of a released picture could also be responded to more rapidly, at minimal expense. Of course even if conventional magnetic tape was used for distribution, this can still be argued to be a simpler solution than splicing together 2000-foot projection rolls into a monstrous wheel of over 10,800 feet of film or more (platter systems), depending on the length of the film. The particular and detrimental feature of satellite distribution, though, is the more than likely use of compression to reduce the necessary bandwidth. Thus the use of compression for transmission and storage, which inevitably would be part of the process, will cause a reduction in the quality of the projected image.

In current practice, these systems are essentially just paradigms for what will likely come in the near future, and thus they remain somewhat proprietary in their operation for the time being, a hybrid system like many others currently used, creating a bridge between the worlds of film and digital data. While the inevitability of electronic projection can still be debated at this point, one must admit that the outcome of the vast changes caused by this seemingly magical word—"digital"—will almost certainly produce a turning point in the film industry in the very near future. In a similar state as high-definition video remains today, it is not really a matter of how this can be achieved, but when it will be achieved. Ultimately what form digital cinema will take and who will provide it remain to be seen, adding an element of anticipation to the whole process. As the technology matures and becomes less costly, more theaters and distributors will likely embrace its advantages.

In pondering these likely changes, one should never forget that film will remain viable as long as the picture quality surpasses all currently applied technology. It is the simplicity and directness of film that has yet to be replicated by any electronic device and, in fact, the most recent digital video cameras continue to strive to achieve a film-like image by means of complex circuitry and increasingly higher resolution CCDs, and thus the situation can be called paradoxical, for one is attempting to replace a medium which is still superior to that which is the implicit replacement itself. The striving force behind the need to improve electronic imaging devices, though, is due in large part to the inconvenience of film. Film technology, while continuing to improve over the years in all respects, remains antiquated in its physical form. The simplicity of its design is both its advantage and disadvantage.

The latest advances may allow faster and more precise work to be accomplished, and even in some cases at reduced cost, but the fact remains that a degree of complexity is naturally being added with each direct implementation. In this way there is both a positive and a negative result, where one is constantly striving to keep up with changes, and simply assuming such changes are necessary in the first place.

Many elements influence what reaches the screen. Logistics play a crucial role in any production, and admittedly little has been addressed on this topic due to the specific nature of the studies at hand, yet this salient and often underestimated factor cannot be regarded lightly when quality is to be attained and maintained, regardless of the medium. The logistics of film production could, in fact, fill another entire volume.

In the end, regardless of the equipment at one's disposal, individual skill is still far more important. An advantage is to be gained by using the latest device only if that device can justify its application in the eyes of the user. Irrespective of changes in equipment and technology, the basic underlying ability to produce compelling and fitting images will always be the key issue.

NOTES

Several sources were invaluable in completing Chapters 12 and 14. For Chapter 12, Glenn Kennel's *SMPTE Journal* article "Digital Film Scanning and Recording: The Technology and Practice" was the primary written source. Its author also took the time to answer some questions about the technology, and specifically how it was practiced at Kodak's Cinesite in Los Angeles.

For Chapter 14, William P. Bleha's *SMPTE Journal* article "Image Light Amplifier Technology for Large-Screen Projection" was of prime importance in comprehending this technology as developed by Hughes-JVC Technology. Further details on the practical application of the ILA system were provided by Steven A. Morley of Qualcomm, who answered several questions concerning its implementation in theaters. The information made available by Texas Instruments allowed for extensive reading on the DMD and its application, the DLP projector. Most of this material was written by Larry J. Hornbeck.

Here we might also note that ILA is a trademark of Hughes-JVC Technology, and that DMD and DLP are trademarks of Texas Instruments. Likewise there are other trademarks mentioned in the text, and though not specifically noted, each is of course the property of its respective owner.

INDEX

A

Adaptation. *See also* Dark
   adaptation; Light adaptation
   and color 9–10
   general 13–14
   localized 13–14
   simultaneous contrast 13–14
Additive color 147–148
Additive printing 120–121
After-images 3
Ampex DCT 160–161, 162
Anamorphic
   considerations 135–137
   format 132, 134–135
   lenses 100
   prints from Super 35 126–
     127, 138
   projection 135, 146
   scanning 186–187
Antihalation
   dye layer of positive stock 116
   remjet 83
Aperture
   camera 132
   eye 1
   lens 1. *See also* f-stops; T-stops
Aperture plate 22
Automatic exposure (video
   camera) 156

Automatic white balance 10, 155

B

Bandwidth 150–151
   and recording 152
   and resolution 153–154
Behind-the-lens filters 73
Best light video dailies 178
Betacam SP 157
Betacam SX 163
Biconvex 1–2
Black body radiator 52–53, 59–60
Bleach bypass 129–130
Bleaching
   eye 3–5
   film 85, 116
Blow-up
   and optical printer 117, 126
   Super 16 142
Brightness 12–13

C

CCD (charge-coupled device)
   camera 10, 151–152
   film scanners 184
   telecine 169–170
CGI (computer-generated images)
   189–190, 198–204
Characteristic curves

negative 86–89
positive 90
Chromaticity coordinates 148–149
Cinemascope 132. *See also* Anamorphic
Color analyzer 119–121, 124–125
Color balance 9–11, 55–65
Color correction
  digital film systems 181–182
  tape to tape 171, 180
  telecine 180–181
Color film 83–85
Color filters
  compensating 69
  contrast control (b&w) 69–70
  conversion 56, 69, 77
  light balancing 56
Color gamut 148–149
Color matching 149
Color perception 6–8
Color temperature 51–68
  changes during day 54–55
  correlated 59–60, 62
    and monitors 149
  limitations of 60
  meters 63–64
  mixed sources 59, 62
Color timing 119–125
Component analog 157
Composite video 152
Compositing 189–190, 203–204
Compression (video)
  DCT 161
  JPEG 160
  M-JPEG 160, 194, 197
  MPEG-2 160–164, 182
    and HDTV transmission 166
Computers 193–204
  graphics accelerator 197
  memory 196
  processor 196

software 195
Contact printers 116
Couplers 84
CRT film recorder 190–192

D

D Log H curves 85–87
D-1 157–159
D-2 158–159
D-3 158–159
D-5 159
D-6 164–165
D-7 163
D-9 163
Dailies
  film 116
    improving 121
  video 177–178
    problems 178–180
Daylight 53–54
Densitometer 86–87, 120, 129
Density 86
  integral 86
Depth of field 106–108
  circle of confusion 106
  hyperfocal distance 107–108
Depth perception 15
Diffraction 105–106
Diffusion 78
Digital backlot 203
Digital Betacam 160–162, 171
Digital cinema 205–211
  DLP 206–209
  ILA 206–209
Digital film systems 183, 190, 192
Digital video
  quantization 158
  sampling rate 157–158
  sampling structure 159
Digital-S 163
Diopters 102, 109

Distortion 105
DTV 165–168
DV 160, 162–163
DVCPRO 160, 163
DVCPRO50 160, 163
DVD 160, 163–164, 197

E

Editing 193–194, 197–198
Electromagnetic spectrum 7
Emulsion
   dye layers 83–84
   multicoat 83–84
   positive layer order 118–119
   testing 96–98
ENR process 129
Exposure
   assessment 46–50
   defined 85
   formula 30
   latitude 93–94
   range 91–93
   under/over 94–95
Exposure index 29
Exposure meters. *See* Light meters
Exposure time 23–24
Extenders 102–103
Eye
   and color 6–11
   and contrast 12–15
   focal length 15
   pigments 3–4
   receptors 3
   sensitivity 6–7
   structure of 4

F

F-stops 27–28
Film formats
   1.85 133–134
   3-perf Super 35 140
   65mm 142–143
   70mm 142–143
   Academy 132–133
   anamorphic 134–137
   standard 16 141
   Super 1.85 144–145
   Super 16 141–142
   Super 35 137–140
   Techniscope 141
   VistaVision 143–144
Film recorders 190–192
Film scanners 184–187
Film storage and transport 115–116
Film to video transfers
   3:2 pull-down 172–175
   calibration films 179–180
   films used 174–175
   framing 176–177
   hard drive transfers for dailies 171–172
   image modification 180–181
   logging 177
   tone reproduction 175–176
Filming monitors 26–27
Filters
   diffusers 71
   fogs 71
   graduated 71–72
   low-contrast 71
   NDs 70
   polarizer 72–73
   UV 70–71
Flashing
   in camera 128
   negative 128
   print 128–129
Flicker 63
Fluorescent lamps 60–62
Flying spot telecine 169–170
Focus 106–107, 113
Footcandles 30, 37
Formulas

color temperature 65
concerning filters 75
diopters 102
exposure 30
hyperfocal 108
macro 100–101
TVL/PH 154
Frame rate
camera 23–24

G

Gain
camera 5, 156
telecine 181
Gamma
film
determining 89
video
correction 149–150
monitor 149–150
GOP (group of pictures) 161–163
Gray card 38
Gray scale 41–42
Ground glass 20

H

Hard drives
capacity 194
transfer rate 197
Hard matte 133
HDCAM 164
High-definition television
1080i 165–167
720p 165–167
High-intensity gas discharge lamps
mercury vapor 62–63
metal halide 62–63
sodium vapor 62–63
HMI 63

I

Illuminant (defining SPD) 51

Image distance (eye) 2–3
Image processing 3, 172, 183–
184, 187, 192, 195, 198
Incandescent 55, 59
Incident meter 17, 37–41, 44–
45, 48
Interlaced video 150–151,
153, 173
Intermediate films 120
Internegative 91, 122, 126–127
Interpositive 91, 122, 126–127
ITU-R [601] 159, 194

L

Laboratory
printing 116–117
processing 116
special processes 127–130
LAD 119–121
Laser film recorder 191
Lenses
aberrations 105
anamorphic 100, 136
diffraction 106
diopters 102
extenders 102–103
focal length 99–100
macro 100–101
periscope/borescope 103
prime 99–100
shift/tilt 103
slant focus 103
split diopters 102
zoom 101–102
Letter-boxing 134, 137, 139, 176
Light adaptation 4–5
Lighting filters 56, 65, 77
Lighting ratio 45–46
Light meters
incident 35, 38–41
reflected 35, 41
spot 41–46

Luminance
  ratio 46
  video signal (luma) 152

M

Mattebox 73–74
Mesopic vision 4
Meters. *See* Color temperature:
  meters; Light meters
MTF 103–105

N

Negative processing 116
Nonlinear editors 193–194
Nurbs 199–200, 201

O

One-light prints 120–121
Optical printer 86, 90, 116–117,
  126–127, 133, 144, 169, 183,
  188
Optics. *See* Lenses

P

Pan and scan 137–138, 176
Persistence of vision 11–12
Perspective 15
Photopic vision 3
Pitch 117
Polarizer 72
Polygons 200
Printer points 120–122
Progressive scanning 147, 150–
  151
Projection practices 145–146
Pull processing 123, 128
Pull-down claws 22
Push processing 123, 127

R

Reciprocal megakelvin 64–65

Reciprocity failure 96
Reflected light meter. *See* Light
  meters
Reflex viewfinder 20–22
Release prints 126
Rendering 196, 200, 202, 204
Resolution
  film scanners 185–187
  HDTV 165–166
  NTSC 153–154
Restoration 190
Retina
  cones 3–4
  fovea 3–4
  rods 3–4
Rig and wire removal 189, 203

S

Scanners. *See also* Film scanners
  3D 200
Scotopic vision 4
Sensitometer 85
Sensitometric curve. *See* Charac-
  teristic curves
Sensitometry 83–98
Separations 127
Shutter
  angle 23–24
  focal plane 20
  spinning reflex mirror 20–22
Spectral power distribution 51
  fluorescent 61
  tungsten 52
Spectral sensitivity
  eye 6–7
  film 9
  light meter 37–38
Step tablet 85
Step-contact printer 116–117
Step optical printer 116–117
Stereoscopic vision 15
Super 16 141–142

Super 35 137–140

T

T-stops 27–29
Tape to tape color correction 180
Techniscope 141
Telecine 169–170, 172
Theater design 146
Time code 167–168

V

Varicon 128
Video
  component 157
  composite 152–153
  compressed video 159–161
  digital 157–159
  formats 157–166
VistaVision 143–144

W

Wireframes 200–202

Z

Zoom lenses 101–102